SATIRE'S BREW

Mass Media & Coffee Beans

First Edition

D1500961

Brian Dunphy

Brooklyn College

cognella®
academic publishing

Bassim Hamadeh, CEO and Publisher
Michael Simpson, Vice President of Acquisitions
Jamie Giganti, Managing Editor
Jess Busch, Senior Graphic Designer
John Remington, Acquisitions Editor
Brian Fahey, Licensing Associate
Mandy Licata, Interior Designer

Copyright © 2014 by Cognella, Inc. All rights reserved. No part of this publication may be reprinted, reproduced, transmitted, or utilized in any form or by any electronic, mechanical, or other means, now known or hereafter invented, including photocopying, microfilming, and recording, or in any information retrieval system without the written permission of Cognella, Inc.

First published in the United States of America in 2014 by Cognella, Inc.

Trademark Notice: Product or corporate names may be trademarks or registered trademarks, and are used only for identification and explanation without intent to infringe.

Cover image copyright© 2013 by Depositphotos / Les Cunliffe
Cover image copyright© 2012 by Depositphotos / Electra Kay-Smith

Printed in the United States of America

ISBN: 978-1-60927-260-9 (pbk) / 978-1-62661-654-7 (br)

www.cognella.com   800-200-3908

CONTENTS

Acknowledgments   V

Satire's Brew: Media Lectures and Coffee Beans in Europe   IX

Introduction   XIII

Lecture One - America's Jester: *The Daily Show with Jon Stewart,* 1 and The State of Politics and Media

Lecture Two - Killing Cartoons: Violence in Art & Animation   59

Origins - Shadows of Forthcoming Events   95

Lecture Three - South Park and the American Experience   125

Lecture Four - Comedy of Outrage: The Satirical Representation 199 of the American Presidency

Bibliography, References & Influences   241

Image Credits   249

ACKNOWLEDGMENTS

One thing I always wanted to do was an acknowledgments page thanking all those people who have helped guide, and formed who I am. In essence, this is my Oscar speech so please indulge me. While some on this list have remained constants in my life and continue to be so even today, others left an indelible mark that even years later still remains.

Finally, after all this time, this is my opportunity to thank them properly.

To my parents, Tom and Sherri: Who always believed in my work even when I doubted every word, sentence, and page. You always pushed me and were proud even when I was pulling away and decimated from defeat. You made me who I am today with all the flaws and strengths. And lastly, and most importantly, you are still way cooler than I will ever be.

To my brothers, Justin and Colin: Stuck in the middle with you two is the best place for me to be.

To my huge family: Thanks for putting up with me at holiday dinners and sorry about the political discussions. But especially to my cousin Danielle—you know what you did and I can't thank you enough.

To all my friends for influencing this book: From high school, college, University of Amsterdam & PHK, and those outside of school and work. Yes, some parts of this book are about you and yes, I did take liberties about that time with the thing and the other thing but I always said I would write about it some day.

To the students who assisted with some of the research and even with suggestions, there are so many to name so just know I appreciated all your work. I'd list you all but this would end up being thirty pages long!

A special thanks to a few others

Bari for putting up with me and my obsessing over work, being difficult, and constantly thinking about this book and/or another lecture coming up. And to answer your question: Yes, there is something else coming up, because, there will always be something else coming up. But also, for making me laugh more than anyone else has (and probably ever will), for being a wonderful, supportive, and loving partner, and most importantly for having the same sense of humor as I do. We have forever to debate on which one of us is the funnier one in this relationship, but regardless of the outcome, I love you.

Meredith Caraher for being an incredible friend, fellow sufferer, and sounding board to all my ideas and theories. Without you a lot of this work (the book and lectures) doesn't get done in the way I envisioned and you're a major reason for that. Your contributions were invaluable in every way and I thank PS 26, Facebook, and geography for bringing us together. Oh, and thank you for the Jon Stewart/Don Quixote image! It's perfect!

DB Gilles from NYU: The only professor who gave it to me straight and unfiltered when I needed it most and someone I still trust to be honest with me years after I graduated.

Professor Jill Adler from the University of Amsterdam: Who was the first to tell me to become a teacher, introduced me to Professor Mueller, and whom I consider a friend ten years after I left that perfect city.

Professor Jim Miller who while I was at graduate school at The New School for Social Research introduced me to Thomas Nast and allowed my satiric obsession to really take fruit.

Professor George Rodman for hiring me at Brooklyn College, supporting my work, and pushing for the "South Park" course. To the Television and Radio faculty for approving the "South Park" course and their continued support.

Martina van Riel for sending an innocuous email in November 2011 asking if someone else can do a lecture on *South Park* and me offering my services instead. Without her email these lectures never make it across the ocean so I will be eternally grateful. And to Kirsten Krans and the entire Studium Generale team in Groningen for being incredibly sweet, understanding, and enthusiastic about my work.

To the Cognella Team

Putting this book together has been quite a rollercoaster! Beginning with a meeting in my office with a Cognella/University Readers representative named John Remington to changing the focus of the book to its final rendering here.

Thank you to the managing editor Jamie Giganti for allowing the project to go wherever it ended up and was unbelievably patient with me.

A huge thank you to my editor Sharon Hermann for understanding what I was doing here, and helping me understand what exactly I was doing here. Working together and talking me off the proverbial ledge as often as you did makes me forever indebted to you.

Others who deserve mention and cannot be forgotten

Trey Parker & Matt Stone: I've been watching you since I was seventeen and haven't stopped laughing since. Your balanced approach to everything and anything helped form the way I discuss the most important issues of the day.

Jon Stewart & Stephen Colbert: the work you and your writers do is absolutely essential and has enabled me to think differently about issues while being incredibly entertained week in and week out.

Andrew Sullivan: a blogger, who I never met, but over the years introduced nuance, understanding, contradictions, and mental health breaks to my day to day. I never miss a day reading your blog and look forward to your continued insight.

Thomas Nast: an American hero who should be taught to every single student somewhere during his or her educational journey. Nast's influence on my thinking is immense and I apologize profusely for the comparison in chapter three.

SATIRE'S BREW

Media Lectures and Coffee Beans in Europe

AUTHOR'S NOTE

*S*atire's Brew is not a book of complete fiction but a healthy amount of exaggeration, story-telling, real and current history, and media interpretation. Included within this book are ideas that have been popping around in my head for several years and not all are exclusive to satire but a wide range of subjects. Some sequences are obvious fictions, while others are simple embellishments, and others are exactly the way they happened. To keep with the mystery, it doesn't matter which are imagined and which aren't: what matters is and the hope is, as it always is when writing or lecturing or anything produced in media for that matter, that the reader enjoys the journey and process of getting from A to B to Z, or from Crop to Cup to keep with the coffee motif. The lectures themselves are original with influences from so many thinkers, authors, friends, and family. I truly enjoy the visual aspect of them and each sentence or so has an image behind it with a scant amount of wording. I felt that a lecture that all people will enjoy has information and entertainment, and feels "new." A PowerPoint presentation was never my intention nor do I believe that the millennials want that. They've grown up in a sea of imagery, bombarded while being entertained—maybe I can capture that, and I think, from the reactions, I have. Transferring them to the written word while staying faithful to the other is an arduous task, to say the least. What it does allow is expansion in parts that I wasn't able to delve into before. There will also be some repeated notions only because we're covering similar ground for different audiences every time a new lecture is created.

The lectures have a similar structure and were highly influenced by a one-time visiting lecture from Professor Gerhard Mueller while I was in a Constitutional Law class at The University of Amsterdam in 2003. Professor Mueller, his voice raspy from old age and education, started the special lecture with the beginning of civilization and how tribes had to work together for survival. One tribe would have access to the river while the other had the ability to grow crops. Sitting in a Constitutional Law course I had no conception or idea where he was going—I honestly believed this was the ramblings of an old man as he traced civilizations that relinquished some autonomy for tribal survival, using numerous examples along the way. Thirty minutes later, with an umbrella drawn on the board, he said (I'm paraphrasing): "And that's why what George W. Bush is doing to the United Nations with regards to the Iraq War is damaging to the ... " I do not remember EXACTLY what he said after that—I may have passed out from the amazement—but to have the ability to trace what is happening in 2003, Iraq, the US, and the UN to what transpired centuries and a millennium ago was absolutely riveting. To lead us on a journey from the micro to the macro and the macro to micro, combining history and present day in such a way had a tremendous influence on my impressionable young mind. The lectures are influenced from that because if someone can explain the world by taking a journey through history, then that's how I want to do these lectures.

The book's second element of a "character" delivering the lectures was surely influenced by Hunter S. Thompson and Salman Rushdie's "Joseph Anton." But the idea was conjured up while on a flight home to New York from Amsterdam in 2012. I had just been upgraded to first class and had no business being there, and my enthusiasm for the class certainly revealed my lack thereof. The night before, I had checked in, but due to a computer glitch my reservation was missing from the KLM website. The next morning when I went to the service counter, they had NO record of my flight—even though they sent me an email reminder the night before. I held out my paper copy saying: "It's here! See how I hold it in front of you" and immediately remembered a *Seinfeld* episode.

Technology can be interesting, to say the least. The lovely agent apologized, comforted me, and handed me a stand-by ticket. I had just toured The Netherlands for about eight days for a student organization, crossing the country via train, meeting faculty and students, and delivering a *South Park* lecture. Exhausted to the point of delirium and wanting a proper bed, now I have a ticket issue to worry about.

At the gate was a tired person's worst nightmare: forty or fifty college students who just spent their spring break in Amsterdam. I love my college students but that many at once, coming from Amsterdam—that's too much for anyone. Sadly, and to my horror, the only available seat in the waiting area was next to two college kids, who were reliving the night's events as if they were the first to explore Amsterdam's sordid attractions. While amusing for a minute, eight hours of this and my head may explode. My sympathies to the cabin crew that day, who only get paid once the wheels are up and in flight. That has to be exploitation in some way, just not sure how. I may as well be boarding a flight that only serves Coffeemate and Folgers instant coffee because this will be my own personal trip to hell. I know I am going to be seated between these two and will have no choice but to hear every story retold in its supposed epic-ness. They'll laugh and improperly use the word literally four hundred times before my head 'literally' explodes. The passengers are summoned and I'm still on standby—first, business, then economy comfort, finally the back of the plane and every single college student stood up rushing the front entrance. Good riddance. I sat alone with my thoughts. Cursing the airline, hoping for a savior—any kind would do … I'd even consider a false god if there was a promised return. All the passengers are loaded onto the plane and I remain. I look around. They forgot about me. I'm ten years old again waiting for my parents to pick me up after Little League. Then as if all my prayers or complaints were answered, an angel appears, well not an angel, but a beautiful Dutch woman dressed in KLM's uniformed blue approaches me with a ticket in hand. She smiles and wishes me a pleasant flight. Confusion creeps in as I glance down towards the ticket.

So here I sit taking photos, downing champagne and orange juice, thinking about those two spring breakers. I wonder who is being tortured sitting next to them right now—another glass? Sure! Why not? Don't mind if I do. And that's where I am now: first class. A place I certainly don't belong but if I could stay, I'd probably never leave.

A man next to me snores loudly, eh, enjoy it my good man—this is first class. I take some more photos. The entire experience fundamentally changed my travel limit. Now, every time I fly, I do my best to get into first class or business. I still don't belong here, and I don't believe I ever will, but for a fleeting moment, I am in first class. But my advice to you: don't ever sit there. I've been dreaming about first class every night and it will not stop. It's an unhealthy obsession, to put it mildly. Instead, sitting in first class I decided to recount these lectures along with the (mis) adventures I've had while conceiving, rehearsing, and delivering them. My hope is with each lecture created comes a new chapter and with that, a new adventure, but for now the flight attendant needs my order: I'll have the white wine with my salmon dinner, and of course a coffee afterwards, thank you.

Extra Note

The reader will notice there are no foot or endnotes because the person delivering the lectures and engaging with a copious amount of coffee is a fictional character. You cannot footnote or source a fictional character. However, at the end of the book there is a bibliography of all the books referenced throughout the story and lectures.

INTRODUCTION

The shadows of my forthcoming events were about to reveal themselves piece by piece and step by step, when suddenly the iPhone's alarm pierced the dream and snapped me awake, ruining any advantage gained by the incoming premonition. 6:45 AM, an unacceptable time for a night owl but hope remains as the coffee calls out to me. But right now, the real question is: To snooze or not to snooze? Maybe I can re-create the situation, find out exactly what is on my horizon. An eight-minute snooze it is, a ticking time bomb for sure, the pressure cooker of choice in cinema and television. Either way, it's not going to work, too much anxiety. Dreams fold under the pressure of reimagining, at least mine do. Maybe this time it'll be different. Eyes close, nothing—eight minutes pass quickly, one more snooze? No, the moment's gone, I'll have to wait for the answer another time. 6:53 AM.

Time for work, but before anything, coffee is a necessity. When I make a cup of coffee for someone, they always ask me about my love of a French press. I smile, pour in one scoop too many, and explain it has NOTHING to do with love of any sort or what works better. Basically, the French press is a survival tool. I remember numerous blackouts in New York City over the years, while having "La Pavoni" or as I lovingly called it: La Machine. She's beautiful, complicated, and you wouldn't be surprised if she was also plutonium powered. Yeah, it's that involved and the machine was used every morning, always making sure to scoop the right amount. Weighing the grinds so that there is the perfect amount, one too many as always, but the extra makes the coffee just where I need it to be. There are books and articles on how to not make a mistake with your coffee and brewing the perfect cup. All I care about is getting the cup the way I want it. I slowly take the time to clutch the handle ever so gently, working the piston just right. Yes, I know what that reads like and I know what it looks like but I took more care in making this cup of coffee than I put into most relationships. What does that say about me? Even worse, what does that say about those who got into relationships with me? I've done this so often I could tell almost exactly how much I needed to make a flawless cup. I'm searching perfection wherever I go—La Machine delivers but I do wonder if I'm going all *Breaking Bad* on a cup of coffee. Are there others out there like me?

La Machine did her job, and she did it well. I loved the work involved, the care plus the exact measurements. Everything seemed to jive with the meticulous nature I had evolved into as I aged. But then a power outage, and this thing, this extravagant europiccola espresso machine of epic proportions sat in my apartment: UNUSABLE!

And, the stress that came with it, thinking:

"When will the power come back on? Is it safe? What will happen? Wait ... will La Machine work? NO. It won't!"

The panic sets in. I scrambled out to the neighborhood stores to get a cup of coffee. I was sure of the insane fact that Brooklyn has over thirty coffee shops within a few miles but wait—they didn't have power either. This is madness! What can be done? What was done before La Machine? What has happened to me? How far have I come with my fascination from that first cup while sitting with Professor Adler (who I was attempting to impress) to this panic mode I am in right now? How was I to know that cup of coffee would frame my existence? Have I lost touch with reality on how to make a plutonium-free cup of coffee? I walk into a shop and there on the shelf, illuminated by God it seems, only one remained: a French Press.

I pick up the French press box and study the foreign contraption. Does it need batteries? Does it need power? NO! You press it by hand—hence the name! All is needed is hot water. So as long as there is heat or some flame, coffee can be mine. Genius. Even during the power outage my gas still worked, so I was still able to have hot water. La Machine, you are now a simple paperweight that is used only for impressing people when having a dinner party. So, I'm now using a French press—for safety and sanity's sake. There's a bit of sacrilege attached to this, but if I were truly honest, this is about survival and when the power goes out, the French press will survive.

There's the French press all cleaned and shined. Ready to go. The coffee of choice, so many choices, are all sealed fresh in containers so I can have options over a set time. The containers are lined up, silver, suctioned at the top, it's as if I'm keeping a deadly chemical agent from being released into the atmosphere. Top care is taken here. More than most relationships, apparently. If only I could meet someone who understands the coffee's care as much as I do. I look at each container labeled with a date, and the sun's glare reflecting on one container. The answer to the morning riddle has been solved: This is the coffee I will have today. 7:03. Ten minutes have been spent debating on which coffee I will be starting my day with. The decision: "Uganda Bugisu Washed Arabica" from Crop to Cup in Brooklyn on 3rd Avenue.

The water boils and I'm finally ready for the day. The morning routine and the process of getting a day started ... knowing what's ahead, before the check of the first emails, messages, news of the day, Skype, instant messenger, social media, and anything else to distract from actually going outside. God this coffee is good. And no, I won't reveal how I take it. Black? With milk? With sugar? The Dutch call coffee with lots of milk "Koffie Verkeerd," which translates to "coffee wrong." Talk about a hint. Then again, the Dutch are quite direct.

Back to the morning routine—all the means of connection have to wait. My steady diet of *The Daily Show* and *The Colbert Report* is why I wake up so damn early, to find out if something is worth discussing and studying. What will their topics be today? They're the only shows I can watch more than twice a week. I like my mornings with Jon and Stephen—old friends I have never met. However, today seems different than other days. It could be the meetings, the extra office hours, or maybe that just before bed I read Hunter S. Thompson's November writings in *Fear & Loathing on the Campaign Trail '72*, where Thompson seemed to put down the Gonzo and did something incredible and seemingly unheard of: reported the truth about politics and campaigning. But I'm extra agitated at the morning headlines, I know it's not a shocking statement but still, something is stirring. Maybe it is the frustration my grandfather spoke about and my father confirmed later in life? Maybe we're all doomed to disappoint ourselves, and each other? Yet, neither of them did anything of the sort.

Everything in media is a scandal and scandalous, everything is a controversy and controversial, it makes me tired all over. From the president's statement on rights for a persecuted minority or a major policy blunder to the celebrity birth or nipple slip or some fashion faux pas—everything is treated as a world-changing event. The coffee begins to kick in and soon my thoughts go with it. How can a revelation that the CEO of a Fortune 500 company is stealing funds and a successful release of a new book both get the same bold letters, right next to each other? Who is running this website? How can Dick Cheney go on a promotional book tour and advocate torture and no one question him about it? And no, you shouldn't be over it either. Why does it seem that every time a whistleblower is in the news his personal life is attacked? Is he A or is he B? It's always easier to destroy the messenger than the message. Who cares! Tell me the story! Concentrate. "Ask the question, ask the question, ask the right question" dominates my thoughts during every newscast. Don't let the coffee overtake you. It was just outside of 7:30 AM when the caffeine began to take hold.

Part of me misses newspapers where the space was finite and the editors had to make choices. Now, the Internet allows EVERY story to be put on the front page—now it's just a matter of how high or low on the screen, but the room seems infinite. In a sense, there is no page two unless you want a specific story or category—wonder what that's doing to us as information consumers. Then again, the finite choices have a drawback too. And in full disclosure, I haven't had a physical newspaper subscription in years. Random thought—why is my iPhone in my bed? It's the last thing I look at before bed and the first thing I look at when I wake up. Am I in a relationship with my iPhone? Yes, the caffeine has officially put itself into fifth gear and I have to admit it feels good. But one more bit of caffeine and it would be too much, shocking the system into an uncontrollable and unstoppable rush.

Focus. What's on today's agenda? Preparing a lecture to present in The Netherlands, exactly two months from today and even though the deal was finalized weeks ago, nothing has clicked. During the Skype conference call, the organization asked for the go-to stuff: "Just make it 'American' and 'help us understand America more.'" And lastly, "Comedy is a must." In all honesty, the conversation was more helpful than that but that's what has stuck out in my head—America. Last hit of my go juice. Finished. During the conference call, I also agreed to an interview with their in-house journalist who happens to be passing through New York next week. He wants to watch me work and make an entire feature on the lecture and my preparation. I better have something for him; otherwise this is going to be a disaster.

The coffee was an ideal choice for the day as I watch Stewart on *The Daily Show* and how exasperated he looks after ripping apart Fox News, yet again. The poor guy, and I don't mean that sarcastically, he looks exhausted. The show's fighting something that will never change, that keeps spinning, turning, that won't stop—yet at the same time, Jon keeps charging and going to battle. It seems like a fool's errand, a crazy-man's pursuit of justice, tickled with a touch of insanity that makes us feel sane. He looks fried. No wonder *The Daily Show* airs only four times a week for twenty-two minutes a pop. My eyes drift for a moment at my bookshelf—all the mainstays are there, with some others trickled in, the bottom shelf is dedicated to the classics: Shakespeare, Dante, Cervantes, Twain, Marlowe … Wait! Back up one or two … I think I got the hook. This could work but before I can get started, I definitely need another cup of coffee … . Maybe the answer is within reach and closer than I believe.

LECTURE ONE: AMERICA'S JESTER

The Daily Show with Jon Stewart, and The State of Politics and Media

ONE WEEK LATER

The hook is there but re-reading Cervantes's *Don Quixote de la Mancha* truly is an impossible dream. Was it always this long? I read the book as a kid but nothing penetrated. I do, however, remember Sophia Loren in the film. I also remember that Johnny Depp and Terry Gilliam were supposed to make a movie out of Don Quixote, but the two had their film shut down after too many production issues. There's a documentary about it called *Lost in La Mancha*. I'd love to be able to break down the book further but there's an element of "get to it, already!" Stop stalling. Today's coffee choice was easy: Kobrick's, a family-owned place in New Jersey since the 1920s. I must admit, I thought it was Kubrick's, as in Stanley, and had to drink their most expensive roast on the off chance I would find the answers to *2001: A Space Odyssey*. No such luck.

The coffee isn't for the caffeine rush or anything like that. This is all about routine, rhythm, schedules, and transition. These four elements are essential in this all-too-distracted world. So, after a healthy debate I select their Sumatra Mandheling fair trade from Indonesia. I had it before and the word "smooth" came to mind. It keeps me focused, keeps me on target. Hit this benchmark, make this transition—stay on point, remain on schedule. Been drinking this brand a lot recently and the words have flowed. Once you hit a rhythm, why mess it up? Like an athlete who won't change his socks because he's on a winning streak, coffee is my streak and Kobrick's deserves some credit for the roll.

Worst part, it's a really warm day in New York and living on the top floor of a brownstone, while the views are beautiful, an apartment with east- and west-facing windows will get absolutely brutal in a few hours. It'll be an effort to just move around or to even think.

The buzzer rings. Who is here this early in the morning? I walk over and press the talk button on the intercom.

"Hello." I hit the listen button.

A garbled voice with way too much static comes over the intercom, "I have an appointment. My name is Olli Van den Bosch, I'm here for the interview."

It's today! The interview completely slipped my mind. I do a quick glance around the apartment, somewhat acceptable for company and too late for any real housework.

"Yes, yes, of course. I've been expecting you." It's so easy to lie over an intercom. "Come on up. Top floor. Just knock when you get here." I hit the buzzer just long enough for Olli to get through the two doors.

I put the second air conditioner on. One will not be enough—I got to move out of here. I put as many undesirable materials into the closet, fold a few shirts, and turn the television off. Then the knock on the door.

"Just a minute." I give the place an once-over, then stop. Who cares how it looks! Just open the door.

Olli is standing in the doorway. He's blond, tall, and just everything about him says: My name is Olli and I am a Dutchman. And I mean that with all compliments. He carries a Brooklyn Industries bag and wears a suit. He's going to be warm in five minutes. I would feel bad for him if I didn't have to suffer through this myself.

"Come in please," I say, inviting him in. We shake hands and exchange greetings. Olli glances at the apartment and walks in. We're standing in the hallway and I lead him to the living room/work space area.

"Very nice place you have here. The staircase reminds me of Amsterdam housing," Olli says with a hint of a Southern Dutch accent. "But those gentlemen outside the apartment—"

Great. I hope they didn't harass him. Then again, their harassment is usually only reserved for women. "Yeah. Sorry about that. I found this place on a rainy Tuesday. Olli, let me tell you, never look at a place when it's raining, you never know who really hangs around the apartment complex."

"Are they always in front loitering?"

"Yeah. I'm convinced these hobos were reborn on my street and not the Jack Kerouac *On the Road* hobo, where there's a mission without a cause or some 'raison d'être' but no, these guys are just characters with no character. Side shows without the show or a semi-interesting story to bother listening to."

"They seem quite interesting to me," Olli says as I invite him to sit on the chair. I sit across from him.

I smile at him, hoping to convince him otherwise. "If they were, I'd speak to them. I'm sure they have stories but one simply hangs out in front of the corner shop, all day. He has this long, flowing white hair, with a face too young to have white hair—I'd think something happened to him that's tragic but he has this look of dirtiness, like it used to be a nicer white, and he used to do something, now who knows."

"Yes, he was there on a bike."

"Of course he was. He's always there on that bike. Sadly, there's nothing memorable about them, nothing worthy. I really do wish there was." The temperature begins to rise in the apartment. I turn the air conditioner to high.

"Can I get you some water? A cup of coffee?" I ask, immediately regretting mentioning coffee because the Sumatra is almost finished. Remain calm. Don't panic. Grab a towel.

"Yes, a cup of joe, as you call it, would be wonderful." There goes the Sumatra, next time just offer water. Olli stands up and walks over to the wall. Hanging throughout the apartment are twelve framed political cartoons by Thomas Nast, the father of American political cartooning and a hero of mine.

I head over to the kitchen to make the coffee. Olli remains.

He calls from the other room, "These are quite remarkable. Are they originals?"

I yell back, "Yeah, the Nast pieces are all originals. I've been collecting them." I walk back into the room. "Been collecting them for about ten years now."

"Remarkable artwork. And they're in excellent condition."

"Yeah, there's a place online I order from; an old friend of mine introduced me to Nast's work and I've been buying them up ever since. It's certainly an expensive hobby to have."

"This one." Olli points to Nast's cartoon titled "Emancipation." This piece was released after Abraham Lincoln freed the slaves across the South. "Very inspiring."

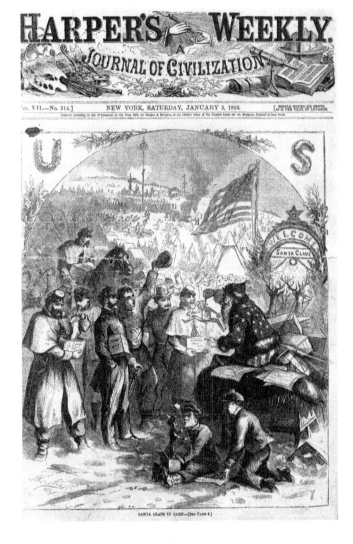

SANTA CLAUS IN CAMP.—[See Page 6.]

"Nast is pretty special. On many different levels."

"Seems as if you have a lot."

"I only wish, there are hundreds, maybe thousands. I haven't been able to get my hands on a certain Santa Claus print. I have this online company, Prints Old and Rare, keeping a lookout for me. Maybe one day with some luck."

"Remarkable."

Olli is unlike any Dutchman I've ever met. He's surprisingly friendly and adept at making himself comfortable. The kettle calls and I excuse myself as Olli remains transfixed on the Nast pieces.

I bring back the coffee and set it down on the coffee table. I give him all the options: milk, sugar, cream. Whatever he needs. He's already sitting down with a recorder and a notebook out. He's checking the audio levels; everything seems to be in order.

I motion to the options, and Olli places his order, "Black is fine."

I serve him his coffee and the interview starts. Olli hits the record button on the digital recorder. "So, I'm here to cover your process and everything else before the lecture in a few weeks."

"Yeah. You want to see the food prepared."

"Exactly right. My job is to understand how you create the piece you're going to present but also to present a human side to you. This will be printed in a few of the newspapers, mainly online, and this will bring attention to our event."

"Sounds like a plan to me. Fire away."

Olli takes a sip of his coffee nodding in satisfaction. "Wow. Very nice." I think: "I know, Olli, I know," as he clears his throat and checks his notes. "You'll be discussing *The Daily Show with Jon Stewart*."

"Formulating the approach took some time but the way I see it, Jon Stewart is a modern Don Quixote: slightly mad, honorable, willing to take on injustice … and Stephen Colbert is his Sancho Panza. I had to establish that, but once it was in place, the idea really started flowing. The rest began to make sense."

"Don Quixote. I must admit, rather embarrassingly, I've never been able to finish it."

"You're not alone in that, my friend." We both laugh. "Going to University in Amsterdam, I was taught that everything old is new again and we've seen this all before. I remember intense debates with a professor on this. They formed who I am as a thinker. This thought process allowed the lecture writing to commence as ideas are put on paper. There's a circular nature to art and criticism, to everything it seems. But I also see that there's a connection from the past through the ages to where we are right now. The past is prologue, for sure, but the past, successful or not, inevitably leads to a sequel, which leads to a trilogy—and we deal with the same issues just slightly altered, some examples being gay and minority rights, and prohibition of alcohol in the 1920s to the eventual decriminalization and public acceptance of marijuana. I could give other examples of course."

Olli takes notes and drinks the coffee. He's an excellent interviewer. He wants to interrupt, but knowing we're going to be spending a few hours or possibly longer together, he allows me to speak unencumbered by follow-up questions. I continue.

"The lecture takes its form from this singular thought, as the focus becomes *The Daily Show with Jon Stewart* and its impact on American democracy, media and politics, and the show's role in the 2012 presidential election. But to truly understand the traditions of the show, I needed to discuss some of the origins, and how the show became an essential part of America. One of those traditions is the court jester from the earlier European centuries—kings and queens would have the jester there to add levity to courtly gatherings. The jester, also known as the royal's fool, the joker, or the clown, was stationed in the palace to keep those in power entertained. We've read the jester from Shakespeare in *King Lear*, Touchstone in *As You Like It*, Feste in *Twelfth Night*, and to a different more ironic degree, Falstaff from *Henry IV Part I & II* and countless others in literature. Though there has been some debate on the jester's power, its place in history, the myth, is solidified in our mind. The jester's satirical targets were the clergy and the nobility, or as they were called 'the first estate' and 'the second estate,' respectively."

Olli's excitement is evident as he straightens up, though the heat in the apartment is beginning to takes its toll on both of us. "I find it remarkable to focus on the jester especially because Stewart is a product of today's media environment."

"Not sure I agree with that, because we had David Frost, who, sadly, recently passed away, and the show *That Was the Week That Was*. In essence, isn't this what Jon Stewart and Stephen Colbert are? The jester uses, as Stewart and Colbert do, a sharp tongue and quick wit to make those at court laugh. The jester's court was the monarch's palace. Stewart and Colbert's court is cable TV and the Internet. Openly mocking but always in 'jest,' the jester worked for the monarchy but the subtext of what he was saying was for the people, the commoners or the third estate. Stewart and Colbert both work for Viacom, part of a huge conglomerate but still mock the institutions that supply the stage. Stewart once said—"

I try to remember what he said word for word but instead, I go for my notes. Olli nods in understanding. "Stewart once said, 'It is settle law, satire is settled law. Governments have realized that jokes—if your regime is not strong enough to handle a joke, then you don't have a regime. Because it is not, you have to be able to handle anything—a joke is a joke. You may say that is an insult and they say, you know there's an expression, I don't know if you have it 'adding insult to injury.' Yes maybe it is an insult but it is not an injury. A joke has never ridden a motorcycle into a crowd with a baton; a joke has never shot teargas into a group of people in a park. It's just talk.'"

I pause to let Olli take some notes.

"So, the jesters rarely held back as they created a new perspective about the politics of the day by balancing humor and truth. They knew their place and the regime were certainly established, so a little insult would not contain much injury. The jester's point of view crossed the moat, penetrated the palace walls, and moved into the halls of power as they punctured the royal isolation bubble. The jester was one of us, a surrogate of the people, no matter their success or access—the same as Stewart and Colbert are. And as the scientist and author Isaac Asimov said, 'that, of course, is the great secret of the successful fool—that he is no fool at all.'"

"I must assume it is quite problematical taking a jester seriously without that knowledge, especially here in America with no monarch or royal family."

"America does not have a monarchy or royal family per se except the Clintons. The Kennedys. The Bushes. That is something similar, no?"

"I read once that all the presidents are related in some distant way." I laugh because the thought is so absurd that it has to be true! Olli continues, "But I do find it challenging to take a jester or clown seriously and considering the jester is all but extinct from our modern culture, how does—"

"Ah, but that's the thing, the jester isn't extinct but instead he's evolved from the bells and whistles on the hat or the cap n' bells we've grown accustomed to, to a suit and tie ready for power's destruction. However, the jester's antics, humor, satire, and honesty remain perfectly intact. The United States has jesters and of course, satirists speaking truth to power, as Jon Stewart and *The Daily Show* lead the way. Others are there but this lecture focuses on Stewart's satire but even before Stewart, America had a litany of jesters and satirists taking on the powerful. One of my first introductions to satire was a fascinating book: *American Satire: An Anthology of Writings from Colonial Times to the Present*, edited by Nicholas Bakalar. And contained within the anthology were several pieces by Ben Franklin!"

"I was unaware of Mr. Franklin's comedy." Olli interrupts me for the first time.

"Yeah, I never knew he was a satirist though reading his autobiography, I found him quite amusing. Franklin wrote numerous satirical pieces, mockingly writing a letter of recommendation, something a college professor has a wonderful relationship with. I have it here."

I hand a photocopy to Olli who reads it to himself, he laughs a bit. "Olli, read it out loud. It's hilarious."

"OK." Olli clears his throat. "'*Model of a Letter of Recommendation of a person you are unacquainted with*. Paris, 2 April 1777. Sir, the bearer of this, who is going to America, presses me to give him a letter of recommendation, though I know nothing of him, not even his name. This may seem extraordinary, but I assure you it is not uncommon here. Sometimes, indeed, one unknown person brings another equally unknown, to recommend him; and sometimes they recommend one another! As to this gentleman, I must refer you to himself for his character and merits, with which he is certainly better acquainted than I can possibly be. I recommend him, however, to those civilities, which every stranger, of whom one knows no harm, has a right to; and I request you will do him all the good offices, and show him all the favor, that, on further acquaintance, you shall find him to deserve. I have the honor to be, &c.'" Olli puts the letter down and smiles. "Remarkable. Absolutely remarkable. Even then."

"Classic Ben Franklin for sure because all a person wants is the name on the letter. Who actually reads a letter?"

"Right, do recommendations really matter?"

"I'm sure they do but this is just—every word is, it's flawless! Besides the 'letter' being quite amusing, the one satirical piece that I was able to relate this lecture to was 'Rules by Which a Great Empire May Be Reduced to a Small One,' where Franklin tears into the British Empire. In the essay, Franklin lists twenty things the British are doing to the American Colonies that would eventually lead to their demise and the colonies' secession. The prophetic Franklin writes the piece as 'how to become powerless' in the age of the British Empire. It's not a laundry list of grievances, as the piece's effectiveness stems from Franklin's restraint while tackling a difficult subject—tone here is everything. So, if you allow me."

Olli stops me. "I must admit, I didn't think you would be so prepared." Little does he know I thought he was coming tomorrow.

"It's been a good week." I pick up another photocopied page. "This is rule number eleven but he writes it in roman numerals to make it seem that much more important: 'To make your Taxes more odious, and more likely to procure Resistance, send from the Capital a Board of Officers to superintend the Collection, composed of the most indiscreet, ill-bred and insolent you can find. Let these have large Salaries out of the extorted Revenue, and live in open grating Luxury upon the Sweat and Blood of the Industrious, whom they are to worry continually with groundless and expensive Prosecutions before the above-mentioned arbitrary Revenue-Judges, all at the Cost of the Party, prosecuted tho' acquitted, because the King is to pay no Costs … . If any Revenue Offices are suspected of the least Tenderness for the People, discard them. If others are justly complained of, protect and reward them. If any of the Underofficers behave so as to provoke the People to drub the, promote those to better Offices … all with work towards the End you aim at.'"

I put the copy down as Olli is laughing out loud, his awkward laugh is like half hiccup, half cough. His laugh makes me laugh, and finally it subsides for the both of us.

I continue, "All of the rules are written in this manner ending with some form of 'this is what you're doing and why you will no longer rule America.' By the 1773 publishing date, Franklin's legend was already cemented and his record as a thinker well known but it was these twenty reasons that began the first moments of secession from Britain; Stephen Koch notes in the introduction to American Satire that three years later, 'Thomas Jefferson transposed many of the abuses listed in Franklin's inventory of ridicule into another list of abuses, writing not satirically but in the most elevated political discourse of the ages: The Declaration of Independence. If the Declaration is America's greatest piece of Enlightenment prose, Franklin's Swiftian raillery captures something essential to all the philosophies: In it we hear the laughter of minds setting themselves free.'"

I take a breath and wonder if I'm talking too much, giving too much away on our first meeting. Olli writes in his book and then checks the recorder, he looks to me. "Remarkable." That's his word for sure. "Franklin helped author the Declaration of Independence, that I know, but are there other examples—better yet, would this begin a tradition of jesters?"

"I'd call them satirists only because that is just their lineage. When you think of the jester, your imagination springs towards a type of clown. This new jester isn't a clown but their humor is there."

"Remarkable," he says, yet again. I'm now beginning to wonder whether this is actually remarkable or not. There's now pressure to usurp the word from his vocabulary and force him to use a different adjective. Who am I to talk though? I love the word "impressive."

"In the nineteenth century, Mark Twain, someone who I believe should be mentioned in anything American, wrote about the injustices of slavery in *The Adventures of Huckleberry Finn*, a favorite of mine—though I do find more of a comparison of Colbert to Twain than to Stewart. Christopher Hitchens would disagree with me. Aha! I do feel another lecture idea coming on! One second."

I take out a note pad and write down a few quick thoughts—Stephen Colbert, power, Twain, and Hitchens. "Sorry needed to do that. So where was I?"

Olli is about to speak but I figure it out before his assistance is needed, "Right. Twain. Well, during Twain, there was Thomas Nast, the father of American political cartooning, whose work you were just asking about that is hanging all over the apartment. He created and popularized iconic American imagery and took down some of the most powerful politicians in America, all by the age of 31. A short list of Nast's creations and popularizations were The Republican Elephant, the Skeleton Army representing an underfunded military, Uncle Sam, and he created the modern-day Santa Claus.

"You mean the Coca-Cola version?"

"Exactly right, Nast was from Germany, so he knew about Sinterklaas. All Nast did was look at his fat self in the mirror and he created the Santa you know today."

"Remarkable."

"Yes, remarkable. Nast was a 'King-Maker' who had such influence in American politics that if he preferred and supported your candidacy, the odds of your election were greatly enhanced. Nast was a man whose power is worthy of an entire lecture for sure. I have plenty of ideas how to approach that one. After Thomas Nast, there's the emergence of sensationalism with William Randolph Hearst and Joseph Pulitzer."

"As in the Pulitzer Prize, of course."

"You know, Olli, I'm still amazed, years later that even though Pulitzer helped get America involved in the Spanish American War of 1898, we recognize our best journalist of the year with an award called The Pulitzer. It's like naming a journalism prize, 'The Bill Kristol' for his honesty towards the Iraq War and Sarah Palin's competency."

"Who?"

"Oh, Olli, if only everyone in the world said that."

"I could cover so much more here—but a refill is needed. Would you like another? Better yet. Would you want to go for a coffee?" I should share more of my coffee with him but he hasn't earned it just yet. I'm selfish. I know.

"That would be wonderful. I'd love to see more of Brooklyn. I'm staying in the New Yorker Hotel." My sympathies. "And this very well may be the only opportunity I will have to come to Brooklyn."

2

Olli and I are walking along Fifth Avenue in Park Slope, passing several coffee shops along the way. I know where we're going so I only give the others a cursory and loving glance.

"You have quite a system for the coffee," Olli says.

"I call them my precious hermetic silver containers. They're designed to keep out air, light, and anything else to contaminate the process." Olli writes down what I just said and continues walking. "You know, we're going to walk for several blocks. If you want to take out your recorder, that's fine."

He nods, puts his notes away, and takes out the digital recorder. "I can tell you're a man who takes his coffee seriously. When did that start?" he asks.

"Years ago, living in Amsterdam, actually. But finding the right place to go out for coffee has been the most difficult challenge of them all. 'Difficult' isn't the word; 'disaster' is more apropos to my suffering. The small shop across the street made it too weak, and with little variety throughout the week but the convenience was its draw. Drinking more than once a day, you need to figure out what plan works best, and the system was expensive and inefficient."

Olli stops at Kos Kaffe on Garfield and Fifth Avenue. He looks inside. "No good?" The huge windows allow him to see inside. Almost every seat is filled and there's a line but it's moving quickly.

"Very good. Israeli owned. 'Kos' means 'cup' in Hebrew. Good owners. Good service and be sure to try the Costa Rican roast. I dig the windows, let's me observe the clientele. However, today I'm in the mood for something with a bit more kick. Have to show you a place like that on your first trip to Brooklyn."

We continue strolling along Fifth Avenue, passing all kinds of bars, restaurants, shops, and of course, the strollers. Olli notices the babies and nannies, "Is it always like this?"

"You're lucky it's only Wednesday and mid-morning. You should attempt to navigate the streets on the weekend as seemingly every two- to six-year-old is on the avenue complaining, crying, or screaming. If that image is not an ad for birth control, I don't know what is."

Olli laughs a bit, he stops at Goorin Brothers Hat Shop, takes a quick glimpse inside, but it's not open yet. A shame too because that blue fedora would go perfectly with the new suit I just bought—I'll be back. We keep walking. "You take your coffee seriously."

I can't help but smile at the thought. "I noticed that was a statement, not a question. But yes, my friend said to me once, 'I like my coffee like I like my satire: with variety, slight complications, and its history.' While I think there are undrinkable blueberry-flavored coffees, I refuse to be a java-snob, and believe I know what's best. I know what I like and what works for me. Those who believe only this coffee is best and the others are less than zero, I have no time for them. Coffee is the currency of understanding and anyone who attempts to be above that currency is not worthy of discussion. I guess that makes me a java-snob snob."

"I think it does. You said coffee is the currency of understanding and there's another coffee shop." Olli points to Konditori that hangs a Swedish flag that is faded from too much sun. A detail I always seem to notice even though I pass the shop every day.

"Yeah, this is a Swedish one, as if the flag doesn't give it away. I tried their roast once. Very nice but not the gear we're looking for. A pound of coffee is not always worth the same but the weight is. I've always equated satire and comedy with coffee—it has all different varieties, flavors, appeals, and uses, but no one is the authority on what is funny. It depends on timing, on you, where you are in life, the zeitgeist, or better yet, your own personal zeitgeist."

"My sister mixes her used coffee grounds with almond oil as a body scrub. Apparently, there are people who use grounds for enemas."

"So many uses. Some more understandable than the others," I remark with a grin.

We arrive at our destination: Gorilla Coffee on Fifth Avenue in Park Slope. We stand in front of the entrance, as the line is almost out the door.

"When my coffee dedication first started, there was great care taken in searching for an ideal shop, but not a 'perfect' cup. The odds of finding that in a neighborhood, Brooklyn or otherwise, is not impossible but is a fool's errand. Why bother even attempting that, when just something purchase-worthy will suffice? I started walking up and down the two popular avenues without going into any shop, but then The Gorilla called out to me. The ape on the front, daring you to walk in, and the inviting red had no hint of 'caution' or 'stop,' only 'go forward.' The gorilla's black silhouette only enhanced the mystery and the sign's colors led to the most accurate assertion—this coffee is heavy, powerful, and of course organic and fair trade, so don't feel bad for drinking it."

Then I think, isn't that the way—eat or drink this organic/grass-fed/fair-trade fare and you won't feel guilty about doing subjecting an entire race of people? It's rare to get a weak cup of coffee there. It's as if we've evolved to a weaker sensibility—hence calling the place "Gorilla Coffee." Peering inside, I know my decision to just visit is right; to get any meaningful work accomplished in the shop is rather difficult. The place is always so busy and rightfully so; the coffee is a swift kick in the ass. Sometimes it is too much. The long lines and the constant flow of people along the avenue make this a quick-stop shop, hard to work in. I tried all the brands and each one has their strengths and flaws but whenever I walk by, the gorilla calls me. Most of the time I resist, but today, with Olli here, I felt it was necessary. The aromas are intoxicating and my thoughts go to the lecture, which while I say it to Olli, seems to be more in focus than I thought. I'll start panicking soon. It's coming along, surprisingly well. Cue the panic button in T minus … .

We finally reach the counter. I ordered a small cup of coffee from Guatemala with a nice elevation and Olli takes the same. The process is fine (patio-dried) and with tastes of baker's chocolate, plum, and mango. I pay little attention to how the coffee's described, because truthfully, the plum or mango or any other flavor they describe escapes me. Wish I had a nose or a palate for that sort of thing, but no such luck.

"Elevation is my go-to and never cinnamon or something that'll overpower my sensibilities," I tell him. We go outside and sit down on the worn wood bench as the sun shines down. It's a distracting day, to say the least. The coffee helps me focus on things, while the entire borough of Brooklyn seemingly passes us by.

Olli takes a few sips nodding in approval, "You were discussing Twain and Nast, Hearst and Pulitzer."

"Right, but if we fast-forward about fifty years, other political cartoonists injected their satire and used truth to chip away at power. Nast's pioneering influence took hold of Herblock, Harold Maudlin, and Theodor Geisel, aka Dr. Seuss, as they tackled America's biggest issues without uttering a word. Using Nast's creations and some originals, the artists commented on 1950s America during the height of the Cold War and Red Scare era. The cartoonists challenged the government's motives and the legality of their actions during one of the most difficult times in our history. Around the same time, comedians and entertainers began what author Stephen Kercher would term in his book *Revel with a Cause: Liberal Satire in Postwar America* as a way for liberals to speak to those in power. The US had a conservative president in Eisenhower, and a conservative military outlook as the US was combating communism around the world. Leading the way during Kercher's age of liberal satire was comedian Lenny Bruce who pushed the bounds of good taste, conformity, sexuality, and race relations with coarse language never heard before in public. Bruce was actually arrested in New York for using raunchy language at a comedy club.

Olli interjects, "Wait! You're telling me a comedian was arrested in New York for using offensive language?"

I nod and continue, "Yet while listening to his material now, his work does seem outdated, but he laid the all-important track for those who would follow. This cause would continue into 1960s and the 1970s, and primetime American audiences were confronted by the Smothers Brothers' variety show. In the variety hour, the Smothers Brothers commented through song and comedy on all facets of the Vietnam War, the protests, and the actions of President Richard Nixon. They used comedy to diffuse a violent situation in America as the fabric was being torn apart by factions of dissent throughout the country. *The Smothers Brothers Comedy Hour* was groundbreaking in its obvious leftist slant but due to political, advertising, and organizational pressure, the show was canceled even as it connected to a generation of young Americans. And there is the emergence of iconoclast comedian George Carlin as he followed in the footsteps of Lenny Bruce by challenging the system, using language to explore and tests the bounds of reality by battling the Federal Communication Commission (FCC) and the notion of free speech. His use of the seven dirty words made it all the way to the Supreme Court in *Federal Communications Commission v. Pacifica Foundation*, where the court ruled to create 'safe harbor' hours when indecent words can be said on radio or TV with the minimal risk of children listening."

"I know this case, I learned about it in my law class. 'Shit, piss, fuck, cunt, cocksucker, motherfucker, and tits,'" Olli says, and kind of loud, too. Several nannies with strollers turn to us, giving Olli and me a dirty look. Get over it, lady. The kids are mere months old, they're not going to remember what was just said; I guarantee it. If only I could say that aloud.

"Well done, Carlin would have been proud that his influence crossed the Atlantic." The nannies take their children away in a huff. I motion for Olli to ignore them and move on. "So, after the rights of what can be said, or in this case, not be said during a specific time were established, we have *Saturday Night Live*. This show, another groundbreaker fueled by genius and drug use disparaged social norms, relished in their addictions, and satirized the presidency as they impersonated Richard Nixon, Gerald Ford, and Jimmy Carter. The show commented on the state of American politics during their weekend update segment to highlight the farce that had become American democracy, especially during the Nixon Administration. Though I'd like to discuss this further, presidential satire has its own place and its own lecture. Maybe if this goes well, they'll invite me back."

"I am sure a return visit can be arranged."

"Political cartoonist Garry Trudeau—owing his success to Nast, Herblock, and those who sketched the trail of success—illustrates the cartoon 'Doonesbury' and wins the Pulitzer Prize, scrutinizing Washington and national politics on a weekly basis. In fact, Trudeau's cartoons have been the target of the targeted as George H.W. Bush fought back against Trudeau for portraying him as nothing but an empty helmet that changed with what personality he was attempting to convey. In 2010, *The Chicago Tribune* and other newspapers banned 'Doonesbury' for mocking former vice-presidential candidate Sarah Palin, as Trudeau illustrated bits of Joe McGinnis's book, *Going Rogue*. In the 1980s, Trudeau joined forces with celebrated director Robert Altman who directed *Nashville* and *M*A*S*H*, and together they created *Tanner '88*, an HBO mockumentary. This was actually one of HBO's earliest forays into original content where the American electoral system was satirized. *Tanner '88* added a much-needed voice to the presidential nomination process by having a fake candidate interacting with real candidates on the campaign trail. What made *Tanner '88* unique was that it was satirizing not presidential candidates and politicians, but the process, political messaging, and the inner workings of what makes a candidate win or lose. Actually, a sequel was made in 2004 titled, *Tanner on Tanner*."

"Remarkable." OK! Now, I'm starting to get frustrated. Not everything is remarkable. I mean, I think it is, but I would never continuously and consistently use it. To say it's distracting is a bit of an understatement. Is it even possible that he really means it? "So every generation has their satirist or jester and their fight against those in power coincides not just with the time, but technology would play a role, too," Olli says, as he finishes his coffee. His eyes widen as if the strength is finally hitting him.

"Absolutely," I respond to him. "While other shows had some interesting thoughts, fighting those windmills, as I said earlier, wouldn't come out in full force until the 1990s as political comedian Bill Maher gives the television world *Politically Incorrect with Bill Maher*, a weekly television show where he fused politics and entertainment in a way unseen before and beginning a trend of 'entertaining politics.' Jeffrey Jones edited and contributed to a book called *Entertaining Politics: Satiric Television and Political Engagement*. Each week Maher would have politicians and pundits but also stars of stage and screen discussing the day's news. While not a completely 'new' way of discussing the day's news, the collection of diverse thinkers and influential stars made the show incredibly relevant, funny, and watchable. After some moves and a forced hiatus from TV because of some 9/11 comments, Maher now resides comfortably on HBO for his weekly show, *Real Time with Bill Maher*."

"Wow, this coffee is quite strong."

"It's a gorilla they've got as their mascot. Expect nothing less, my friend." Olli was just outside Gorilla Coffee when the caffeine began to take hold.

"One of the things this feature has to do is to find out your sources, your influences. We're hoping that the Dutch press read about you and want to come to see you. So, besides the lecture itself, which seems to be coming together remarkably well …" I should do a shot of espresso every time he says, "remarkable" or any variation of the word. Olli continues, " … you seem to believe that people understand satire. That's a bold choice especially if some do not."

"Absolutely, it would be. I understand that satire needs to be defined in a basic way. This is essential and it's something I'll no doubt do in the lecture. Regardless of background or lack thereof. Satire comes from the word *satura* meaning 'mixed dish' or 'medley.' This is why satire is used so frequently—it has no master and it applies in other forms. Terms such as broadside, caricature, invective, lampoon, parody, and travesty can all be used to describe it. Satire's tones can be gentle and affectionate to out-and-out furious to ice-cold and vindictive. The targets are numerous but all in all, it's always there to ridicule. The hope with satire is conversation and a controversy to follow."

"In University, I read Jonathan Swift's *Modest Proposal* where he 'solved' the food shortage and Irish population problem. I've never laughed so hard. It was remarkable when the professor went over the details about what was happening," Olli adds to the conversation. One espresso. "I never thought a writer could discuss such things and in such a way as he did."

I stare into the warm sun, remembering the first, second, and twelfth time I read Swift's *Proposal* and seemingly memorized, "'I have been assured by a very knowing American of my acquaintance in London that a young healthy child well nursed is at a year old a most delicious, nourishing, and wholesome food, whether stewed, roasted, baked, or boiled; and I have no doubt that it will equally serve in a fricassee or a ragout,'" I say with an awful Irish accent. "The limits are never set as a satirist stretches the line out further." I switch back to my normal voice. "As George Carlin said, 'I think it's the duty of the comedian to find out where the line is drawn and cross it deliberately.' He should have said 'satirist.' A comedian crossing a line can be through language or sexual explicitness, but a satirist finds the line, paints over the old and draws a new one that is curved, not straight. Another important facet of satire is making sure to capture the zeitgeist or spirit of the times. The references have to be immediate to have any type of resonance. It's why some people read or hear older satirists and don't fully appreciate the joke but do appreciate the sentiment. While Swift's *Modest Proposal* is disturbing in every way, it does not get the laugh it probably did when it was released. Lenny Bruce was a trailblazing genius during his time but now seems tame after the comedians who have followed him."

"I'm sure there's a text you would assign."

"Gilbert Highet's book *Anatomy of Satire* is one of the best, if not the best source to understanding satire. Highet's main focus was on satirical literature but his words can be applied to new satire, especially political satire. Highet laid out satire and what satire can accomplish as he said, 'it is the most original, challenging, and memorable forms of literature. Satire has the urgency and immediacy of actual life because it is topical and shocks with its informality and, of course, is funny. Highet saw the world in the most accurate way possible—that the history of the human race is a strange succession of light and darkness. Brief and exciting the bright periods usually are, long and stubborn the years of obscurity."

Olli is about to say, "remarkable," but I have to beat him to it. "Remarkable line, I know. I want those words written in calligraphy over the archway in my apartment."

"It certainly is an extraordinary line." Not "remarkable"? Did he notice that I was mocking him a bit? Maybe but it was worth it, as he now has two adjectives. I continue, "Using Highet, I began to think of today, and within these stubborn years, we have a new group of satirists who emerge to lead us back to the brief and exciting light. A good satirist has to describe, decry, denounce the here and now." Olli takes those words down carefully. "Several words fall under satire's umbrella: irony, paradox, antithesis, parody, colloquialism, anticlimax, topicality, obscenity, violence, vividness, and exaggeration. It's all useful for today's satiric creations. The truth is the best satire comes from frustration. Frustration with society, politics, people, life, love, sadness—everything and seemingly everyone."

Olli stands up and shuts off his recorder. "I don't want to keep you all day. So thank you for your time. I'd love to do a follow up but I understand if you're too busy."

"Of course, but you're not keeping me. I get to talk about satire and coffee. No complaints on my end. But I understand."

"Will you be rehearsing the lecture any time soon?"

"Actually, that doesn't come till later on in the process for me. But I do enjoy talking it out. Never had this before. My first draft of this thing was over two and a half hours."

We shake hands and I'm ready to leave when Olli stops. "Before I go, one last question—What are you after?"

The question stops me cold. I am not really sure if I have ever thought about this before. Olli knows he's asked a good question. He takes out his notepad and readies for my response.

"Besides an excellent cup of coffee? I would say I am always searching for answers. But I don't believe in tea leaves. I believe in coffee beans and the coffee grounds. I'd love to say the grounds predict the future, but that would be too bizarre, but if done right and experienced right, I was told they have the ability to definitely form the shadows of all forthcoming events. It's you who has to make out what the silhouette is revealing and what answers lie behind."

"Remarkable." One more espresso to order.

3

Olli called several times throughout the next few days, asking some follow-up questions. I kept working on the lecture. We would meet the day before he left for one final interview. He explained how important the piece is because the organization had never had an opportunity to interview their presenters in this manner. I sent him my notes and where the lecture was headed. He littered the page with "remarkable," yet I didn't seem to mind nor would I engage in the espresso game anymore. I want to sleep occasionally.

Our last meeting was at Four & Twenty Blackbirds in the industrialized zone, but they swear it is the up-and-coming Gowanus area of Brooklyn. Four & Twenty is housed in a white brick building and sells incredibly tasty pies but also coffees, lattes, and sandwiches. Everyone is always so sweet and typically enjoys their job or they're all good actors. I am early, as Olli was coming from midtown, and had no real estimated time of arrival. Sitting on the metal chair at the wood table, I look around the room, which is old with peeling paint but a charm perfect for the menu. I order a coffee and a slice of pie. I am not usually a fan of pie—carrot cake is my confection of choice—but Four & Twenty has convinced me to change my stance on the pastry. First, a sip of coffee and then a bite of the Lemon Chess pie as I look over my work, waiting for Olli to arrive. I read under my breath yet aloud, making sure everything is in order.

In 1996, *The Daily Show* would premiere on Comedy Central as a replacement for *Politically Incorrect with Bill Maher*, as Maher migrated to ABC, a trend worth noting, as this would lead *The Daily Show* on a completely new path a few years into its run. *The Daily Show* was created by Lizz Winstead and Madeleine Smithberg and was originally conceived as a political satire show, similar to the way it airs today but it didn't premiere that way. Originally hosted by a smug, sexist former sportscaster named Craig Kilborn, the show was more of a pop culture show with human-interest stories than the groundbreaking show it is today. Kilborn, as amusing as he was, did not have the intelligence required to properly lead the show in this direction. He had the snarky attitude, perfect for the 1990s, borrowing from *Saturday Night Live's* David Spade and his "Hollywood Minute" but Kilborn lacked the gravitas and pedigree to lead us through the disasters to come in the 2000s. A sexist comment later by Kilborn in *Esquire* magazine would lead (or not lead, depending on whom you ask) to the female creators leaving the show, and while the show was successful for

Comedy Central, in late 1998, Kilborn left *The Daily Show* too. In 1999, Jon Stewart was tapped as host and executive producer and the show would forever change comedy and politics.

Craig Kilborn left *The Daily Show* and headed to CBS for *The Late Late Show*. An understandable move for Kilborn going from a small network to one of the Big Four: there's more money and exposure. It's easy to forget that *The Daily Show* was not headed towards cultural iconic status then; if anything it was just another show searching for its place in the cable ether. In the beginning, the show's motto was "Same World, Different Take" and there was a photo of Pamela Anderson, the most famous Playboy model of the 1990s, and next to her was a bicycle pump. Clever, indeed, but nothing that would last; it would have gotten old quickly, similar to all the shows with that juvenile sense of humor. The show was funny, no doubt about that, but it lacked something. Just like this cup, it's missing something. Make no mistake—it's good, but I need more from it for me to buy a bag's worth.

With Kilborn out, negotiations began with Jon Stewart and were officially completed as Stewart came aboard in 1998. One of the immediate changes was the title of the show from *The Daily Show* to *The Daily Show WITH Jon Stewart*. By putting his name in the title, he immediately put his stamp on the show and it became his. The show would be Stewart's responsibility, his success or his failure if the audience did not come along for the satirical ride. The show evolved as Stewart's focus was more Highet than he imagined:

> When a satirist uses uncompromisingly clear language to describe unpleasant facts and people, he intends to do more than merely make a statement. He intends to shock his readers. By compelling them to look at a sight they had missed or shunned, he first makes them realize the truth, and then moves them to feelings of protest. Most satirists enhance those feelings by careful choice of language. They employ not only accurate descriptive words, but also words which are apt to startle and dismay the average reader. Brutally direct phrases, taboo expressions, nauseating imagery, callous and crude slang—these are the part of the vocabulary of almost every satirist.

All we need to do is replace "reader" with "viewer" and this is the new *Daily Show* as Stewart steered the show into the political world with the occasional pop culture story. In essence Winstead and Smithberg's original concept for the show, a parody of a news show, has been achieved but only after Stewart's arrival. Since the Stewart years began (as if anyone really remembers the Kilborn years), *TDS* has been mentioned next to such iconic names as Mark Twain and George Carlin, as the show has raised the bar for social commentary over the last decade. Stewart follows in the jester's lineage but he wears the jester's new outfit: the suit and tie, which seems outrageous for a jester. So to remind the people where Stewart's tradition evolved from, he occasionally dons a funny hat or spits food out of his mouth while reacting to a story. To Stewart and other satirists, they're in business because of the failure of something: the media, or what Thomas Jefferson and Ben Franklin coined "the fourth estate" as an addition to the first, second, and third estates.

The media, or the fourth estate, was supposed to be on the people's side, not working in concert with the powerful. The media and government were supposed to be in an adversarial relationship, not a mutually beneficial one, and this failure has been well documented throughout the years. When the fourth estate is mentioned, iconic names such as Edward R. Murrow, Walter Cronkite, and for a time, Dan Rather, and others who fought for the people represented what was best for the nation as a whole. With the creation and birth of cable followed by the 24-hour news networks, the trusted name for all has been lost. The trusted name is now reserved for the commentator who says or writes what the consumer already bought and believes. Rush Limbaugh, Bill O'Reilly, for a brief moment Keith Olbermann, and to a lesser extent Rachel Maddow, have all become trusted because they appeal to their core audience regardless of accuracy or integrity. Cable news has morphed into the organizations it covers as the pundits have gerrymandered the audience to their liking, similar to the House of Representatives, where the sides have been over- or under-represented to the public, causing mistrust and chaos. Outside of their respective bubbles, doubt lingers and mistrust consumes the other. This process is known as selective exposure where individuals search for those who share in their tastes and views. It's easier for someone to hear "yes, you're right" as opposed to "no, you're wrong." The big media conglomerates are in the keep-watching-us business, not the you-should-think-differently-because-you're-wrong business. The media world has created a required selective exposure, and in turn the citizenry has split as diversity in opinions has dwindled. Cable's gerrymandering has led to the problems we encounter in society today. This is not to say that society was perfect before CNN, Fox, and others, but there was a difference.

During the 1950s and 1960s, Murrow and Cronkite appealed to American sensibilities in a different way because there was a level of trust to these individuals that is dissimilar than their contemporaries. While there could have been a level of naïveté in the trust of these flawed individuals during that time, that does not take away from their revered status.

Murrow's rise was during World War II, while on the air for CBS Radio. He would broadcast to Americans (and others) every night with his in-depth reporting and comforting tone, and would end each broadcast with: "Good night, and good luck." The American audiences would establish a trust with Murrow as he saw them through the dark times of war. Murrow would then parlay that success from radio to television where he and his team created *See It Now*, a documentary television show that would become the forerunner to CBS's *60 Minutes*. Over the years, *See It Now* reported on the abuses towards migrant farm workers but most famously Murrow's epic battle with Joseph McCarthy. While Murrow gets credit for taking down McCarthy and his red-scare tactics, others were certainly involved in the senator's demise. Murrow was so trusted by his audience and entrusted to report the news in the fairest way possible that he was able to do the work he (or his team) deemed worthy. Murrow not only challenged those who supported McCarthy but also those who opposed the senator.

Murrow's fight with McCarthy has taken on mythical standing as do all media battles, as Thomas Doherty explored further in his book, *Cold War, Cool Medium: Television, McCarthyism, and American Culture*. But Murrow's place was cemented, no matter what "The Venona Papers" or Hollywood films have to say—it's cemented because in times of crisis, Americans gravitate to one person and that person becomes trusted, either momentarily or for the rest of their days, depending on the crises and the news anchor's career.

Walter Cronkite would take over the mantle as a trusted newscaster as he experienced a tremendous loss with the American people: the murder of a president. Cronkite was on air as the call was made announcing John F. Kennedy's death. The emotional yet stoic balance performed by Cronkite made him "one of the people," not just some talking head reading the news. His steadfast approach would endear him to the public, as he would be there metaphorically holding our hands and helping us live through and grieve the shocking assassinations of Bobby Kennedy and Martin Luther King, Jr. Cronkite's famous sign-off, "And that's the way it is" allowed him to tell the public this is the way it is, and they believed in him. Similar to Thomas Nast, my hero, who connected to the people through the tragedies of the Civil War and Abraham Lincoln's assassination with political cartoons, and to Murrow who led the people through World War II and the Cold War, Cronkite would utilize his trust to speak out against the Vietnam War and the turbulent 1960s and 1970s. A majority did not care about who Murrow was as a person or what Cronkite was like behind the scenes or off-camera. There wasn't a concern of: "I have to like him to listen to him" feeling by the American people. Even if they didn't like them as people, American audiences still respected the words they spoke.

This trust built by Murrow and Cronkite slowly eroded over the years as a July 2012 Gallup poll revealed that Americans' confidence in television news had dropped from 46% to 21% over the previous twenty years. Yet as the confidence has dropped, Jon Stewart has risen to the top as one of the most trusted news anchors in the country. Media surveys have shown that the overwhelming majority of men and women under the age of 35 list *The Daily Show with Jon Stewart* as their primary source of television news. Stewart's audiences are more knowledgeable about domestic issues and more informed overall than their counterparts who watch real news programming. A study in 2008 from The Center for Excellence in Journalism concluded that, "*The Daily Show* is clearly impacting American dialogue" and "getting people to think critically about the public square."

While Stewart's "trust" moment is interesting, if we could point a "go-to moment" similar to Murrow or Cronkite, it would be in his heartfelt, post-September 11 show that aired nine days after the attack that Stewart's raw emotion and connection to New York City came out. It's a long monologue but the end is when Stewart chokes up and bears everything. Play video:[1]

> Stewart: You know all this talk about these guys are criminal masterminds, they've gotten together and their extraordinary guile and their wit and their skill, it's a lie. Any fool can blow

---

1   Author's note: For playing a video, I will simply write, "play video" and transcribe the section.

something up. Any fool can destroy. But to see these guys—these firefighters, these police-men, and people from all over the country—literally with buckets, rebuilding, that—that is—that's extraordinary. And, and, and that's why we've already won. They can't—it's light. It's democracy. It's—we've already won, they can't … shut that down. They live in chaos, and chaos: it can't sustain itself. It never could. It's too easy and it's too unsatisfying. The view from my apartment was the World Trade Center. Now it's gone and they attacked it; this symbol of American ingenuity and strength, and labor, and imagination and commerce and it is gone. But you know what the view is now? A statue of liberty. The view from the south of Manhattan is now the Statue of Liberty. You can't beat that.

The pain and heartache Stewart conveyed would enable his rise to power as a series of assorted events beginning with September 11 through the Iraq War and Bush's reelection in 2004 put Stewart in the upper echelon of iconic American broadcasters. Like Cronkite before him, he faced the public and we believed as his heart broke for all to see. During the next decade, Stewart took up the mantle and became the leader of the newly emergent "fifth estate," a term coined by Syracuse University professor Robert Thompson. The fifth estate is an additional check on those in power and in corporate media. The fifth estate's vibrancy is owed to access and the Internet but what makes the fifth estate powerful is that it is an inclusionary organization, and not an exclusionary organization like the fourth estate. Any blogger can join and remain as long as their credentials are notable and their integrity maintained. While there is a flaw with an inclusionary system, the Briebart.com's[2] of the world eventually lose all credibility, as the system usually rights itself. There will be pushback from journalists who will claim bloggers are not journalists, but eventually if the information gets out and is accurate, why does the person's title matter?

The Onion, a satirical "newspaper" can report on what they deem worthy as they remain outside the mainstream by tackling important issues and bringing some much-needed levity to a tense world as their post-9/11 newspaper accurately predicts America's hopes, fears, reactions, and over-reactions to the tragedy. Years removed from the catastrophe, the work The Onion did is no less powerful. The articles are even more prophetic as they anticipated America's reactions and over-reactions to the event. In 2012, the website wrote a short blurb about America not experiencing a gun massacre, but just as that story was posted, a man killed several people at the Empire State Building. The Onion updated their piece with a simple: "Never mind."

The Onion continues to do incredible work day in and day out, although as with any satirical piece, there are ups and downs of genius. One other duo deserves a mention here, and will be explored in another lecture. South Park creators Matt Stone and Trey Parker have a firm position as the most financially successful and most difficult to quantify of the fifth-estate members. What makes Stewart, Stone, Parker, and Colbert unique within the estate is that even though they are

---

2   Check Andrew Briebart's story on Shirley Sherrod as one of many examples of Briebart.com's failings within the fifth estate.

on basic cable and they still work for a corporation, all of them affectionately maintain an outsider status, a rebellious one that is necessary to fall into this category. They truly are jesters invited by the king to mock the court, but the differences are that the king is a big corporation and the court is today's media world.

As one of the weekly leaders of the fifth estate, Stewart attempts to influence debates within the public square and the political world, but resides on the sidelines. His influence expands and shrinks depending on the issue, but his voice is heard. The interview format is one of Stewart's best segments in the show and it features his skills as a satirist. Jeffrey Jones in "Entertaining Politics" breaks down Stewart's interviewing technique by presenting him as a "lawyer" of sorts as he reviews Stewart's famous takedown of Jim Cramer of CNBC and the John McCain interview where McCain shriveled in embarrassment from Stewart's hard questioning. Imagine if you will a duke arriving at the palace who expects to be lightly mocked but instead receives all the scorn from the jester speaking for the people who normally would not have the opportunity. Play video:

Sen. McCain: The war was terribly mismanaged—it was terribly mismanaged.

Stewart: But then why not be honest about that? Why attack the people who question?

Sen. McCain: We are where we are now. We are where we are now. The question is: can we give this strategy a chance? I'm emphasizing a chance to succeed with a great general, and I think—

Stewart: Why should we? Why?

Sen. McCain: Because the architects of failure are ignoring this.

Stewart: If the architects that built the house without any doors or windows don't admit that that's the house they built and continue to say: "No, it's your fault for not being able to see into it," then I don't understand how we're supposed to move forward .... They say that if asking for a timetable or criticizing the president is not supporting the troops—. Explain to me why that is supporting the troops less than extending their tours of duty from 12 months to 15 months, putting them at stop-loss, and not having Walter Reed be up to snuff. How is it? How can the president justify that? How can he have the balls to justify that?

(Later in the interview)

Sen. McCain: Now you're entitled to your views. But the view of the majority of them is that they feel they're doing the right thing and their parents who have also made sacrifices, generally speaking, and they're proud of the services of their sons and daughters.

Stewart: No one's saying that they shouldn't be proud of their service.

Sen. McCain: And I'm proud of them too.

Stewart: Very unfair way to deal with this issue. It certainly is. It certainly is. What's less supportive of them is— Settle down for a second.

Sen. McCain: No, you settle down—that they're fighting in a war that they lost. That's not fair to them.

Stewart: What I believe is less supportive to the good people who believe they're fighting a great cause is to not give them a strategy, that makes their success possible—

Sen. McCain: We now have a strategy.

Stewart: Adding 10,000 people to Baghdad? Add 350,000, then we might have a shot.

Sen. McCain: I don't know that that strategy will succeed, but we do have a new strategy. That's a fact.

Stewart: All I'm saying is you cannot look a soldier in the eye and say "Questioning the president is less supportive to you than extending your tour three months. You should be coming home to your family."

The interview has plenty more to go but this absolutely devastating exchange ended Stewart and McCain's long-time friendship and seemingly derailed the McCain Express. McCain's body language and facial expressions said it all. When challenged with real questions that do not allow for sound bites to be answers, the argument falls apart. Stewart "asked the question" and did not toe any party line or allow for the spin to dictate the interview. These are surprising comments from a comedy show but sometimes a comedian needs to be a bit angry. When a guest is on and Stewart wants to ask more questions than the six minutes allotted for the on-air segment, he asks them to: "Stick around and we'll throw it on the web." MOST, if not all, agree to stay and talk to Stewart. The extended interviews are usually reserved for politicians or advocates, though an occasional movie star or comedian gets to hang around. During the extended interview segment, the show sheds its satirical edge and becomes a real news show, but the humor is present throughout. Stewart would claim otherwise, however, the questions are incredibly poignant, thoughtful, and penetrating. In 2012, Stewart interviewed Florida Republican Senator Marco Rubio who came on the show to discuss his book (of course) and the state of America. Stewart is always friendly to his subject even if he disagrees completely with the person. Stewart begins to challenge Senator Rubio two minutes into the thirty-minute interview. Stewart asks Rubio, himself from a family of immigrants, why his view is different from his Republican colleagues. Play video:

> Stewart: You have deep and heartfelt feelings about it, you have experience with it, uh Dick Cheney, uh has a different view on gay marriage than, uh, many of the conservatives that you would count with. His daughter is gay and she is—. John McCain has a different thought about interrogation because he was interrogated. And, it makes me wonder that, you know there's so much within the Republican Party already that is about these entitlements and these things that happen, is it that if you, if you have experience with something and you understand the complexity of it because you've experienced it, it no longer becomes an entitlement. There's a valid issue that needs to be addressed in a nuanced way. That doesn't seem to be the way the Republican conference generally approaches these, what you would call, special interest issues.

This is the right question to ask a senator! It's essential because it halts the red–blue state dynamic, and the "us vs. them" divide that's occupied our nation. Rubio responds that he wouldn't limit it to just Republicans, but it's just true in politics as he blames both sides of the aisle for rhetorical hyperbole blaming the president for being both the most divisive president and what's wrong with the culture in Washington D.C. He sees the president as pitting people vs. people, men vs. women, etc. Stewart cuts through the talking points jargon and presses Rubio on this innate contradiction.

> Stewart: If the issue at hand is that your sense is that the Democrats are the ones that are divisive, and the conservatives and the Republicans are just trying to protect themselves, it's hard to listen to their rhetoric over these past three and a half years and believe in their victimhood in any way, shape, or form. They have been relentless in their pursuit of submarining even the issues, like you yourself would agree with.

This thirty-minute-plus interview reflects Stewart's skills as an interviewer as Rubio was never let off the hook for his "straw man" examples. Yet they still continued to talk around one another with Stewart pressing and Rubio deflecting. An exasperated Stewart says, "It's so interesting because the world you live in is so different from the world that I am witnessing." Stewart presses on Rubio and the Republican dogmas and the audience receives a real education on Stewart's abilities and Rubio's thought process as the question turns to the economy and what caused the issues and how to get it back on track. Play video:

Stewart: And the Bush tax cuts of 1.7 trillion dollars.

Rubio: The Bush tax cuts did not create the deficit.

Stewart: But do you see what I'm saying? How can you do a balanced approach to solving problems when you just dismissed a large portion of the problem just 'cause, well, just 'cause.

Rubio: Because the way you defined balanced approach, no I didn't say that. You're saying that a balanced approach is both sides get something at once.

Stewart: No that's not what I'm saying.

Rubio: I'm saying the goal here is to solve the problem.

Stewart: Right.

Rubio: And to solve the problem, there's only one way to solve the problem.

Jon: Okay, right there.

Rubio: But it is!

Stewart exposes Rubio for a typical politician who claims he wants to hear both sides of an argument but to him there is only one way to solve the problem. And this only way to accomplish it is to listen to him and his party. Towards the end, Rubio remarks this is one of the best discussions he's ever had about policy. Within the interview numerous philosophies emerge that Stewart and *TDS* follow. To the creators of *The Daily Show*, it is paramount to hold politicians and the elites accountable for any deception to the American people, within that, it's also necessary to hold the media accountable for their complicity with those in power and/or timidity towards the truth. Or even within truth the idea of reality as he says to Rubio. Play video:

Stewart: It's a fascinating discussion because I feel like you and I live in separate universes and it's interesting because here's the thing, 'cause in general, I think you're a good dude. I really like talking to you and I like hanging out with you but we can't even agree on reality. Like it's so funny. I'm like "this water is good" and you're "this Kool-Aid? I don't know what you're talking about." It's like we can't agree on even the most basic, don't you think?

This is Stewart and the show's reality—they understand that there is an actual reality and they use satire to make people see the flawed politician's perceived reality. It's a difficult balancing act because when Stewart speaks to politicians he does not ideologically agree with, he makes an attempt to understand their perspectives. The frustration comes at the end when he says, "I understand your universe a little better and while we may not be in the same solar systems," he at least has made the effort. But for the show to be as successful as it has been there is a crucial balanced approach towards social and political issues, and someone needs to call out both sides when there is hypocrisy. In March 2013, Ohio Governor Rob Portman, an anti-gay-marriage Republican, revealed his son was gay and his views had "evolved" on the subject. Portman now supports gay marriage, proving Stewart's point about the empathetic and apathetic nature of the modern-day Republican. Within these stories and interviews is revealed Stewart's main goal to be truthful and funny, or as Don Quixote said: "it is my duty to redress this wrong with all my might." Quixote's might was his honor and sword, Stewart's might is his intelligence and satire, and this will drive him towards his goal, and towards the windmills in front of him.

4

Olli is lost. I haven't heard from him since he left for Brooklyn. Poor guy, stuck on the New York subways, but hey, I've been stuck on the Dutch rail system. If I could survive that, he can survive whatever is occurring below the city. All I can do is wait for him to arrive. I get a refill and debate about a second piece of pie.

The door opens and in walks Olli, sweaty and disheveled. He spots me and walks over to the table and sits down, absolutely exhausted.

"Your first New York train disaster? Let me get you some water." I get him two glasses of cold water. Olli drinks one and then the other. I could swear he's lost ten pounds since the last time I saw him.

His breathing is labored. "Were you chased by a pack of wolves?" I ask.

"The orange line was stuck in the tunnel and the air conditioning broke. We were stuck for thirty minutes underground."

He's a New Yorker now. To suffer through a New York City summer is an experiment created by some mad scientist, but add in the F train (or the "orange line" as he amateurishly calls it) plus no air conditioner, and local New Yorker status is instantly earned. Should I tell him that he probably could have died if he been down there any longer? Nah, no need to scare him. He knows how close to death he was. It's how New Yorkers feel every morning just crossing a busy street or as a train enters a subway station.

He continues, "I don't know if you have ever seen this but there was an Asian man clipping his toenails on the train." I can't help but laugh. I know exactly the guy he's talking about. "And one nail almost hit me in the face. Finally, this woman yelled at him saying, 'You shouldn't be doing that here, this isn't your bathroom! You don't see me peeing on your lap, do you?' Everyone in the train cheered."

"Did the guy stop?"

"I think he was cutting his last nail when everyone was cheering."

"Well, that's a story to tell all your Dutch friends and family, for sure. It's a real subway story."

Olli takes out his notepad and digital recorder again. No time to waste, so let's begin, "I wanted to start with more about *The Daily Show* and following the outline you sent me. I want to know how the show does what it does. I am certainly interested in the last few months with the presidential elections. We in Holland are genuinely confused on how Mitt Romney has even a chance at the presidency. Does the show explain that?"

"First get yourself a cup of coffee and some pie." I needed him to leave so I can enjoy his subway moment. He really does look like he's been through a warzone. I couldn't laugh right in front of him. With his back turned I let break into this huge grin and it disappears right when he turns around after ordering his coffee and pie. He sits back down. "What pie did you get?"

"Balsamic Strawberry Crumble."

"Very nice choice, I never liked pie until I went into this place." I open up my laptop, ready to present the videos and lecture to him. "So, to answer your question is to avoid one and answer the other. I can't nor will I attempt to read into someone's mind on why they would vote for Mitt Romney or vote for Barack Obama. Neither is my concern. But do they understand why they are voting for one or the other? That is always my concern. When someone has the power of the vote, why do they use it in the way they do, when it could be against their own self-interest? The vote itself to me is inconsequential. I think Obama will win but that's only because Nate Silver of *The New York Times* has a perfect track record and he said Obama is going to win. With *The Daily Show*, they have philosophies that are more like doctrines to follow and they are on full display during each and every episode. Their principles consistently shine during their election season coverage: they've won the Peabody Award for Journalistic Excellence in 2002 and 2005 and the Emmy Award for Best Variety show for a decade-plus straight. This election coverage segment from May 2012 titled 'Mormon, Mo Problems'—obviously spoofing Biggie Smalls' song 'Mo Money, Mo Problems'—illustrates what happens when Republican challenger Mitt Romney's religion, media bias, and public reactions mix with the current media environment. First, Stewart starts discussing

Mitt Romney's Mormon religion but also the media's and the public's reactions to the religion, which is still an unknown and foreign entity." Play video:

> Stewart: Our main story tonight focuses on the man who defeated Newt Gingrich and all other comers for the Republican nomination: Willard J. Romminington the Mitt. As you know, Mitt Romney is Mormon. (DASTARDLY MUSIC PLAYS) No. I don't; that's, that's actually; that's kind of unnecessary. He's Mormon—(THUNDERSTORM SOUNDS) There's, there's nothing frightening about him being a Mormon. (ANGELIC MUSIC PLAYS) Okay, you've overcorrected; that was an overcorrection. All right, I should have qualified that statement. There's nothing frightening about Mitt Romney being a Mormon to me. Apparently some in the Republican Party's evangelical base think otherwise.

The show then examines through videos the overblown and subsequently hypocritical attitudes from the Republicans evangelical base before Mitt Romney becomes the Republican candidate and then after. The audience also is treated to another staple of the show, Jon Stewart's classic Jewish humor. Play video:

> Rev. Robert Jeffress: Mitt Romney is a good moral person but he is not a Christian. Mormonism is not Christianity. It has always been considered a cult, by the mainstream of Christianity.

> Franklin Graham: Most Christians would not recognize Mormonism as part of the Christian faith.

> Bryan Fischer: What this would mean for the spiritual health of the United States of America if a worshiper of a false god occupied the White House.

> (END EDITED VIDEO CLIPS, AND BACK TO STEWART)

> Stewart: YES! You would never want someone in the White House who worshipped a different God than you. If I may, as a Jew—Mm, you get used to it. (LAUGHTER and APPLAUSE) But of course those comments were made while Romney was still duking it out with real Christian candidates. Now that a false god has triumphed, what are you going to do?

> (RESUME *TDS* EDITED VIDEO CLIP)

> Rev. Robert Jeffress: Given the choice between a Christian like Barack Obama, who embraces non-biblical principles like abortion, and a Mormon like Mitt Romney, who embraces biblical principles, there's every reason to support Mitt Romney in this election.

(END VIDEO CLIP)

Stewart: Simple math; I hate Barack Obama more than I love Jesus.

One of the most vital elements in the show is that whether Stewart (or the staff) is liberal or conservative—as vital as some think this may be—is irrelevant because the show still manages to go after left and right. While there may be more ammunition for those they disagree with, most of the time there is a balance. Within this same segment, Stewart explores the "journalism" being performed by the left-leaning media with regards to Mormonism as they attempt to keep with the anti-Romney narrative they've created. The show responds in kind, but also adds a humorous view to religious origin that should stop the madness that is occurring. Stewart runs MSNBC hosts Martin Bashir and Lawrence O'Donnell through the treatment for being reactionary journalists who are not doing an adequate job on reporting what really matters. Play video:

Martin Bashir: Mr. Romney has but two choices, he can either keep lying and potentially win the White House but bring eternal damnation upon himself; or he can start telling the truth.

Stewart: Yes! Those are his only two choices; or he can make the third choice, the one every president and politician has made from the dawn of time. Continue to profess your faith, whilst also lying. Being a Mormon has nothing to do with Romney's conundrum. You don't spit scriptures at him, although it takes a bold man to judge somebody by a book they are simultaneously shitting on. (LAUGHTER) I guess that means Bashir is not saying that Romney belongs to a fake religion and worships a false god. That would be Lawrence O'Donnell's job.

(BEGIN VIDEO CLIP)

Lawrence O'Donnell: Mormonism was created by a guy in upstate New York in 1830, when he got caught having sex with the maid and explained to his wife that God told him to do it.

Stewart: Yeah Mormons aren't the only religion whose origin story can be alternately explained as a convenient alibi. (Picture of Virgin Mary) You can just as easily say that Christianity was created by a knocked-up teenage girl who told her parents an angel had come down and magically (LAUGHTER, a picture of the Buddha) OR, maybe you can say Buddhism was created by some guy who fell asleep under a tree, missed work, and explained he was late because he discovered another state of being. Yeah, yeah, whatever, fat ass, get back to the deep fryer. And stop eating the inventory.

I look to Olli who had managed to calm down from his trip through hell, but now is laughing hysterically, filling Four & Twenty Blackbirds with a loud booming laugh that gives you the feeling of: "I'm onto something here." But back to the lecture:

This is an absolutely hilarious and perfect response to what MSNBC was attempting to do and Stewart sticks it to MSNBC and Lawrence O'Donnell. Stewart is not taking Romney's side or defending him in any way. He's simply doing the work that real journalists should be doing: focusing on the issues and cutting through the spin and distractions. Then Stewart finishes the segment by revealing the truth about policies from the Republican Party and to others in America. He's unfiltered and honest, making it so funny to hear. Play video:

> Stewart: You can't cherry-pick the worst aspects of the religion and then hold every member of that religion solely responsible for it. It's not even relevant. It's not like Mitt Romney is going to enforce policies that are unfair to black people because he's a Mormon. He'll do that because he's Republican.

The crowd cheers loudly because FINALLY someone has said what seems to be the truth. Whether Republicans believe that or not, or are going treat black people as less than—it's certainly the image with which they seem to permeate the public's mindset. But notice that Stewart doesn't care about Romney's religion, and contrary to the mainstream media, the show has NOT attacked Romney's religion. Discussing someone's religion in this capacity is a non-issue to the show because it's not the honorable thing to do. For Stewart, his issues have to do with Romney's policy stances, his messaging, party affiliation, and his hypocrisy from the past and into the present. Stewart, of course, is concerned about what Romney will do in the future as president. However, if Romney used his religion as other politicians do, or where it added to his hypocrisy, they would report on that. Analyzing someone's religion to find verbiage that could hurt his chances doesn't help the media's cause, it makes them look petty. To Stewart each religion has its flaws and strengths, so why bother reporting on the subject? As I've stated before, if Romney made his religion an issue, then that is a completely different story and debate. Attacking Romney was undoubtedly easy as Romney's penchant for flip-flopping allowed for *TDS* to use their method of "going to the video tape." And we'll continue to witness Stewart's methods: Saying something as if someone would NEVER say it, then playing a clip of the person saying the exact thing to show how they've contradicted themselves, as the show does here in a segment called "Bain Damage." Play video:

> Stewart: Romney's week wasn't only about why no one seemed to know when to throw his Bain retirement party. There's also the issue of his offshore investments and tax havens. Explain that.

(BEGIN VIDEO CLIP, "ROMNEY ON THE ED SHOW")

Romney: I don't manage the money that I have. In order to make sure that I didn't have a conflict of interest while I was governor or while I was considering a run for national office, I had a blind trust established.

(END VIDEO CLIP, back to Stewart)

Stewart: Oh. So avoiding conflicts of interest matters so much to Mitt Romney, he actually blinded the man running his money. That's … I'd like you to manage my money. Oh, and one more thing. (JON JABS TWO FINGERS) All right, so Romney's money was in a blind trust, I guess that's a pretty good excuse, unless a blind trust is just a ruse?

(BEGIN VIDEO CLIP, October 18, 1994)

Romney: The blind trust is just an age-old ruse, if you will, which is just to say, umm, you can always tell the blind trust what it can and cannot do. You can give a blind trust rules.

Olli yells, "Remarkable!" getting everyone's attention in the shop. I turn to the patrons and in an apologetic manner, I say, "First time watching *The Daily Show*." Everyone nods in understanding as the lecture resumes.

I tell Olli, "The crowd cheers because Romney's caught in a lie and *TDS* is the only one to catch them. Or possibly because this is what real journalists should be doing instead of focusing on religious dogma. And of course, Stewart is shocked about the comment, even though he knew it was coming, but the audience didn't (though if you frequently watch the show you'll see the joke coming). It's a classic comedian move—he sets the audience up and knocks them down. Or maybe everyone knows the joke is coming but is more impressed with the ability to find the older clips. As host, one of Stewart's gifts is his ability to explain things so everyone can understand an issue—cutting through the political spin and deceptive language. One of those issues is Romney's finances or his lack of transparency with regards to those finances. This became a huge issue through the campaign—Romney's money and tax returns. As Stewart explains, no one cares Romney is rich; most politicians are, but this is something else. Romney uses every trick in the book to pay as little in taxes as possible. But for people who defend Romney, Stewart explains the issue perfectly, first by using Romney's statements about paying taxes and then appealing to Romney himself using basic common sense." Play video:

Stewart: And that really is the point of this campaign. If you're a so-called job creator in this country, even if the jobs you create are in India or China, you are legally entitled to wonderful things like offshore tax havens and carried interest tax rates that are less than half the rate for normal income or 77,000 dollars in business deductions for dressage, horse competition expenses.

Yeah, a 77,000-dollar tax break to send your horse to the [bleep] prom. Here's what he doesn't get. Here's what Romney doesn't understand. Nobody cares that Mitt Romney is rich. It's Romney's inability to understand the institutional advantage that he gains from the government's tax code largesse. That's a little offensive to people, especially considering Romney's view on anyone else who looks to the government for things like, I don't know, food and medicine.

(BEGIN VIDEO CLIP, "LIVE CNN: CANDIDATES COMPETE AT NAACP EVENT")

Host: Romney says the following. You remind them of this, if they want more stuff from the government tell them to go vote for the other guy—more free stuff. But don't forget nothing is really free. It has to be paid for by people in the private sector.

(END VIDEO CLIP, BACK TO STEWART)

Stewart: And horse prom is black tie, mother-[bleep].

"This is where *The Daily Show* and Jon Stewart have found their way—a measured, logical, hilarious, sometimes vulgar but always honorable approach to everything, especially given the media's propensity for dramatic reactions and overreactions. Though there is a level of frustration about those windmills that will never stop turning, through this approach, the audience gets the crux of the show: You can't have it both ways but we can because we're a comedy show."

Olli gets my attention quickly saying, "Say that again, say it again!" He's writing furiously on his notepad, getting more excited as he catches up.

"The crux of the show: *You* can't have it both ways but *we* can because we're a comedy show." I wait for him to finish writing and continue, "Within that crux, the show is able to subdivide these thoughts: The political and media class can't cry foul now, when they didn't complain before. Republicans can't blame the other side while their side is out of power, then turn around and not take blame when they are in power, and the same applies to Democrats. As a person in media or in public life, you can't say something in the present that contradicts your past statements because we will find it and broadcast it to make you look foolish as they did with Romney's blind trust. This sequence fulfills all of Gilbert Highet's requirements for satire, as 'it is a blend of amusement and contempt.' However, that does not mean the progression of thought is forbidden, it means whatever applied to someone else must apply to you. At odds with this 'you can't have it both ways' philosophy is the game of politics and most operating in the partisan media. A majority of those involved within these two structures want to have it both ways as often as they can and assume everyone else suffers from collective amnesia. Sadly, most do suffer from this condition and are probably oblivious to it. *The Daily Show* would never allow amnesia to get the better of them, either from the media or a politician, as the show goes after President Obama and his administration for the Fast & Furious scandal. This is where a government agency allowed guns to be smuggled to Mexican drug lords, oh and the agency lost track of about 2,000 of them and two of the guns were used to kill a US Border Patrol officer. The Justice Department has refused to give the program's documents over to a committee to investigate. Before the committee could take further action, President Obama invoked 'executive privilege.'

"*The Daily Show* responds to Obama's actions with a joke about prima nocta—a law where a medieval lord gets to have sex with your bride on YOUR wedding night—as Stewart claims he was lied to by that executive. Stewart was trying as he said, 'to make this terrible story funny,' and once again, we have *TDS* doing the work of the media. Here, by holding politicians and both parties accountable from the archives of previous statements, he compares the hypocrisy from Democrats to Republicans." Play video:

> Stewart: It turns out that during the Bush Administration, executive privilege was seen by the democrats as a "refuge of scoundrels." A method of obstruction used for anything from keeping the Bush White House Valerie Plame investigation documents secret to preventing Carl Rhode, Josh Bolton and Harriet Myers from testifying about the 2007 Attorney's purge. It upset many, many people back then. Here's one of them chosen at random:

> Senator Obama, CNN Clip: There's been a tendency on this part of the administration to try to hide behind executive privilege every time there's something a little bit shaky that's taking place. And I think the administration would be best served by coming clean on this.

> Stewart: That handsome young high school senior is right. But if the current president ignores this young man's advice, the Democrats are now in the position of having to defend an executive action that they thoroughly denounced during the Bush Administration five years prior, which means we have no choice but to play everybody's favorite game, (on screen) "Differentiate Your Party's Assertion of Executive Privilege from the Previous Administration's."

"In this 'game show,' a device the show uses with some frequency, the Democrats are now going to have to explain why it is acceptable to use 'executive privilege' because Obama is in power, as opposed to when they strenuously objected to the practice when George W. Bush was in power. After dismissing the first contestant, he moves onto the next one." Play video:

> Stewart: Our next contestant, White House spokesman Jay Carney:

> Jay Carney (on video): President Obama has gone longer without asserting the privilege than any president in the last three decades.

Stewart: That's not an excuse. Come on everybody! Obama held out for so long! Executive privilege, it's like virginity. You hold on to it for as long as possible and then one day you're like I JUST GOTTA HAVE IT MAN! Just let me have a little executive privilege, just touch it once! BUT! Is that different from what Republicans said in 2007? Survey says:

Florida Republican Ric Keller: In reality, President Clinton has raised executive privilege five times more than President Bush.

Stewart: (buzzer sounds) Didn't differentiate. Same argument! Sure our guy did it and it's wrong but he didn't do it as much as the last guy. See we get it. You vote for the virgin compared to the slut who was in office before you.

"Always remember the crux of the show: You can't have it both ways. As politicians and people attempt the duplicity, the media's job is to prevent it from happening and they've failed. Stewart and his team continue to highlight the flaws and their exhaustion is evident throughout. *The Daily Show with Jon Stewart*'s job is to emphasize the duplicitous nature of not just politicians and the media but also the people who have been influenced by the two. It's holding onto these tenets and being consistent with their outrage and philosophy that the American people desperately need. The show receives accolades and Stewart has been hailed by individuals doing 'real news' for the work the show does. Tom Brokaw, an award-winning newscaster, deemed Stewart 'the people's surrogate.' *The New York Times* called Stewart 'The Next Walter Cronkite' and CBS News remarked that Stewart has great political power. But Stewart says his job is to 'throw spitballs from the back of the room' and that he's just a guy in the stands yelling things to those playing the game. But if Stewart is only throwing spitballs, the public's reaction has been, "Who's that guy in the stands with the huge spitballs and incredible accuracy, hitting everyone right between the eyes?" A lot of people want Stewart to join in the game and get out of the stands, but I do not see that happening. Stewart is quite comfortable where he is and his work is better served from the bleachers yelling the necessary obscenities about our world at large. So, is *TDS* a news show or a comedy show? Stewart considers *TDS* a comedy show and continues to claim that he's not a journalist, no matter what people say. For years, I disagreed with Stewart and his critics whose frustration was with Stewart's plea: 'I'm a comedian.' They didn't see this disclaimer as fact; it was seen as noncommittal cowardice. However, my thought process and argument changed when I looked at radio shock-jock host Rush Limbaugh. If people consider him to be an entertainer, then Stewart is as well. If Bill O'Reilly is a commentator and commenting on a news show, then Stewart is a comedian comically discussing the news. But when did this all begin? When did Stewart become such a vital entity in the media world?"

I pause as Olli checks his watch for the fifth time in the last three minutes. "I guess you'll have to see the rest in Amsterdam."

"Yeah. I'll make sure to come in right where the lecture left off. It was a pleasure meeting you and I look forward to seeing you again soon."

Olli and I shake hands as he walks to the door, "Good luck on the F train!" I tell him as he waves goodbye and heads towards the underground orange hell.

5

The lecture dates are here, the rehearsals have gone well, as well as can be expected. I read the piece from Olli. It was remarkable. But in all seriousness, he did really capture everything about the lecture and wrote up a wonderful preview of the preparation, but also gave it the human element. I was told the lectures are sold out. With this being so close to the election, it makes sense that there's a palpable excitement in the air—even if it's in Amsterdam and other cities in The Netherlands. The election or reelection of an American president is always on Europe's radar.

Overall, Olli said the relation to Don Quixote has worked even though he apologized profusely for not having read the book in its entirety. For me, it was getting comfortable with the lectures. That will come with time. However, that wasn't my main concern. I had to consider all the ways to pack the coffee and the French press, and nothing seemed to work. TSA rules are so confusing and the beans were going to be confiscated. With the lecture dates here and plenty of work to do, the last thing that should have occupied my time was how to transport coffee across the Atlantic Ocean. Transportation or better yet, smuggling, seemed as if it was lost cause because as I sit in the emergency row exit of this plane, we are experiencing a terrible streak of turbulence. The movement has gotten so bumpy that I looked at the person next to me, he looked back, and we both thought—"I'm going to die next to you, aren't I?" I think my deathmate's name was Jim. He wasn't a typical tall Dutch person; I can tell by how high his knees are when he sits and they're nowhere near his chest. Besides the fact that his skin was pale, he had dark eyes, dark hair, and the typical Dutch pronunciations that made him easy to identify as a Dutchman. I'm calling him Jim.

The plane drops a few feet, or was it a few thousand feet? Jim taps me on the arm, "Bet you never thought you'd die next to a goat cheese manufacturer."

I wasn't sure what he had said. I was too busy making a list of all the things I'm never going to do in life. "What?" I ask him and realize I never went skydiving.

"I make cheese from goats' milk," he says. As if that is the last thing I want to hear before—oh man, that's a huge drop. I can't take much more. I never spent a ridiculous amount of money on a pair of pants. Like an offensive amount that makes people question your sanity.

"The goats—"

"I'm sorry but are you serious? You're telling me about your goats." I never went to Vegas for a bachelor party. I'm going to regret that one.

"You look nervous. I thought this would calm you down. I make goats' milk cheese and I'm doing quite well."

"How in—how is that going to calm me down?! We're going to die and the last thing you think I want to hear is about goats and cheese and that you're doing well for yourself?" I say, raising my voice. I never played in a tree house. Why can't I meet a coffee purveyor on a long cross-Atlantic flight and she has samples for me and we fall in love and then die in a nosedive into the Atlantic? The turbulence ceases and the captain comes on the intercom apologizing for the bumpy ride and saying it should be smooth sailing from now to our destination at Schipol airport in Amsterdam. I never met a coffee purveyor or broker outside a coffee shop who wanted to pay me to drink their coffee.

Cabs in Amsterdam are overpriced. Makes sense for a city with one million bikes for 750,000 inhabitants. They need to make their money somehow. Fortunately, I know the route and instruct the driver to take it. I re-read some notes I made on the plane, occasionally glancing up to make sure the route is being followed. We arrive at The Movenpick Hotel named after an ice cream company, though there's nothing sweet about the place. It's an all-business hotel (which is certainly not a complaint) and close enough to Centraal Station to be considered the center. This is the "new" part of Amsterdam that has sprung up over the years. Amsterdam can't really build up so they build out—with its flat lands and bikes plus new tramlines, it's a good city plan. Though I'm sure there are flaws. Not even worth exploring, just an observation.

Check-in is smooth as I snag an apple from the bowl on the desk, and take my messages. The organizers and Olli want to have dinner before the lecture. I haven't had my coffee yet so I can't even start to think about dinner. I have seven hours till the lecture. My room overlooks the water and Centraal Station. It's a good size, super clean with an absolutely shit coffee selection, but I brought my own for these types of emergencies. An "I do come prepared" smile crosses my face, the smuggling was worth it, as I fill up the electric teakettle and unpack, unwrap, and put together my small French press. Everything flows. It's the one bit of normalcy I'll encounter this week. The taste is perfect; could have been the altitude. I'm ready for the day knowing the jet lag will eventually overwhelm me.

The lecture is ready and I chose the gray suit jacket with a white shirt and blue jeans. A less formal city, hence less formal attire, this is more Amsterdam's speed and style. Dinner was a blur, couldn't even remember where it was. I think there were four of us but it honestly could have been twelve. Don't get me wrong—I was coherent and everything penetrated that needed to, but all I could think about was the lecture and yet I was still forced to maintain some level of conversation. That's always the most challenging aspect of doing these tours—knowing you have to perform but dinner and drinks are first. Claudia, one of the organizers and a friend of Olli's, kept asking me questions about politics. She was different looking than most Dutch with her red hair and freckled skin. The other guest was her girlfriend, Annelieke, short hair, piercings, and tattoos. They were openly affectionate, but asked for permission first. It was sweet and kind of them, but made me loathe being an American abroad. Is this what they think of us?

They both saw my first lecture on *South Park* and gave their reviews. I was waiting for the typical Dutch reviews where they would compliment and insult at the same time. I think the reviews were

positive: I wouldn't be here if they weren't. They were both quite pleasant and very inquisitive as each had numerous questions about America. Talk about pressure. All I want is a coffee. Just like a typical couple they would switch off asking questions.

First up, Annelieke. "Why would President Obama not stand up to Republican obstructionists?"

"It's an election year."

Now it's Claudia's turn. "Why would the Tea Party be allowed to thrive in your country yet Occupy Wall Street fail?"

"It's an election year. Presidents tread lightly and follow safe ground during an election year. Obama wasn't going to lose Democratic votes so he can play it towards the middle for the independents." I really don't want to discuss this because there's no explaining this to someone who is not suffering from jet lag, turbulence, a case of the "I nevers," and who has to work in a little while.

"Why are Americans not up in arms about American foreign policy?" Claudia says, cutting

off Annelieke before she can ask her question.

"The Tea Party had some worthy ideas but seemingly lost its way when it became popular and funded by powerful forces. And Occupy Wall Street was up against titans and didn't have enough Goliaths, and too many Davids. However, they did change the conversation about financial reform and others. While it'll take a—" I felt myself rambling and I just stopped, smiled, and said, "Maybe the lecture will answer each question." Probably not, I was half lying. I never attempt or want to answer questions, because this is all theory mixed with some facts and fictions on the ground.

"Does *The Daily Show* have the ability to change things in America?" Claudia gets in the final question.

"*The Daily Show* is a powerful show, but enough to change the course of history? Of course not." Both look disappointed. I always felt modern Europeans longed for that cultural influence. They experienced or have seen the consequences after World War II with the Marshall Plan, so the sentiment is understandable. They love and hate American culture in Europe. Some have embraced it, while others rejected it. Amsterdam and the Dutch in general have embraced the culture.

We finished dinner early and Olli suggested we walk over to Bar Italia to order coffee and dessert. Sadly, we missed the Espresso Bar by two hours. Bar Italia's Gran Caffe is on the Rokin side or the front side. It's a bar with open windows on the off chance there's good Dutch weather—however improbable or unlikely. There are high wooden tables, stools, and an open space. It's after work so it's a tad crowded. If this were after the lecture, I'd grab a drink. All the classic Dutch are there—basically everyone is tall and that's all that registers. The bar is directly in front as you walk in; up a few stairs and to the right of the bar is a back corridor where dinner is served. Bar Italia's restaurant is a surprise—while the joint looks like just a bar, the dinner area is the real jewel. There are two floors with a staircase to get down to the lower level and diners surrounding the metal railings and wall. The ground floor is an open space consisting mainly of dinner tables and a huge wine rack along the wall. We're seated in a corner with a view of the back street. The conversation continues, and for as much as I enjoy this, I know it's only tonight. Tomorrow is a travel day to another city in The Netherlands and a few more cities to follow. Not until the end of the week do I get to meet the organizers and spend some time with them. Tonight, these are more single-serving friends except for Olli who will follow me throughout the country. The coffee is served and the jolt hits—this was not a blur. An unadulterated cup of exceptionally brewed Italian coffee.

Olli motions for our attention, "I must refer everyone to try the Sgroppino Classico Dessert Cocktail. It has Grey Goose vodka, Prosecco, and lemon ice cream. Best of all, the waitress makes it at the table. I think there's something about the process that you will all enjoy."

"I'm sure it's great. How about after the lecture?"

"Yes, of course." Olli doesn't seem disappointed but I do feel like I disappointed him. "I cannot wait to hear the rest of the lecture. I'll come in where you left off."

"It took some time to get together but it's done. Considering where it was to where it is."

"Like fighting windmills?" Olli smiles at me.

"Yeah, just like fighting windmills or surviving the F train in the heat."

6

During the lecture, I catch a glimpse of Olli walking into the lecture hall picking up exactly where we left off in New York. We're halfway through and the audience has connected to the content, laughing at the right spots. I think they appreciate the glimpse into the American psyche.

"With *The Daily Show*'s new direction and host, the Clinton presidency ending, and their 'Indecision 2000,' the show began carving out its cultural identity. They accurately covered the Bush–Gore absurdity by mirroring the frustration and confusion of the time as Stewart remarked, 'Calling this whole thing "Indecision 2000" was at first a bit of a light-hearted jab, perhaps an attempt at humor. We had no idea the people were going to run with that.' But it wasn't until 2004 where the real groundbreaking time for *The Daily Show* occurred as Stewart started attacking the broken structure of politics, media, and the 24-hour news machine. Stewart would remark years later during his Rally to Restore Sanity and I quote: 'The country's 24-hour political pundit perpetual panic conflictinator did not cause our problems but its existence makes solving them that much harder. The press can hold its magnifying glass up to our problems bringing them into focus, illuminating issues heretofore unseen or they can use that magnifying glass to light ants on fire and then perhaps host a week of shows on the sudden, unexpected dangerous flaming ant epidemic. If we amplify everything, we hear nothing.' End quote.

"Stewart was tired of the amplification and that nothing of use was penetrating. He did not distinguish between politics, media, and the twenty-four-hour news cycle; instead he views the three as engaging in a twisted symbiotic and parasitic relationship that is hurting the country's progress. That year, Stewart's theory was presented to the American people from outside the comfort of his own studio and into theirs as he appeared on CNN's *Crossfire*. There to promote his best-selling book, *America: The Book, A Citizen's Guide to Democracy Inaction*, Stewart seized the opportunity to repudiate the show and the two hosts Republican Tucker Carlson and Democrat Paul Begala for 'hurting America' and 'being part of the system.' He called the hosts 'partisan hacks,' but when challenged by Tucker Carlson on the questions Stewart asked presidential candidate John Kerry on *The Daily Show*, Stewart interrupts him and gives a scathing assessment of not only *Crossfire*, but also the 24-hour news networks." Play video:

> Stewart: You're doing theater, when you should be doing debate, which would be great … It's not honest. What you do is not honest. What you do is partisan hackery. And I will tell you why I know it.

> Carlson You had John Kerry on your show and you sniff his throne and you're accusing us of partisan hackery?

Stewart: Absolutely.

Carlson: You've got to be kidding me. He comes on and you …

Stewart: You're on CNN. The show that leads into me is puppets making crank phone calls … . What is wrong with you?

Carlson: Well, I'm just saying, there's no reason for you—when you have this marvelous opportunity not to be the guy's butt boy, to go ahead and be his butt boy. Come on. It's embarrassing.

Stewart: I was absolutely his butt boy. I was so far—you would not believe what he ate two weeks ago … . You know, the interesting thing I have is, you have a responsibility to the public discourse, and you fail miserably.

Carlson: You need to get a job at a journalism school, I think.

Stewart: You need to go to one.

"This unexpected critique continued for several minutes, and if you have an opportunity, watch all fourteen minutes of Stewart underscoring the problems with CNN, the 24-hour news machine and the show *Crossfire*, and that the thirty-five-year-old Tucker Carlson was wearing a bowtie. Stewart's indictment of the show was so powerful that one of the network's producers agreed and CNN canceled *Crossfire* a few weeks later. Sadly, I recently learned the unfortunate news that CNN is bringing *Crossfire* back with different hosts. Lucky us. But on to Carlson's counter-indictment of Stewart's lack of interviewing or hard questioning skills, which would lead to changes in *The Daily Show* set a few months later. The show scrapped the comfortable informal living room/couch staging for a large bean-shaped conference table in a drab grayish white, at which both Stewart and his guest sit upright in rolling chairs across from each other. This setup gives the interview segment of the show a more formal feel than before, like a Sunday morning public-affairs show. Dana Stevens of *Slate* questioned why change the set 'if it ain't broke' because 'the new conference table makes *The Daily Show* set a more serious place, closer to the world of news than entertainment; granted, the balance between the two is difficult to strike in a satire.' But this coupled with *The Daily Show* website and extended interviews enabled Stewart to alter the direction of the interview segment. He was no longer going to be a 'butt-boy' as Carlson put it; instead, Stewart will ask the hard questions and school Carlson on how an interview should be done. I explored the interviews a bit earlier but if you have a chance, watch these interviews in full. There are so many incredibly poignant interviews but the best are when ideologues stay and Stewart destroys some of their arguments using basic math. Scarily enough, Carlson was right! Stewart needs to teach a journalism course and do a better job at interviewing his guests, especially those who are on the other side of the ideological spectrum or even those he agrees with in theory and practice.

"Before the studio switch occurred, *The Daily Show* assault continued during their Indecision 2004 coverage where they had their spitballs aimed and ready to fire. During the Republican Convention, *The Daily Show* used one of their tried and true techniques: cleverly editing a speech for maximum effect illuminating the audience on what the speech was truly about. They savagely tore apart former NYC Mayor Rudy Giuliani for his excessive use of the September 11 terrorist attacks as the speech is cut down into Giuliani saying and constantly repeating the words: September eleventh. The crowd laughs and we cut back to Stewart adding to the fun by telling viewers 'sometimes there was a preposition' before the reference as the video cuts back to the former mayor saying, 'Before September 11, After September 11, Following September 11, Since September 11.'

"We all know these were not the only words out of Giuliani's mouth but to *The Daily Show* and many others, they may as well have been. This in essence was the speech and the convention: 9/11, George W. Bush, 9/11, Republicans, and fear everything and everyone else. And the 9/11 references would continue throughout the week as the Republicans attempted to own the exclusive rights to the 9/11 tragedy as New York's governor George Pataki blamed the Clinton Administration and others BUT never those in charge ON September 11. Pataki reminds the convention members of all the incidents that happened before 9/11 and he says, 'how I wished the administration had done something then.' Stewart then sarcastically tries to remember other 'warnings' that had occurred during the Bush Administration. The show cuts to Secretary of State Condoleezza Rice testifying in front of Congress haphazardly recalling a document's title saying: 'I believed it said bin Laden determined to strike inside the United States.' We cut back to Stewart smiling and the crowd cheering as he says, 'Yeah, that's it.' This is *The Daily Show* at its best—not allowing a politician to get away with saying something that while partially true that Clinton was president during several terrorist attacks, the major event can and should be blamed on the Bush Administration as well. Or as the show always does: simply go back to the archives to prove their point against what the person is saying. Remember, you can't have it both ways and while you're at it: be truthful and funny.

"This is the show's formula and it has worked for the past decade-plus but never more effectively than during the conventions and election season. In 2012, Stewart and *The Daily Show* continue their work on both parties as they reveal the hypocrisy from people on the left and on the right. First with the Republicans' convention in Tampa, Florida, *The Daily Show* reveals the biggest defect with regards to a major Republican philosophy that government should be run more like a business. During this segment the correspondents interview convention-goers from several states in the Union who all have the same mentality." Play video:

South Carolina Man: I think government needs to run more like a business.

Delaware Man: These aren't easy conversations to have but if it's not working, you have to end it. It has got to go.

Mississippi Man: Always letting the market decide is the best thing to do.

Jason Jones: Where you from?

Man: Mississippi.

Jones: Mississippi, whoa, whoa. Dead last in per-capita income. You are costing the federal government 20 billion dollars. That is, you know what, I think we're going to have to let the market decide.

"The rest of the piece, the show breaks down several states and how much the states are taking in and how much they're giving back to the country in taxes. Instead of pandering to the people like the other media outlets, not responding to statements properly or worse yet, reaffirming their sentiments by the audience via selective exposure, *The Daily Show* takes the people to task for their rigid shortsightedness. The correspondents reveal what the states are costing the US, and if they want to run the country like a business, well, the states they're in are the ones that are causing the most problems for the country. Wisconsin is failing, Georgia has to be let go, Wyoming should be kicked out, South Carolina is in the red, and West Virginia would rather discuss their hats than their debt forced on the American government and people. If the Republicans want the country to be run like a business, *The Daily Show* will treat them like a business. This is done to accentuate the slogan's hypocrisy as the people who are normally not used to justifying their beliefs now have to contend with cold hard facts. If the country were to be run like a business, representatives from struggling states, in this case Mississippi, Wyoming, and Minnesota, would be brought in front of a boss played by correspondent Jason Jones. Jones becomes a Donald Trump-wannabe and the representatives have to convince him why their state should be allowed to remain in the Union, especially if government is to be run like a business." Play video:

Jones: All right. You three are here because you are the worst three fucking states in the union. So we're going to have a contest, okay? First prize, you get to keep your job. Second prize, anyone want to see second prize? Second prize: CD, third prize is you are fucking fired. You, Minnesota, why the hell should I keep you?

Minnesota Woman: We have a land of 10,000 lakes.

Jones: Fuck you. Go water ski. Wyoming, what do you got?

Wyoming Man: Least population in the union. Wide-open spaces.

Jones: Who gives a shit—go fly a kite. Mississippi you think this is funny?

Mississippi Woman: Yes.

Jones: You see this watch? This watch is worth more than your entire fucking state.

Mississippi Woman: We know what hard work is and we're good at it. And we grow cotton and we're the most hospitable people that you'll ever want to meet.

Jones: I got to be honest, her state is a piece of shit and she is outselling you two. Take the CD (throws it at Minnesota), (to Wyoming) get the fuck out, you are fired.

"One of the show's irreplaceable and vital elements is when normal people are exposed on camera for their flawed ideology. In this case, social Darwinism, where only the successful survive, is given *The Daily Show* treatment, revealing how the philosophy doesn't work in an economic depression and applied to everything. Add to the fact that those who believe in it are the ones who should be most affected by the practice. What makes the piece so relevant is conventioneers' utter shock when they realize what is occurring. Whether or not they change their views is not the issue; in all likelihood, they will not but for a moment, *The Daily Show* takes away the power by those who have ingrained messages into people, chipping away at their carefully constructed reality. If only for a moment, the people pause and actually THINK about what they're doing and what they believe—this is enough for the show to continue. Satire is the comedy of shaping and molding with the zeitgeist not OF the zeitgeist. While satire can certainly add to and alter the zeitgeist, it works best when fighting the current climate. And always remember, the best satire comes from the creator's frustrations—it fuels everything.

"Not to be ignored, the show also visited the 2012 Democratic convention in Charlotte, North Carolina, and points out that while tolerance is what the Democratic Party is all about, they call themselves the Big Tent Party—turns out that's not exactly true. Not everyone in the "All-INCLUSIVE" party is well, all-inclusive. They claim to represent and want everyone in their party except, well, let them explain it." Play video:

Man #3: Except … Unless you own a corporation or if you're a hunter, a gun owner, white males …

Jason Jones: Really? You want to lose all the white males?

Man #3: They're a bunch of gun-toting hillbilly Tea-Partyers, that's all I have to say. Bang, bang, bang, bang, bang.

Jason Jones: Right. What jerk-offs, right?

Man #3: Definitely.

Jason Jones: How open are you?

Man #1: Well, open enough to include everybody.

Jason: Oh, really? Who wouldn't you include?

Man #1: We wouldn't include those beer-toting fakers down in Florida. The Tampa Convention guys.

Jason (narration): You know the types.

Man #1: Pot bellied.

(*Cuts of attendees labeling those "types" to exclude.*)

Man #4: Church going.

Man #5: Small minded.

Man #4: Anti-science.

Man #3: Bunch of Yosemite-Sam hillbillies.

Man #6: Wackjob, Evangelical, gun nuts.

Man #7: They don't wanna hear a message of difference and of hope.

"Weren't the Democrats supposed to accept everyone, no matter who they were and where they were from? One woman even believes that the Republican base doesn't have a clue about science or 'any kind of thought that involves more than two or three sentences.' The Democrats flaunt their all-inclusive mantra, but what about those who carry guns, a major social and personal issue in American." Play video:

Woman #2: We are the Big Tent Party and we will let most anybody in unless, of course, they're carrying guns.

Jason Jones: Right, who needs that 146 million people in your party?

Man #8: The Democratic Party, we don't stereotype, we don't generalize.

Grandma: The TeaBaggers generalize because they're very narrow-minded people.

Jason Jones: Right.

Man #6: This has been historically the party of tolerance.

Grandma: The TeaBaggers are the least tolerant group I have ever seen and they're destroying us.

Jason Jones: Can you say that more dismissively?

Grandma: … Uh. How was that?

Man #6: I've always called them Nazis and evil, even before it was appropriate, actually.

Woman #2: These Christian Evangelicals don't get it because I don't believe they've ever actually read the Bible.

Jason Jones: I have a feeling they have read it.

Woman #2: Well possibly, but—

Jason Jones: —No, more than possibly.

"We are all watching and thinking: Do they even notice what they're saying or how they're being presented? Of course, the cynics can say they edited the piece or as Bill O'Reilly once said, 'gerrymandered' the clip to their liking but this is a comedy show, NOT a news show. They're supposed to reveal humanity's flaws and deceptive editing, if it is needed, can come in handy. But here I do not believe it is used. However, the segment was created to simply to make a point about American culture and similar to the Republican convention where the conventioneers had their philosophy challenged, the Democrats had theirs. What makes this so important is Gilbert Highet's *Anatomy of Satire*, and the rules he set forth are alive and well—as *The Daily Show* holds up the satiric mirror to all Americans hoping to fix all the problems. The first step in the round to recovery is admitting there is a problem with your philosophy. The joke continues as the correspondents continue to make their argument that the people supporting the Democrats are not as progressive as they believe themselves to be, not as tolerant or fully invested in their philosophy. But all *The Daily Show* is really trying to do is keep with those core philosophies: you can't have it both ways and if you're being a hypocrite, they will call you out and hopefully make you see the flaws. The segment continues":

Woman #1: This is so inclusive. You know, we even invite the redneck freaks in.

Man #2: We don't judge.

Jason Jones: What don't they get about tolerance?

Man #1: I would never call a redneck a name.

(Later in the piece)

Grandma: The world would be very beautiful if we could just accept everybody's differences.

Jason Jones: Exactly. Accept everyone's differences.

Grandma: Mhm.

Jason Jones: *Everyone's* differences.

Grandma: Yes.

Jason Jones: We need to accept *everyone*.

Grandma: You mean, I should accept them? Is that what you're saying?

"By revealing both sides are at fault, *The Daily Show* is hoping this will bridge the gap created by politicians and the corporate media who have benefited from this division, and that the audience matures with that newfound knowledge that no one and no philosophy is perfect. However, Stewart cannot achieve this success and knowledge all by himself. He has the news correspondents to assist him, as they're the ones out on assignment taking Highet's satirical tenets to the people. All the correspondents possess comedic gifts that enable them to catch the interviewee off guard or make them feel inadequate during the interview as they ask the questions that the media does not, for fear of seeming partisan. They also possess the ability to improvise and keep a straight face while asking outlandish questions. The reporters look like real news correspondents, a suit and tie, a cameraman, lighting, a microphone, and a notepad—yet sometimes by the end of the segment, they end up more jester-like than anything else. The questions are sincere, hard-nosed, but with the jester's sharp tongue posing them.

"One example of this is when Aasif Mandvi investigated Florida's Republican governor Rick Scott who just instituted a law that all poor people who are receiving money from Florida taxpayers submit to a mandatory drug test in order to receive funds. The law was targeting welfare recipients because, according to Governor Scott, studies showed people on welfare were on drugs more than those who weren't on welfare. The bill passed by more than a 2-to-1 margin because of this evidence, which turned out not to be one hundred percent NOT true. Aasif interviewed one of the bill's sponsors, Representative Scott Plakon, who attempts to explain the bill and it's revealed that only two percent have failed the drug test and the program 'has saved the taxpayer, negative $200,000.' Plakon's main issue is that the Florida taxpayer should not be paying for people who are on drugs. As Plakon says, 'it's the freedom of the taxpayers that are working day and night, sometimes two and three jobs and they won't even do this simple thing to help their family, I just don't get that.' He also says anyone receiving money from taxpayers should submit to a drug test. Then, Aasif shows why the correspondents are so essential to the show." Play video:

Mandvi: So, who pays your salary?

Plakon: Uh, the taxpayers of the state of Florida.

(Laughter, applause as Mandvi looks at the camera)

Mandvi: I'm sorry, I think I'm going to need you to pee into this cup.

Plakon: I'm not going to submit to a drug test because, Aasif, Aasif is, has one in my office—

Mandvi: Uh, there was somebody who said anybody who's receiving hard-working Floridian taxpayers' money should submit to a drug test, and I believe that somebody was … uh, Representative Scott Plakon.

Plakon: If a law passed requiring legislators to do it, I'd be happy to.

Mandvi: So, would you be willing to be the first person to put that bill forward?

Plakon: Uh, well this year I have all my bill slots filled, but, you know, we get six bill slots so if you ask what's on the high priority of my list, that's not it.

Mandvi: So can I—can I say that you being drug tested is priority number seven?

Plakon: No, what I'm saying is—

Mandvi: Priority number eight?

Plakon: —fourteen months from now—

Mandvi: So I'm gonna put you down for … "go (bleep) yourself." That's what you're saying to the Florida taxpayers.

"The crowd, watching the segment from the studio, begins to cheer as Plakon answers: 'the taxpayers of the state of Florida.' Aasif looks at the camera, as if to say, 'I've got him!' and takes out a cup and tells Plakon: 'I think I'm going to need you to pee into this cup' to prove Plakon is not on drugs. Aasif doesn't allow the politicians to have it both ways and Plakon's horrified face says it all—he's caught, he knows it, and there's nothing he can do about it. By using politicians' own words against them while seated in front of them is exactly what journalists are supposed to do, yet that seems to be missing from the major media networks' news. This goes back to the power struggle—Plakon has the power to make this program a law and Aasif takes the power of righteousness away from him by not cowering to the fact that he can MAKE a law. However, far from satisfied from calling out Plakon's hypocrisy, Aasif goes after the 'kingpin' and architect of the bill, Governor Scott. In one of the more daring displays of satirical theater, Aasif crashes Governor Scott's press conference. And we are treated to another *Daily Show* staple: putting the politicians on the spot in public to see how they react, knowing a politician has to remain in control, especially with the camera rolling. This satirical theater allows for a bit of revenge from the little guy and Aasif accomplishes it brilliantly. Governor Scott allows Aasif to speak during the question-and-answer session and we get an incredible exchange." Play video:

Mandvi: Governor, you benefit from hundreds of thousands of taxpayer dollars every year, so would you be willing to pee into this cup to prove to Florida taxpayers that you're not on drugs—you're not using that money for drugs?

Scott: I've done it plenty of times.

Mandvi: You would?

Scott: I've done it plenty of times.

Mandvi: Would you pass this forward to the governor—we can all turn around, it's fine, we can all turn around—

Scott: There's a longer explanation I could give you …

Mandvi: Governor I hate to be—can you pee into the cup?

Scott: Excuse me a second—okay, just a second. I'm going over here. You don't get to run this. Gary.

Mandvi (voiceover): While we wait for the governor's urine, a federal judge has temporarily blocked mandatory drug testing.

"The segment also shows a clip from a local newscast proving its authenticity as the hysterical moment zaps all of Scott's power—not in the legislature but in the public forum, an important forum, no doubt. By embarrassing the governor in front of reporters and on the evening news, *The Daily Show* shines a bright satirical light on the injustices going on in Florida. Fortunately, the mandatory drug testing was blocked, but it'll surely come up again when the publicity dies down. The correspondents join Stewart as 'the people's surrogates' in speaking truth to power by embarrassing those making the laws. Once again, here we see *The Daily Show* having it both ways, making us laugh but also holding politicians' feet to the fire.

"In one of the most hilarious and surreal segments, Al Madrigal travels to Oklahoma to report on a bill that determined that life begins at the moment of conception between sperm and egg, and should have all the rights and protections of a human. Yet some in Oklahoma don't think that went far enough, as Senator Constance Johnson wanted to add an amendment banning the 'depositing of sperm anywhere other than a woman's vagina.' Her point is to have the men who are for this personhood bill to understand what it is like when someone tells them what they can and cannot do with their body. Of course as expected there are opponents of the bill, like Republican Senator Ralph Shortey, a pro-life advocate, who explains his reasoning for opposing the amendment. Here's a prime example of the work *The Daily Show* does: letting the politicians explain themselves in more than a ten-second sound bite and realizing that they hold a contradictory position to how they are voting on something." Play video:

Shortey: I think the Johnson amendment is an egregious attack on personal liberties from the government, and quite frankly it's embarrassing that this was even brought up because it's just—it's a ridiculous notion.

Madrigal (voiceover): And you're not going to believe this pro-life state senator's reasoning.

Shortey: One, it would be a huge free choice issue. Basically, the government is telling the man what he can and can't do with his body. (Laughter)

Madrigal (in disbelief): Okay. …

Shortey: There's not another individual that knows what's better for you than you.

Madrigal: And who are women to think that they can control our bodies? (Laughter)

Shortey: Right, just like who is a man to think they can control women's bodies?

Madrigal: Um … you?

Shortey: Uh … well, you know, that's the—that would be, uh, you know, uh, it's not about the government trying to control a woman's body. It's about protecting a life. When you have life inside your body, it should be the government's place to protect that life, even if it does infringe on your liberties.

"The crowd is already laughing, cheering, and applauding, as they know the punch line before it is deliver and add in Madrigal pointing at Shortey saying 'you' certainly lands the satiric blow to the argument. As an audience member or a viewer, you begin to question Shortey's thought process: How can he be for an individual's right to their own body then turn around and be a pro-life supporter and restrict women's rights? Shortey then explains what the Johnson bill is really about and what the real intention is as it will restrict men from doing—I won't ruin it for you, but watch the entire segment. Madrigal's performance alone is worth the view."

7

"Effective satire elevates the discourse and brings those in power down to the commoners and allows us to laugh at them. They're all jesters on *The Daily Show* and they are carrying on that tradition in fine form with an undefeated record against the powers that be. But every jester needs a target so obvious, so ridiculous, that they just cannot help themselves. For Stewart and *The Daily Show*, their villain is the 24-hour news channels, such as CNN, MSNBC, and FOX. Fox News is their favorite target because of its constant shredding and spinning of the truth. *The Daily Show* sees the media a two-headed monster feeding off itself, devouring those who watch it and splitting them into left vs. right and liberal vs. conservative with no room for nuance or understanding. That's not how we function. It's a new phenomenon ushered in by strategies of major corporations and businesses. Stewart points out the political and media insincerity on a nightly basis by deconstructing the 24-hour news coverage and the selective outrage machine housed at Fox News. As he said to MSNBC host Rachel Maddow during an interview, 'I think the brilliance of Fox News—they delegitimized the idea of editorial authority, while exercising incredible editorial authority. It's amazing. And they also have the game that they're all out to get us. Any criticism of them can be filtered through the idea that it's persecution. This isn't criticism, it's persecution. That's a tough distinction to make. Nobody likes to be criticized.'

"The brunt of Stewart attacks against Fox News may seem constant or more numerous than the other networks. The reason for Stewart's attention is that as Fox's unspoken narrative of 'anyone who disagrees with us in an enemy' becomes more and more obvious and detrimental to the country, the more Stewart feels the need to respond as only a jester could. But somehow Stewart sees Fox as ideological not partisan and *The Daily Show* just wants real, fair, and balanced reporting from the network. The way to do that, according to the show, is whatever was a controversy five years ago is a controversy today, and vice versa. His work attempts to 'articulate an intangible feeling that people are having, bring it into focus, and say you're not alone.' Chipping away Fox News's armor is the jester poking the hand of the king, not the king himself, though the king certainly gets his just desserts. This is where *The Daily Show* takes its rightful place next to the greatest of the satirists and jesters where its sharp and cutting commentary forbids the other side to change the debate in their favor. The show frames their argument in a way that seems to stick as Stewart becomes a modern-day Don Quixote for the modern media age, hoping to right the wrongs of the current times with his trusty writers as his lance, and Stephen Colbert as Sancho Panza following close behind. Stewart stabs at the powers that be, hoping to make a difference in today's world.

"To exemplify this balance sans Colbert was in September 2012 after the infamous 'Romney 47%' remarks. As a reminder, a videotape was released by *Mother Jones* magazine, which Fox News immediately dismissed because they don't like the 'liberal' *Mother Jones* having Romney say to a small group of millionaires that 47% of the country will vote for Obama and they believe they are victims who are entitled to food, medicine, and housing. Not surprisingly, this can and probably should be interpreted that Romney was calling almost half the country freeloaders. Never before in presidential election history have a politician's true feelings been revealed and in such a shocking and modern way. It's a breathtaking display of how far our technology has come and where our inequality is currently. If you would like to watch the entire unedited secret tape, go to *Mother Jones* online and watch for yourself.

"The absolutely devastating comments touched off a huge firestorm in every media outlet, but nowhere worse than as Stewart says: 'Romney Campaign Headquarters' as an image of Fox News comes on screen. Stewart calls the segment 'Chaos on Bullshit Mountain' and since the video was released, 'turd containment crews have been working overtime on Bullshit Mountain.' The show effectively splices together clips from Fox News's hosts reacting to the damaging videotape." Play video:

Hannity: Keep in mind it was posted by a left-wing website.

O'Reilly: Mother J—Mother Jones, by the way, put this tape out.

Male #1: Mother Jones, the magazine no one reads.

Male #2: We're getting word that Jimmy Carter's grandson might have played an instrumental role in getting this video.

Stewart: Oh, my god! Your campaign got blown up by Jimmy Carter's grandson? Oh, the Habitat for Humanity! So, word one from Bullshit Mountain is, well, yeah, he said it, but you only found out about it because of people that are … We don't … like.

"A common Fox News maneuver and plenty of other outlets: attack the messenger and not the message itself. This is certainly an effective tool to get public opinion on your side and away from the issue at hand. It's much easier and more powerful to attack the messenger than the message. This technique is not reserved for one side or the other—it's common business practice. When Michael Moore released his documentary *Sicko*, some questioned why a man who is overweight is discussing health care. Or focusing on WikiLeaks's founder Julian Assange's background and life story as opposed to what the leaks contained and the information that was in them. *The Daily Show* segment continues with the show's deconstruction of Fox's narrative as the network attempts to spin the Romney statements, saying it's a dirty liberal smear and the worst type of politics. The hope is if the spin works, this will give Romney an edge against Obama. And those on the network are seemingly willing to say anything to make this happen. Once again using a Fox News video montage to illustrate its point about the turd containment crew's work." Play video:

Hannity: This is factually accurate, what Romney is saying.

O'Reilly: If I'm Governor Romney, I'd run with this all day long.

Female: It was the truth.

Host #1: He's a boss that says the truth, but the truth often hurts.

Host #2: I think this will be seen as a win for Romney.

Stewart: Let me—let me sum up the message from Bullshit Mountain, if I may. This inartfully stated dirty liberal smear is a truthful expression of Romney's political philosophy and it is a winner. Let me tell you something, you don't summit Bullshit Mountain unless you know your way around a turd or two.

"This is Fox News desperately trying to change the discourse by swinging the pendulum to Romney's side. Then Stewart cuts to other Fox News shows as they all say we're harping on a videotape because no one wants to talk about the serious issues afflicting our country. So the show cuts to the same day of Fox News's coverage where they 'uncover' an audio tape from Obama discussing the redistribution of wealth. To Fox, it's now Obama's turn to be haunted by something he said, to which Stewart responds by asking, 'Are there NO rules on Bullshit Mountain?' Stewart continues to charge at Fox News, not because he is anti-Republican or against conservatives. No, Stewart's anger stems from Fox News's lack of honor, as he watched the 'turd containment crews" foolish endeavor to spin Romney's statements and distract the electorate in any way possible. It turns out the Obama tape was made in 1998 but the Romney video was made in May 2012. Fox News and Sean Hannity attempt to dismiss that by spinning time and space because the Romney tape was from 'WAYYYYYYY back in May,' so we should not take it seriously. But fortunately Stewart is on the case, and in classic satirical fashion, he demonstrates Hannity's absurdity." Play video:

Stewart: Oh! This video is from WAY back in May. May. Oh my god that was like before June. Who even remembers May? "Grandfather, may I sit on your knee and hear you tell tales of what life was like way back in May?" (Using an old man's voice) "Well Timmy ... I ... hold on. Timmy hold on. I remember like it was yesterday. The iPhone 5 was but a glimmer in the iPhone 4's eyes. It was an incredible time."

"Yes, Stewart is poking fun but you can see his exhaustion, his frustration, like Don Quixote fighting windmills that will never stop spinning and believe me when I tell you: Stewart and *The Daily Show* will never stop fighting. But Stewart feels like he has to respond to statements that are made by Fox News. He does the same when the other networks fail but Fox seems to do it more often and with more audacity than the other networks. As Fox News continues to spin the numbers in their containment, the network reveals that 49% of the American population is on some kind of handout by the government and Obama enabled all of this. Stewart jumps on his valiant steed, grabs his shield and lance, and charges at the windmill armed with the weapons needed to stop it from spinning. In this final bit, Stewart shows why he becomes that trusted voice in America. All the work he does leads up to this section. He breaks down the barriers and cuts through the talk like no one ever has. Like a lawyer making his case, he finally appeals to the jury or a Don Quixote convincing not just Sancho but everyone to join his quest, Stewart has given his audience the knowledge needed not just to make their own decision but to understand that this is more than just talk, spin, or distraction; what he is saying is truth. The jesters of old would be proud." Play video:

Stewart: This is the core of Bullshit Mountain. The forty-nine percent entitlement society Obama enables. That is the core of the bullshit nation fiction. That somehow, only since Obama, the half of Americans who love this country and work hard and are good have had the fruits of their labor seized and handed over to the half of this nation that is lazy and dependent and the opposite of good—I'm sure there's a better term for that. Now in that 49% Hannity is including those on social security and Medicare or as I like to call them: his audience. DEMOGRAPHIC TV AUDIENCE SLAM! But perhaps Mr. Hannity is understating the problem, for there are many more of those on the government dole than even his 49% accounts for. Like those welfare queens at Exxon Mobil, AT&T, GE, and two hundred fifty corporations that from 2008 to 2010 got nearly a quarter trillion in federal tax subsidies. *(Graphic of the tax subsidies)* Although, to be fair, at least Exxon Mobil and AT&T give us back cheap gas and reliable cell phone service. Or how about this? Here's one: The Wall Street firms who are given access to the discount borrowing window at the federal reserves. Or the five billion in direct federal payments to America's moocher farmers or the incredible tax breaks the government gives the investor class whose money is taxed at a capital gains rate of 15%, as opposed to ordinary having-a-job income, which can be taxed up to 35%. Boy I wish we had a poster boy for that element of the moochocracy. (Picture of Romney pops up) Oh right. In 2010, Governor Romney had an adjusted gross income of 21.6 million dollars yet paid only 3 million dollars in federal income tax or 13.9%. Without the preferential investor tax code, Romney would have paid 7.56 million dollars of government subsidy of four and a half million dollars. Or to put that absolutely fair tax break, given to a job creator, in moocher-class dependency terms, enough food stamps to feed Mr. Romney through the year 4870. By the way, that's no bullshit that's the math. The biggest problem with the denizens of Bullshit Mountain is they act like their shit don't stink. If they have success, they built it; if they fail, the government ruined it for them. If they get a break, they deserve it; if you get a break, it's a handout and an entitlement. It's a baffling, willfully blind cognitive dissonance best summed up by their head coach in what is perhaps my favorite sound bite of all.

Actor Craig T. Nelson on *The Glenn Beck Show*: I've been on welfare and food stamps. Anybody help me out? No.

"That Mr. Nelson of *Coach* does not realize welfare and food stamps ARE helping people out gets to the core of the problem! Some people simply do not understand elements of what government does and how it functions. Stewart uses the clip to tear away Fox News's entire agenda piece by piece but he isn't ONLY anti-Fox, there are other windmills spinning as he attacks other news outlets if he feels that they are failing. CNN can certainly attest to that!

"But Stewart's greatest victory was in December 2010, when the show criticized Congress and the media for the September 11th Health Care Bill known as 'The Zadroga Bill,' named for fallen policeman James Zadroga. This is a bill that would give all 9/11 first responders health care for working at Ground Zero. The media didn't cover the story enough because apparently The Beatles were released on iTunes that week so they had other priorities. Congress had not passed the bill after eight years and the only news service to cover the story was al Jazeera! Or as Stewart reminds us and them declaring, 'you got out-scooped by the network Osama bin Laden sends his mix tapes to!' Stewart, born in New Jersey but very much a New Yorker, took this as a personal insult to the heroes of 9/11. He held the media and Congress to blame for not passing what he called 'the no-brainer act of 2010.' For one week, Stewart used his power as host to eviscerate the media and the Republicans who were holding up the bill and called them out by name to highlight their duplicity as they cared more about tax cuts for the wealthy than about 9/11 first responders' health. That week he wasn't throwing spitballs, these were grenades and they were doing damage. This was about real honor and righting an egregious wrong as he and most of the country agreed. On one of the last segments of the year, Stewart interviewed four 9/11 first responders who are all suffering from terminal cancer to give a face to the tragedy—a common trick used by all the other media outlets to garner sympathy for a cause. Stewart talks to them about how they are feeling, what they think of the media and Congress, and then reveals to everyone why he's truly an honorable person by apologizing for something he had nothing to do with. It's an honest moment and reflected Brokaw's sentiment when he said that Stewart is the people's surrogate. A few days later, due in large part to *The Daily Show*'s work, and the media's newfound coverage of the issue, the Zadroga Bill was passed. A few weeks after, the 9/11 Memorial Fund named Stewart to their board because of his advocacy on the Zadroga Bill. It was the zenith of Stewart's power affecting legislation and calling out the hypocrisy of those who give only lip service to 9/11 and all that it entails. Stewart's ascent to the throne of most trusted newsman occurred in the era of Republican dominance in government, and a time when dissent was stifled. But as the US has emerged from that time period, Stewart has managed to hold the Obama Administration to the same standard as the Bush Administration, especially with regards to the 'war on terror.' Stewart has criticized the Obama Administration's NSA wire-tapping program, the controversial 'kill list' of suspected terrorists by drone strike, and Obama's healthcare and stimulus plan. In an interview with Obama in 2010, Stewart questions Obama's claim that his administration has 'done things that some folks don't even know about.' A surprised Stewart responds: 'what have you done that we don't know about? Are you planning a surprise party for us, filled with jobs and health care?' But even with this critique, Stewart supports Obama, as he did in 2008 when Obama won the youth vote by a 33% margin, and a majority 18- to 35-year-olds watch *The Daily Show* for news and information. So Stewart certainly has influence. Stewart plays an important role as a media watchdog and a jester, but he will not openly support a candidate, because once he does that, he is no longer the jester, he is part of the media, and his outside status changed. If that happens, Stewart wouldn't be able to have it both ways, essential to the work the show does.

"In a fascinating display of reaching across the aisle, Stewart 'debated' Fox News's Bill O'Reilly in 'The Rumble in the Air-Conditioned Auditorium,' with all proceeds going to charity. While some of the debate was classic comedic humor, some even Chaplinesque, the banter between the two friends was real. The most poignant part of the show was during the Q&A segment when an audience member asked, 'why should I vote for Obama again?'" Play video:

> Stewart: (at a loss for words) I don't know what to tell you, kid. Uh, you know, it's a race between him and Mitt Romney (crowd cheers) that would. … It's not, here's what I would say: Turns out Lincoln ain't running this year. …

"Stewart never advocated for Obama but obviously he supports him over Romney. His tactical refusal to give Obama an endorsement or admitting he donated $1 million to his campaign gives Stewart the protection he needs. But he will not 'carry the water' for Obama and will criticize him when he feels it is necessary. In the summer of 2013 when Stewart visited his Egyptian counterpart and friend Bassem Youseef, he made interesting comments about Obama and satirizing power, and I quote: 'I don't like assholes and so, I try to speak out against assholes. Isn't that all government is? We all get together and decide as a majority who the assholes are. That's all it is. Government is always a lottery you put your money down, it's a bet. I'm gonna put down some money on this guy in the hopes that he'll turn out to be something good and a lot of times he doesn't—as it appears to be in this case.'

"This is Stewart and *The Daily Show*'s driving force because to simply mock is easy; the show takes the satire further by really questioning how serious people can do such unserious things. How are these people in charge—how is this system so broken!? Or how can these people be winning the battles that seem so obvious—to him—they shouldn't be. What makes Stewart tick and why *The Daily Show* has been a success and so well received over the years was revealed in an interview with one of Stewart's heroes, journalist Bill Moyers." Play video:

Stewart: It's very serious people doing a very unserious thing and a lot of times, we're watching the government in action or some of the media representatives in action, we feel like those are very unserious people doing a very serious thing.

"Serious people understand that you can change your mind; you can alter your thought process but the constant double-speak, code words, fake outrage that we've seen throughout the lecture comes from all parties in politics. It's scary that a comedian has to point this out, but Asimov was right when he pointed out that great secret of the successful fool. And that is the necessity of *The Daily Show*, even though he is a comedian, making us laugh, giving the audience pop-culture references, and having his audience feel that there is someone out there holding people to account—he is NOT a journalist. Stewart is a comedian, it's the only way he can do what he does. He does act like a child occasionally, doing impressions or spitting food out of his mouth, but he's exceptionally intelligent. He can have real and meaningful conversations with heads of state but also he can have a conversational debate with those who disagree with him, as we've seen with President Obama and Florida Senator Marco Rubio. Stewart's politics are progressive; he looks to tomorrow and sees that it can be better than today, hoping that we can improve because the future is coming whether we like it or not. A conservative looks to yesterday and says: 'That's my preference, it was better for me then so why change it?' It's not a fear of the future but more of a preference for the past, hence the root word 'conserve' in their name. Stewart sees this discrepancy between the two with nuances—the media frames it as right and wrong with no room for nuance. But as the next election cycle and faux scandal rises and falls, *The Daily Show* will continue with their 'Indecision' coverage and irreverent humor. And during this, the American people will NEED Stewart and *The Daily Show* to go right to the heart of the arguments being made by President Obama and others involved. We'll need his ability to tear through a political statement because the corporate media will do it only to serve the narrative bubble that garners them the highest ratings. Stewart will bother with the narrative bubble only to puncture and deflate it or to stop the windmills from turning against progress, understanding, and hope. Like the jesters mocking the monarchy to their face, Ben Franklin setting down the wrongs of the English crown that led to the American Revolution, or the works of Lenny Bruce, George Carlin, Gary Trudeau, and others questioning our elected leaders by elevating our national conversation, educating the masses, and making us laugh in the interim. In the end, Isaac Asimov was right when he said the great secret to the fool is that he is anything but. He wasn't talking about Stewart, but could have been, and Stewart is no fool even if he plays one on TV. He's on a noble quest as *The Daily Show* charges the windmills: to tear away the façade, speak truth to power, stop the fake outrage machine of the 24-hour news networks, and conquer the slippery and repugnant Bullshit Mountain. Because to Stewart and *TDS*, fighting these windmills is necessary for the good of the country; it's an honorable fight against those in politics and in corporate mainstream media because to this very sane Don Quixote, the way those in power and in control are behaving, Stewart's suit and tie is justified and they are the ones who should be forced to wear the jester's hat and endure a lifetime of ridicule."

8

That went well as I'm sleepwalking through the question-and-answer session, snapping in and out of consciousness. The jet lag is nothing less than brutal; it's as if the jet lag is a virus taking over my body and senses. The Q&A started slowly; as per usual, no one asked a question, perhaps because the Dutch don't like to call attention to themselves. Has to be remnants from World War II. However, once one person raised their hand, the rest followed suit. Hopefully, no one is offended with the answers. But they have me there for—I just yawned, and Claudia steps in. She sees my energy being depleted by the second and tells the audience this is the last question. Claudia singles out the tall Dutch girl in the back, she stands up and everyone turns around. One of those. She thanks me for being there and proceeds with her question: "My name is Natasha and I would like to know, when will satire become irrelevant in America?"

"Thanks for the question, a tough one to end the evening." I think for a moment. "When we get it right. So never." That gets a good laugh from the crowd. "But in all seriousness, as long as there are those who oppose a system that is corrupt, flawed, or inherently unjust, satire will not survive, it'll thrive. There's a real correlation between the unjust and satire's potency. There's the ebb and flow but it's still a fight. Satire's the weapon of choice for those who refuse to pick up a gun or take out their anger or frustration in an uncivilized way. They're defending and fighting a different kind of war. Guns are not necessary in these battles but insults are. Of course, those who create satire hope their words have as much effect on the status quo as a bomb dropping or a grenade being thrown. My hope is that I never have to speak about satire again because that means everything is fixed. Satire is useless in Sweden because they have it pretty good up there. Though I haven't seen that much Dutch satire—so you must be doing a pretty good job as well. But in America it ain't going anywhere. So what I'm saying is—I'll see you next month."

The crowd laughs again as Claudia steps forward. "We would like to thank you for your lecture tonight. It was most informative. As a token of your time here, and we all read from Olli's piece revealing that you're a coffee—." She searches for the word, "Fan—fanatic, is that the word?"

"I'd prefer 'enthusiast' but 'fanatic' is fine," I say with a smile as Claudia hands me a gift bag.

"Hopefully, you'll like our choice here. Thank you again."

There's applause but I don't hear it. I give a small wave of appreciation as the audience files out. I'm approached by several people who have some questions, some too shy to ask in front of the crowded theater, others who have a follow-up. The Dutch are always so warm to me, always asking if I would like to go out with them for a drink or a cup of coffee. I'd love to, but I need some sleep. I politely decline and put away all my materials. Claudia, Annelieke, and Olli are the last to leave and ask if I know where I'm going—of course I do. Amsterdam is a breeze to navigate, only a ten-minute bike ride. I open the present—DUTCH COFFEE!! Douwe Egberts! And the beans are ground up for the French press. Perfection achieved.

LECTURE TWO: KILLING CARTOONS

Violence in Art & Animation

1

Where do we begin when the topic is violence? In the only place we can, with the acknowledgment of violence in not just American society but every society. We need to acknowledge that we are a violent species who has not yet managed to eradicate this aspect of our nature and probably never will. How do we acknowledge violence and society? How do we attempt to document the two? We won't begin with animation and violence—that would be too easy—but instead with a scene from a film that encompasses everything we need to know about violence, human nature, and society.

Let's set the landscape: Europe. Vienna, Austria. Post–World War II. The Allies are victorious against the Axis. Europe is in the early phases of reconstruction after the war's devastation and British director Carol Reed starts filming the 1949 film *The Third Man* on location. *The Third Man* stars Joseph Cotten as an American out-of-work pulp fiction novelist named Holly Martins, who arrives in post-war Vienna, which has been divided into four sectors by the triumphant allies. In Vienna there is a shortage of supplies, which leads to a flourishing black market for medicine and goods. Martins arrives at the invitation of an old friend from school, Harry Lime, played by the iconic Orson Welles. Lime had recently offered Martins a job, but Martins discovers that Lime died a few days earlier in a peculiar traffic accident. From talking to Lime's friends and associates, Martins soon notices that some of the stories are inconsistent, and determines that he needs to discover what really happened to Harry Lime. Once Martins realizes Lime has faked his own death, he's able to get a message to Lime requesting a meeting in the Communist-controlled side of Vienna. The pivotal and iconic scene takes place at the amusement park where the two old friends exchange pleasantries and head up into the Ferris wheel. While in one of the Ferris wheel's cars, the two friends exchange wonderfully written dialogue fraught with suspense and exposition that only the most skilled actors can pull off. The two actors, at the top of their game, are probing, manipulating, and challenging the other. Finally, Martins asks the question he needs to have answered. Play video:

Martins: Have you ever seen any of your victims?

Harry Lime: You know, I never feel comfortable on these sort of things. Victims? Don't be melodramatic. Look down there. Tell me. Would you really feel any pity if one of those dots stopped moving forever? If I offered you twenty thousand pounds for every dot that stopped, would you really, old man, tell me to keep my money, or would you calculate how many dots you could afford to spare? Free of income tax, old man. Free of income tax—the only way you can save money nowadays.

If the final line does not capture American and capitalist economic sentiment, find me a better one! But Lime laughs off the tension, masking his disdain for the situation. He walks over to the car's door, opens it, and surveys the people below. Martins get closer to the open door, we get the foreshadowing of the violence and dangerous events to come as Lime tells Martins that he would be "easy to get rid of" and "the police wouldn't look for a bullet wound" after he hits the ground from this height. The tension builds then breaks as Lime laughs off the anxiety, and he says he would never hurt Martins nor would Martins hurt him. The two old friends leave the Ferris wheel as Lime pitches Martins about joining his black market operation. As the scene comes to an end, Lime rationalizes his crimes by telling the disappointed Martins the truth about society, violence, art, and his philosophy on life. And here is our working thesis for the lecture. Play video:

Harry Lime: Don't be so gloomy. After all it's not that awful. Like the fella says, in Italy for thirty years under the Borgias they had warfare, terror, murder, and bloodshed, but they produced Michelangelo, Leonardo da Vinci, and the Renaissance. In Switzerland they had brotherly love—they had 500 years of democracy and peace, and what did that produce? The cuckoo clock.

Rumor has it that Welles improvised the line but regardless of that, this is our thesis—not just that violence and instability produce greater works of art, as the quote implies, but also that violence has been prevalent in almost every society, and great artistic works have been produced because of that violence. We can say with some certainty that violence births iconic works of art. Within that, we will witness how a work can alter the path of a subject, and lead society through an unexpected journey. According to Harry Lime, the most memorable works are created under the worst circumstances for a society—war, bloodshed, corruption, etc. And sometimes a work can change the trajectory of an art form and what a civilization will accept, whether we realize it or not. Violence coupled with art isn't new: it is our basic humanity. Humans are a violent species but we're also a creative species. The two are in our DNA. As singer Beverly Sills said: "Art is the signature of civilizations." And today, we will look at some of those signatures. From the earliest civilizations, such as the Egyptians, the Greeks, the Romans, and the Native Americans, art and violence are connected through the ages. Art—ancient and current—reveal our fears, our nightmares, our instincts, our frustrations, our beliefs, our faiths, our opinions, and our happiness, as artists witnessed the end of monarchies and the worst tragedies befallen societies in the twentieth century. While these tectonic events occur, humans have had to grapple with the horrors that come with society's evolutionary shifts. However, we can't just look at a society or society's evolution; we need to look at humankind's evolution within a country and a people. We have to study the sadistic and seismic acts we partake in and the amount of carnage that our art reflects.

The violence and art of Europe has been studied for years, and their history is fraught with atrocities and creativity; as Harry Lime perfectly pointed out, it's also not my forte. But today our attention gazes west to the New World as America's revolution and evolution have coincided with depictions of art and violence. America's evolution as a country and its progress as a people continue and the art will parallel that development. Where the citizenry stands at a given point in time, debating whether we've become more sophisticated or less, is dependent on the viewer. It's also dependent on those who are engaging in the critique. It's what the viewer chooses to see. To quote artist Edgar Degas, "Art is not what you see, but what you make others see … ."

To make you see where America is as a nation, look no further than our illustrations: from paintings and drawings to modern animation and everything in between. And that's what we will do here: we will also discuss the violence and animation in the last decade of the twentieth century through the rise of computer animation into today. First, we have to get there, from where America started, and then move forward, seeing several incarnations from various time periods leading us to where all the violent work comes together in an episode of the hit animated television show *South Park*.

But to have an understanding and to truly see how it's all connected, or as TED lecturer Kirby Ferguson surmised that, "everything is a remix." To Kirby no idea is new; we're constantly remixing media, and borrowing from older ideas, then reinventing things to make new ones. We can apply this to America, how it began and where it is now. The Founding Fathers looked towards European scholars and authors when crafting the documents that would shape America. These men borrowed, remixed, and/or tossed out concepts that did not appeal to their goals while creating a new nation. The Revolutionaries—though I agree with the Hannah Arendt argument in "On Revolution" that it was more secession than revolution—borrowed and continued Europe's propensity for violence and war. The US is no stranger to carnage, genocide, and violence towards each other and the state. Our history, though brief compared to Europe, is steeped in bloodshed but similar to the centuries of growing pains endured in Europe. The only real difference is the US grew up in the age of mass media. This media explosion has certainly forced America and its citizens to mature quicker than other empires, all the while living under the world's microscope. However, it's America's inception that began with massacres and since then we haven't learned how to alter the path of destruction. To a modern and foreign audience, it's striking to witness and difficult to comprehend. From an outsider's or a European view, we seem to be more violent than ever before. William Lutz, professor of English at Rutgers University said, "the problem is that we live in an age where we see violence as a solution. You see it in our foreign policy, you see it on TV shows and movies, you see it in the home. In the movies, the hero is always that meek, mild-mannered guy who's pushed too far and suddenly pulls out an AK-47 and blows away a dozen bad guys."

Contrary to that, Harvard professor Steven Pinker says in his book *The Better Angels of Our Nature: Why Violence Has Declined* that we are in a time where our species is less violent than ever before, that people living now are less likely to meet a violent death or suffer violence from others than any other time in history. We are in a time known as the "long peace," as there has been a decline in all kinds of organized conflicts as the chart shows: war is at an all-time low. While we've evolved as a species, violence has not been completely eradicated, as events in Connecticut and Colorado, and Boston and numerous other cities have revealed. However, with the rise in violence in film and media, there has been a drop in real-world violence. In *Foreign Policy*, Charles Kenny wrote in his article, "There Will Not Be Blood," that America is at a low of 404 violent crimes per 100,000 people. Combined with that, a study by the *Quarterly Journal of Economics* suggests violence dips when a blockbuster movie is in theaters. Which leads us to wonder: if we see more violence on screen, will we be less violent everywhere else? Is our audience reveling in the catharsis theory, which came from the Greek word meaning "cleansing" or "purging," or having an emotional release?

The catharsis theory states that the execution of an aggressive action in mass media will diminish the need for real-life action by those watching or reading it. In essence, if violence in the fiction world rises to give the viewer their emotional release, the real-world destruction or violence will drop because there is a purge or a purification attached to the entertainment. The theory holds but maintains that media has a tremendous effect on the individual and population as a whole. This can be argued for and against both sides make valid and exceptional points. But violent imagery has been rampant throughout American history, and yet the cathartic release wasn't mentally activated—if anything, the imagery made us prone to more violence. The colonists favoring secession from England used the Boston Massacre to further their cause in the name of America's independence. The newspapers and magazines speak volumes and no one viewing the drawing could feel anything but disgust towards the British. While the tragedy was anything but a massacre, especially today's interpretation, the bloodshed and the imagery plus the emotion that comes along with the killings were powerful and potent agents. This image and the brutality it depicts stirred the public and altered their opinion towards the cause. It's propaganda in its truest form, using emotion and imagery to promote the independence doctrine. Images and the headlines from the massacre convinced those who were indecisive about secession to agree to its necessity regardless of the bloodshed that will inevitably follow. The imagery and other elements such as pamphlets and demonstrations changed the trajectory of public opinion as the newspapers ratcheted up the propaganda machine to support the war. The art drew the audience in and America subsequently declares itself independent in 1776. And then the colonists fight the British for seven long years and ultimately gain their independence in 1783.

The newly formed country attempted to govern itself, struggling to find the right balance between local, state, and federal powers. Even today, the struggle for balance continues to be a contentious debate. Instead of solving the most challenging problem that had been ingrained within the country's fabric—slavery—the country remained split in two with industry in the North, and farming and slavery in the South. This split, as well as other factors, led to the predestined Civil War in the nineteenth century. As the war engulfs American life, dividing the country and families, we have the rise of the father of American political cartooning, *Harper's Weekly's* Thomas Nast.

A German-born immigrant who moved to New York City at the age of seven had already developed a reputation as an artist by the time the Civil War tore apart the nation. He was an original Lincoln Republican, an advocate for emancipation as well as women's equality. Obviously, he supported Abraham Lincoln but also believed the Civil War was a useless war instigated by the treacherous South. However, while he did not believe in the war, he understood the need to fight it: a subtle yet vital distinction between a realist and a warmonger, and as a Lincoln Republican, he was very pro-military, yet anti-war. This philosophy stemmed from his earlier experiences in Italy as he covered the Sicilian War for Independence. Nast embraced the "speak softly and carry a big stick" ideology before it became a phrase and policy used by Republican president Theodore Roosevelt.

You see here Nast's drawing of the unfunded military and the iconic Columbia representing America and Liberty, scared and hiding, with no gun to protect her. The tree trunk masquerades as a cannon to fake military supremacy and crows dominate the sky waiting for the death that's surely to come. Notice the American flag flies upside down, representing distress to an unprepared nation and the skeleton solider, representing a famished military. While there is no outward violence, the piece screams of the possible violence to come. And then to counter that image, on the other page of *Harper's Weekly*, Nast draws "Peace Secure—Safe & Protected" and there is a stark difference: Columbia isn't frightened, the tree trunk has been replaced with a HUGE cannon, and doves

replace the crows, as they represent peace and security. The American flag is flying confidently and the soldier, no longer a skeleton, is standing at attention prepared for battle. This violence is altered and contrary to the other, it's a proactive threat of violence, not the meek situation Columbia endured in the previous drawing.

Nast was a Lincoln supporter through and through and helped explain the president's policy to the public and why fighting the South was essential to the Union's survival. His cartoons were indispensable because a majority of Americans were illiterate at that time—Nast would take it as his civic duty to educate the public. One of most important pieces, certainly filled with propaganda, was from September 1862, titled "A Gallant Color Bearer." The piece graced the cover of *Harper's Weekly* and lifted morale for a mentally defeated North, as the South had more success in the beginning. The people and soldiers viewed this drawing and felt a visceral connection to the sentiment Nast put forth, and in turn, the Northern cause. President Lincoln would call Nast his best recruitment sergeant for the war effort and General Grant, leader of the Union army, who became president several years later, said: "Nast did as much as any man to preserve the Union and bring the war to an end."

To continue his own private war against the South, Nast depicted the Southerners as barbarians, exposing their "Southern Chivalry." This piece was the centerfold, measuring 40 × 56 centimeters, and divulged the atrocities by the rebellious South. The drawing has slaves being massacred and Southern soldiers granting no quarter to injured Northern soldiers, throwing them onto the road to die. Nast was effective at eviscerating his enemy with astounding renditions and the public understood his work, connecting to the cartoon on a deeper level than they would to a speech or the written word. This two-fisted approach is a necessity if one is to portray violence against another party, as Nast also portrayed the Southerners as pompous debutantes:

a common stereotype used to gin up support for the Northern cause. As the tide of the war swelled towards certain victory for the Union, rumors began circulating that parts of the government were negotiating with the secessionists to end the war. Nast, still upset over the war itself, disagreed with compromise and continued his assault on the Southerners to remind people who started the war and the suffering that was endured by the Union soldiers fighting it. This powerful September 1864 political piece, "Compromise with the South," was so popular that Lincoln used it in his presidential reelection campaign. Once again, Nast employed the imagery of Columbia weeping over a grave and the upside-down American flag revealing distress, and juxtaposed with the Southern soldier shaking hands with a crippled Union solider. The Southern debutante solider breaks a sword in two that reads "Northern Power" and a tombstone that is engraved "In Memory of our Union Heroes Who Fell in a Useless War" reminds the public who is responsible for the fractured nation. It's a moving, provocative, and violent cartoon and accomplished its goal as the compromise talk was abandoned and Lincoln is reelected. The war begins to finally wind down, the South's defeat becomes more and more inevitable, and then the tragic events of April 15, 1865. President Lincoln is assassinated and Nast has Columbia weeping over the slain president's grave. Sometime later, Nast illustrates another piece: "Victory and Death," in honor of his friend and fallen president. This time Nast sketched Columbia being consoled by her European equivalents and the citizens still weeping for the murdered president.

Nast and the American people would move on together as Nast created some of the most iconic imagery in political cartoon history. As we viewed in earlier examples, Nast depicted with the gruesome image of a skeleton army what would happen if the military did not receive adequate funds. The skeleton would be his preferred image for horror as he explained Communism to the public in the piece. While not against Communism for religious reasons, Nast did not like the idea of paying more taxes and felt the ideology lacking. The skeleton was also used as a warning to those fighting the Russo–Turkish War that erupted in 1877. Nast believed the war involved no real principles or cause and he saw it as only a macabre invitation to death, as he created "Into the Jaws of Death" in 1878. Even a decade after first finding this political cartoon, the power has not waned as Nast brilliantly captures the impact, brutality, and profound statements made about the true costs

of war. Nast knew how to reach an audience by tapping into their inner demons, their fears of death and carnage, as America had recently experienced a bloody war and the murder of their leader. His skeletons represented the impending doom of where we were headed as a species and a people.

Nast would portray politicians and criminals as grotesque animals, as he attempted to create imagery that would connect with his viewers and vilify those he opposed. Nast drew the Irish as monkeys, as they were considered to be the lowest of the low, and politicians as violent simians to show their lack of evolution. Nast's influence can surely be felt, as the public's perception of those politicians would worsen the more Nast caricatured them. In fact, politicians would send photographs, a new invention, of themselves to Nast to be sure he lampooned them properly. Nast's cartoons were violent, holding no sympathy for those who go against his version of America. He showed his belief that liberty is not anarchy in the piece titled "Dynamite and Panic in the Air!" This reactionary piece exhibited his anger towards several conspiratorial anarchists after they were caught trying to overthrow the US government. His drawings were frightening as he advocated for the murder of President Johnson, the man who replaced Lincoln, whom Nast dubbed in 1869 "A bogus Caesar." He also said treason is a crime and must be punished because Johnson was working openly with the South to curb any assimilation of the newly freed slaves. His cartoons were impactful as Nast almost single-handedly (with help from *The New York Times*) brought down the corrupt political party in New York City's Tammany Hall. Nast challenged the voters with a slogan: "What are you going to do about it?" and this cartoon was released right around Election Day in 1871. Nast's work is timeless. Nast draws my favorite cartoon revealing the risk of Catholicism could have on American soil—and if you lean your head to the side, you will see those crocodiles coming on shore are not really crocodiles at all. But as Nast's influence in politics waned, his mark on political cartooning was secured and still thrives today.

THE AMERICAN RIVER GANGES.

2

As we reach the end of the nineteenth century, a new technology and medium emerges as Eadweard Muybridge originates film by photographing a horse to prove that all four hooves are off the ground when it's galloping. Soon after, the earliest films are created and violence would be a main feature, especially in DW Griffith's black and white film, *Birth of a Nation*, where the racist KKK was glamorized and the newly freed slaves were savages. However, Griffith also perfected the montage, the close-up, and the flashback, even as he created a piece of bigotry unseen before and probably since. However, the overt use of animals by Nast would be used throughout the twentieth century, as film and animation became a dominant medium in America. During World War II, Walt Disney used Donald Duck and others to remind Americans what the world will come to if they don't pay their taxes or contribute to the war effort: a Nazi-dominated world where Donald Duck reads *Mein Kampf* at the breakfast table while eating stale bread. In the 1942 cartoon, "Der Furher's Face," Donald lives in a world ruled by the Nazis—where everything is a swastika: the fence, the trees, and the clouds. Even the house Donald lives in is a representation of Hitler, as Disney used subliminal imagery to show Hitler's attempt at total world assimilation. The chimney is a hand in a Nazi salute, the shadow from the sun is Hitler's hairdo, the window shade and the space below are his nose, and the opened window is Hitler's infamous mustache. Donald Duck is living inside Hitler's brain, a wonderful metaphor to show the effects of Nazism. The cartoon is startling and also extremely funny, as Disney assists America to win the all-important propaganda war by having Donald Duck head to the Nazi factory to help build Hitler's army. The violence is powerful as Donald is put through the impossible forty-eight-hour workday but thankfully in the end, it's a

dream, as Donald realizes he's still in America. Cartoons like this rallied America to believe in the necessity of sacrifice (from soldiers to food rations and taxes) to fight against the Nazis and Adolf Hitler, just like Nast did with the Civil War.

Animation and violence will forever be linked, but the animated violence was, of course, cartoonish with no consequences, as Looney Tunes led the way and still does for many young children: Elmer Fudd, Daffy Duck, Bugs Bunny, Wile E. Coyote, and the Roadrunner could get hurt, beaten, or blown up, but will be as good as new ready for their next adventure. As we moved further away from the Saturday morning cartoon violence, we're introduced several years later to another kind of cartoon violence, definitely less cheery than a Saturday morning cartoon, but registering the same level of grotesque imagery as Thomas Nast. Cartoon artist Ralph Steadman finds an audience as he represents the volatility of the 1960s as the war in Vietnam rages on and the battle for the American soul takes center stage. There are protests and riots and Steadman catalogues the tumultuous period of the sixties and seventies with drawings to match. Steadman's rise to fame came when he joined forces with Hunter S. Thompson to illustrate his *Fear & Loathing* pieces and added to the madness of the gonzo journalism being pioneered by Thompson. And as if connected to Thomas Nast by some cosmic entity, Steadman would be asked to contribute drawings to the 50th anniversary edition of George Orwell's *Animal Farm*, adding his own macabre touch to the iconic fairy story as the villainous Napoleon is given the "Steadman treatment."

Animation, art, and violence did not take a holiday; there was plenty during the late 70s and into the 80s. However, it was the revolutionary work of Robert Zemeckis and the hybrid 1988 film *Who Framed Roger Rabbit?* which was part animation and part human, that the audience entered a world where animated characters and humans interacted in a real-world setting. They intermingled in ways that would seem, well, risqué, to say the least, but also brought up feelings of a permanent underclass represented by the cartoons. The "toons" are servers, entertainers, and cabdrivers. In fact one is a cab! And thanks to Jessica Rabbit, the toons are also love and lust interests. The toons are alive for humanity's pleasure and endless servitude. This unique approach made the film starkly atypical from anything seen before in the mainstream. But what made the film groundbreaking was the violence in the film. A toon's actions and a human's actions against one another had real-life consequences where death was a reality. In the film, a safe falls on a man's head, decapitating him; people are shot in the back; and the weasels patrol the streets, threatening innocent civilians and sexually assaulting Jessica Rabbit. Though she manages a nice booby trap to keep the weasels at bay. Nevertheless, there is a scene in the film that changed modern animation onto a course that no mainstream audience could have imagined. In the scene, the aptly named Judge Doom, played by Christopher Lloyd, "dips" a cute little shoe from the old animated days of Disney and alters what an audience (adult and child alike) will accept from their cartoons. Play video:

Judge Doom: [*while putting on a large black rubber glove*] Since I've had Toontown under my jurisdiction my goal has been to rein in the insanity, and the only way to do that is to make Toons respect … [*lets the glove snap back onto his arm)* … the law.

Eddie Valiant: What's that?

Lt. Santino: Remember how they always thought there wasn't a way to kill a toon? Well, Doom found a way. Turpentine, acetone, benzene. He calls it "The Dip."

Judge Doom: I'll catch the rabbit, Mr. Valiant. And I'll try him, convict him, and execute him. [*dips shoe in poison, and cremation smoke starts sizzling out*]

Eddie Valiant: Geez.

Greasy: [*laughs*] That's one dead shoe, eh, boss?

Judge Doom: They're not kid gloves, Mr. Valiant. This is how we handle things down in Toontown. I would think you of all people would appreciate that.

Watching this scene play out is absolutely brutal, frightening, and sad; it's as if Zemeckis and the writers were killing off Disney and Warner Bros' Looney Tunes by having Judge Doom execute the animation of yesterday. Zemeckis and company ushered in the new era of animation and violence, whether they realized it or not. The audience has watched animated characters be tortured and killed before, but never an innocent one. Villains, such as Ursula from *The Little Mermaid* and Charles F. Muntz from *Up* receive their comeuppance but never a harmless little shoe, whose only crime was cozying up to the wrong person. *Who Framed Roger Rabbit?* was not the animation of your Saturday mornings; while under the guise of being a kid-friendly film, there are adult themes of the classic film noir: adultery, sex, alcoholism, murder, blackmail, greed, power, and capitalism run amok. But Judge Doom's executing the shoe was a huge moment in animation and this scene changed everything for the future of animation. But why would this scene be so important that it altered the animation trajectory? Because *Hanna Barbera's Tom and Jerry* will recover no matter what weapon is selected to hit them with. Donald and Daffy Duck will survive regardless of the size of the cannon used to blow off their feathers—the two ducks will always return without a scratch on them. Wile E. Coyote—my personal favorite—no matter WHAT happens to him, no matter how bad it gets, no matter how high he falls from a cliff or into a canyon, he'll come back in the next scene ready to kill The Roadrunner. And when the Coyote tries again, he'll fall off an even higher cliff. He'll still continue his quest against The Roadrunner, this time with a bigger rocket and more determination than before.

The world Zemeckis and the writers created is radically unique—the toons can be murdered and there's nothing an audience can do about. Judge Doom EXECUTED a cute little fun cartoon show in front of a mainstream audience just to prove that he has the power and ability. As a screenwriting choice, it's also brilliant because the stakes are now much higher than your typical animated film. Now, no one is invincible in this world. Despite a PG rating, there were no complaints from the family organizations or concerned parents of America. *Who Framed Roger Rabbit?* would gross $330 million worldwide, and the audiences accepted the violence towards the "good" toons. For years, we had been watching cartoon characters get beat up and tortured, but we knew at the end, they would return. Judge Doom changed the rules forever. And with a huge box office, Hollywood took notice, and so did animators. They realized their audiences have grown up or maybe our society had evolved to a higher level of acceptance of violence. From the innocent times to a new reality, mainstream Hollywood helped usher in this era but realized it would take some time for everyone to accept it. We can draw a line between the radical violence of *Who Framed Roger Rabbit?* with the emergence of *The Simpsons* in late 1989, and the creation of MTV's Liquid Television in 1991, audiences started accepting more real-world violence against and within their cartoons.

Liquid Television, in co-production with BBC2, introduced us to off-beat characters, such as *The Head*, where a normal guy wakes up one morning to an abnormally sized head with an alien named Roy inside. We are brought into a dystopian future created by Peter Cheung in *Aeon Flux*, introducing the audience to a scantily clad heroine who is a skilled warrior and has a bizarre relationship with the totalitarian leader Trevor. Aeon kills anyone and everyone who gets in her way. Though not anime, the cartoon was definitely a new form of violence and animation. Of course, the most popular of the animation from Liquid TV: Mike Judge's groundbreaking *Beavis & Butthead*. With two adolescent boys—awkward looking, unintelligent, incredibly funny, and incredibly violent—Judge brings teenage angst, teenage rebellion, and destruction home to the viewer, but with real consequence. Whether it's playing "frog baseball," or attempting to have sex with any girl in sight, *Beavis & Butthead* were a cultural phenomenon that brought the lives of the ignored into our living room. They are unsuccessful in almost any sexual endeavor, or even the most basic one: stopping Beavis's nosebleed. Play video:

Beavis and Butthead are in the living sitting on the couch in front of a TV. Butthead punches Beavis in the face and laughs.

Beavis: Ow! That's not what I meant, you butthole. I meant punch yourself in the face.

Butthead: Uh … OK.

Butthead makes a fist and reaches his arm backwards to wind up, but hits Beavis instead.

Beavis: Ow!

Butthead: I missed.

Beavis pounces on Butthead, attempting to choke him, his nose now starting to drip with blood.

Butthead: Whoa.

Beavis: What? What?

Beavis notices the blood, which is now gushing out of his nose.

Beavis: Ah, I'm bleeding! Ah! I'm bleeding, oh no.

Butthead: Beavis, this is the coolest thing you've ever done.

Beavis: Oh yeah …

They chuckle for a few more seconds, and then the scene fades out for a commercial break, and then returns where it left off.

Beavis: I'm bleeding. Oh, oh. I'm still bleeding.

Butthead: Yeah, well if I kick your ass, you'll be bleeding from both ends. Now shut up.

Beavis: Ah, I'm bleeding. Make it stop! Make it stop!

Butthead slaps Beavis twice, causing more blood to spurt across the room and all across Beavis' face.

Beavis: Thanks … thanks I needed that.

Butthead: Dammit, Beavis … now you've got blood all over my hand.

Butthead's right hand is covered in blood, which he starts to rub onto Beavis' chest.

Beavis: You're wiping blood on me. Ah, ah, I've got blood on me. No, no, no!

Butthead: Hey Beavis, I've got an idea. Look at me.

Butthead stands up, and then yells in Beavis' face, which causes more blood to pour out of his nose, some of which lands on Butthead's face.

Around the same time as *Beavis & Butthead*—although not airing on MTV, but on Nickelodeon—the duo of *Ren and Stimpy* surfaces as a counterpoint to *Tom and Jerry*. They played by more perverse standards while still singing "happy happy joy joy," but the basic cartoon rules still applied to the torture the two characters endured and dished out. But Roger Rabbit undoubtedly changed the rules—you can kill the good guy to move the story along. Disney takes notice and the violence reaches the mainstream in 1994's *The Lion King*. The audience suffers through the death of King Mufasa by his younger brother Scar and a stampeding herd of antelopes that finish the job. While we don't see Mufasa hit the ground, we're forced to deal with his son Simba's loss. It's an adult theme for sure, both tragic and disturbing, as animation has now evolved into a serious platform for adult storytelling as Disney used the Bible story of Cain and Abel and Shakespeare's Hamlet to push the story forward. Over the past two decades, Pixar has led the charge in adult animated mainstream storytelling, as the studio continues to deliver critical and financial hits for the Disney Empire. The studio tackles mature themes, usually centering on abandonment, and overall storytelling to a new level as their violence in the first fully computer animated film, 1995's *Toy Story* was truly frightening but thankfully for most—hilarious. In this scene, which occurs late in the film, the toys rise from the dead in a scene reminiscent of *Night of the Living Dead* as the toys settle the score with their tormentor, Sid. Play video:

Sid is holding Woody in his backyard, which is full of other toys.

Sid: It's busted.

Woody: Who you callin' busted, buster?

Sid stops winding up to throw Woody across the yard and starts examining the toy in fearful awe.

Woody: That's right, I'm talking to you—Sid Phillips! We don't like being blown up Sid ... or smashed or ripped apart—

Sid: We?

Woody: That's right, your toys!

Several other toys start acting on their own as well, rising from the sandbox in a creepy manner. Buzz Lightyear looks on in amazement. Dismembered army men rise up out of a puddle of mud and start to corner Sid. A three-eyed alien comes out from hiding under a water bowl and also starts inching closer. Sid is backed against a post, from which a toy with the head of a baby and body of a mechanical spider slides down and closes its arms on Sid's head. He shrieks and backs away. Another toy, a jack-in-the-box with a hand inside, grabs Sid by the leg, causing him to scream again. He is now completely surrounded by toys who continue to close in on him.

Woody: From now on, you must take good care of your toys, because if you don't we'll find out, Sid. We toys can see—everything!

Woody's head begins to revolve around and Sid is at the height of his fear. Suddenly, Woody comes to life and speaks directly to Sid.

Woody: So play nice.

Sid finally loses it. He screams at the top of his lungs, throws Woody directly up in the air, and immediately runs inside. After this, all the toys "break character" and start to celebrate.

Woody: Ha-ha! We did it! We did it! Yeah!

Seeing Woody's head turn around, while it's funny, there is something horribly creepy and disturbing about it. The violence isn't overt, but scary enough to have an impact on Sid, probably for the rest of his life. Sid is going to be in therapy for a long time and probably still is. In fact, if Sid ISN'T in therapy today, I'd be surprised and the person who cured him deserves an award. After *Toy Story*, Pixar animated a home invasion, though it took place in the ocean, the audience is shocked in the opening scenes of *Finding Nemo* by the murders of Coral, Nemo's mother, and all but one of her eggs. Marlin, Coral's husband and protagonist of the film, is mentally destroyed by the trauma he endures and is so damaged that he is unable to handle letting his son even attend school. Marlin is incapable of processing the guilt associated with surviving the attack that ninety-nine percent of his family didn't. The audience is left stunned as well and, adding to the drama, there is a real fear that the ocean is a dangerous place. This tension remains throughout the film for our heroes Marlin, Dory, and Nemo even up to the last shot. Pixar would continue to experiment with violence but in alternative forms as they animate humanity's violence towards Earth and their own physical bodies in *Wall-E*. This violence is represented through a destroyed and garbage-filled planet that is uninhabitable and forcibly abandoned by the human race. The protagonist Wall-E travels to outer space and witnesses what violence humans have done to their own bodies as they've devolved into a new species: one that has abandoned any form of movement, effort, and physical contact with one another—the key to maintaining one's humanity. Hence why Wall-E is the most "human" character in the film and his love of Eve saves the human race from itself. Or their follow-up film, *Up*, which I see as a sequel to *Wall-E*, because Pete Docter contributed the story to *Wall-E* but left the project to write and direct their next film, *Up*. The couple in *Wall-E*, Wall-E and Eve, are the robot and future versions of the couple from *Up*, Carl and Ellie. *Up* asks the question—what happens when Wall-E loses Eve? In the opening and almost silent montage, we are treated to Carl and Ellie's life together. By the end of the ten minutes, the antagonist is revealed as life itself. There's no villain here except bad luck, misfortune, and time. Never shy about pushing the bounds of animation, Pixar gives their viewers the first miscarriage, and ultimately barren woman, in animation history, and Carl has to recover from the loss of his wife. There is some debate about whether she was pregnant or unable to get pregnant, but considering they're creating a nursery and then the tragic doctor scene follows, I always felt they had received the good news but ultimately something had gone wrong. Pixar has managed to capture this real world of life, society, and violence; the studio has the preeminent animators working today. In truth, Pixar is the only movie studio that movie-goers actively go to see in the theaters—rarely do you hear, "I'm going to see a Warner Brothers movie" but you will "go see a Pixar film" and ultimately trust you're going to be treated as an adult because Pixar has carved out a unique place in the animation universe.

Animated films and shows have come and gone since raising the bar of social issues and revealing the core of American society, as Harry Lime spoke of, or lowering the standards of what their predecessors had created. But one show has managed to do both. They've decreased the animation benchmarks set by their predecessors but advanced the technology in an unexpected way. The show ingeniously merged the higher standards of tackling issues more complicated than an average Saturday morning cartoon and coupled that with the audience's appetite for wanton destruction. *South Park*, created by Trey Parker and Matt Stone in 1997, understands that even though "The Simpsons already did it," they have to bring their art further and deeper in order to remain relevant in today's media world. The violence in the show has been a mainstay since the very first episode, as Cartman received an anal probe and Kyle played kick-the-baby with his younger brother, Ike, sending him through the school bus's window. In the episode "Death," the classic version of the Grim Reaper visits South Park, not to kill Stan's Grandpa, as he begs for in the episode, but instead to continue a theme of the show—killing Kenny (you bastards)—as *South Park* established early on in the show, even as Kenny is killed, the next episode he will return without a scratch on him. This, of course, harkens back to Wile E. Coyote and others in the animated universe where death is not permanent even though eventually they tried with Kenny, only to bring him back a few seasons later. And yes, even though *The Simpsons* already did it, so had others, and Matt and Trey know this as they go to the annals of literature, film, and television for inspiration. It's as if what Kirby Ferguson said, that everything is a remix, makes more and more sense. Borrowing ideas from Shakespeare and his most violent play, *Titus Andronicus*, Cartman feeds Scott Tenorman's parents to him in a bowl of chili. The moment is still considered one of the most violent in the show's history. In another episode, Matt's and Trey's alter egos Terence and Philip re-create *Hamlet*'s climactic scene where everyone dies a horrible death. They've spoofed the creepy futuristic violence of *2001:*

A Space Odyssey in "Trapper Keeper," as Cartman fuses with his trapper keeper and Kyle tries to stop him from destroying the world, but the show has never shied away from characters' bowels being released after dying. Some even kill themselves. In the *24*-inspired episode "The Snuke," the Queen of England commits suicide and then her skull falls out onto the floor. Or in "Night of the Living Homeless" the homeless population overruns South Park as the episode turns into a *Night of the Living Dead* spoof as Randy is forced to kill a fellow citizen who has morphed into a homeless person seeking spare change.

It's carnival grotesquerie at its finest, even as the animation is anything but. It hammers home both Harry Lime's belief that exceptional art is produced in violent society and how Roger Rabbit allows the audience to accept real-world consequences in violence perpetrated against cartoons. We could examine the prophet Muhammad episodes that explore the fear of Middle Eastern violence against America, the do's and don'ts of religious law, or the *South Park* movie from 2000, which was a land war against Canada. Or how real world clubs and violent "Kick a Ginger" days were created in response to their ginger episodes, featuring violence against those with red hair and freckles. Or we can list almost any other episode where violence plays a major role in the show, but when did *South Park* represent not only violence against each other but also reflect our society from today and yesterday? How do we connect that bridge we've built? How do we make Harry Lime's philosophy and Roger Rabbit's reality co-exist? The episode that typifies violence against people, all the while revealing who we are as a society, is one of the darkest episodes *South Park* has ever done, Season Twelve's "Britney's New Look." The episode aired in 2008 around the height of "Britney Spears Mental Breakdown Mania," when a large portion of America and parts of the world were watching Britney Spears slowly spiral out of control. She was caught on TV shaving her head and bets were being taking on when Britney was going to kill herself for the entire world to see. The media had their claws in Britney and Matt and Trey decided to add to their voice to the mix, not to reprimand the poor girl but instead make humanity realize what Harry Lime spoke about: we are a violent species and through that Matt and Trey created an incredible work of art. Ironically, we discussed earlier America maturing under the media's watchful gaze and how they've failed on numerous occasions; the same can be said for Britney who started as a child star and attempted to become an adult as everyone criticized her every move. In each case, animation and violence have catalogued the journey.

In the audio commentary for the episode, Matt and Trey said that this is the episode that polarized many fans, just like Britney had and just like a piece of art that is outside the norm or offensive in some way. As they said with regards to the episode, "you are either on the train or you were left in the station." Either you loved it or you hated it. It is one of the most sadistic, revealing, and honest episodes *South Park* has ever done. During the episode, Randy is watching the Democratic presidential debate between then-senators Barack Obama and Hillary Clinton. The boys are seated next to Stan's father Randy and are understandably bored out of their minds until an emergency bulletin interrupts the debate. The bulletin is not about a terrorist attack or some vital information, but it's about Britney Spears and it's titled: "Britney Watch." Britney has been spotted vacationing in the woods near South Park and she gets photographed peeing on a ladybug. So, I guess it is vital information! The media also comments about her body, embarrassing her by pointing out her acne. During the newscast it's revealed that the Colorado resident who photographed Britney received $100,000 for his intrusion. This, of course, gives the boys an idea: get a photo of Britney peeing on a squirrel and it'll be worth even more! How to find a squirrel? No problem with that—just dress up poor Butters! The boys arrive at the hotel where Britney is staying and the paparazzi are swarming, hoping to get their own $100,000 Britney shot. The boys manage to convince the guard that they are Britney's kids there to see their mother, and they're allowed to enter the hotel. Britney is on the phone upset about the news coverage and that people think she hates ladybugs, but perks up when the security guard tells her that her boys have arrived. Her elation turns to disappointment as she realizes Stan, Kyle, Cartman, and Butters have tricked her into a false happiness. Then Britney comes to the harsh realization that the media will never leave her alone, and there's no way out for her. Play video:

A hotel room. Britney is painting her toenails while on the phone with someone

Britney: But now everybody thinks I hate ladybugs. I didn't even know it was there. I can't take it anymore. I'm just sooo—*[several knocks are heard at her door]*

Guard: Excuse me, Ms. Spears, but your kids are here and they've brought you a squirrel.

Britney: My boys? Really? Send them in. [to the caller] It's okay. My kids are here. I feel better now. *[hangs up. Stan and the others enter the room]*

Kyle: We did it guys!

Stan: I told you that would work!

The Boys: Yehehahah, all right!

Kyle: Alright!

Britney: *[walks up to them]* You mean, it was just a joke? My kids ain't here?

Kyle: Alright. Butters, go get next to her.

Butters: I ain't doin' it! We tricked her and it wasn't nice!

Stan: Butters, do you want your share of the hundred thousand dollars or not?

Britney: [walks back to the table] You're never gonna leave me alone, are you?

Butters: It ain't right to take advantage of somebody no matter who they are! [Britney opens a drawer and pulls something out]

Kyle: All right, fine! We don't need you, Butters!

Stan: Yeah, we'll just get a picture of her doing something else.

Cartman: [aims his camera] All right lady, just flash us your crotch or somethin'.

Britney: I've got a better idea.

Stan: You do?

Britney: Yeah.

[Britney takes out a big shotgun, shoves the nozzle into her mouth, and pulls the trigger]

Stan, Kyle: NO!

[The gun goes off and she falls to the ground. The gun falls away from her. All four boys stand there, stunned and speechless. Cartman does not take any pictures. After a bit, Cartman turns and runs out. Butters looks at Stan and Kyle, then heads for the door]

Butters: [stops and looks back] You killed her!

Guard: Hey, everything all right u—. Oh.

It's absolutely shocking—something *South Park* is known for—as Cartman runs out the door and Butters follows. This is what the audience who were watching the real Britney expected and in a sort of perverse way wanted to happen. But *South Park* won't let us off the hook that easily. Somehow Britney survives the gunshot wound, and Stan and Kyle visit her in the hospital, feeling awful about what happened and hoping she is all right, but Britney is anything but, and as Matt and Trey said, "you're either on the train or you're left in the station." Play video:

Stan: We should have just left her alone. So we just had to push her.

Kyle: How could we know she would … Aw we suck so hard.

Doctor: *[walks up to Stan and Kyle and faces them]* She's … alive.

Kyle: Whew.

Stan: Oh, thank God.

Doctor: But, we almost lost her. Why couldn't you boys just leave her alone?

Kyle: Doctor, could we talk to her for a minute?

Doctor: I don't want you making her upset.

Stan: We don't wanna upset her, we just want to tell her that we're sorry.

Doctor: *[sighs]* All right.

[Inside Britney's recovery room]

Doctor: *[enters with Stan and Kyle]* Ms. Spears, these boys wanted to say something.

[Britney gurgles something. Only her lower jaw and the base of her skull remain of her head]

Kyle: Oh my God!

Stan: Oh no!

Doctor: *[by Britney's side]* The boys are just shocked at how good you look, Britney. *[glares at Stan and Kyle]* Right, boys?!

Kyle: Oh, yeah. Yeh-yeah. It's a—it's not even noticeable. *[Britney gurgles something back. The boys join the doctor at her side]*

Doctor: Well, I'll let you boys have your say. *[walks off. Britney gurgles something]*

Stan: *[his voice shaking]* Ms. Spears, uh ... we're ... really ... sorry for making you want to kill yourself.

Kyle: Oh, God, what have we done??

Now the episode has moved away from shocking and into an entirely new level of grotesque—something Thomas Nast or Ralph Steadman would have enjoyed. Britney has NO face and the top of her head is completely blown off. As I said, it's violent and dark but the metaphor is clear: her mind and head are completely destroyed. Also the doctor trying to console Britney, pretending like she is perfect and nothing is wrong. It's as if no one can tell her the truth about how she looks or what she did because everyone wants a piece of her. Instead, her handlers continue to lie to Britney. Everyone seems oblivious to Britney's mental state, represented by her lack of face and head; instead the paparazzi continue to stalk her and focus only on her body issues by pointing out that she may have plastic surgery for breast implants. After a few more scenes, Matt and Trey re-create Britney's infamous MTV appearance where Britney is once again criticized for her minor body issues and those who are closest to her don't realize what she has endured as the child star lost on her way to adulthood. The boys feel they are the only ones who can "do something" as they and everyone else are partially responsible for her physical and mental deterioration. This is *South Park* at its best—somehow within the disgusting and gruesome imagery, the violence, and the harsh reality of Britney possibly killing herself, the creators manage to evoke sympathy and empathy for the fallen idol. This approach and these emotions are absolute necessities when dealing with violence; otherwise, it's inhuman and the audience will not care as much when the character experiences cruelty. Play video:

Reporter: Disaster at the MTV Awards. People are ridiculing Britney Spears. Her performance was awful, Tom. She looked tired, she looked fat, she didn't have a head. It was just completely phoned in. No doubt, Tom, that girl has major issues.

[A green room. Britney, her manager, and the boys are watching the news report]

Manager: Don't listen to 'em, Brit! They're all just jealous. And we can put you on SlimFast tomorrow. *[walks over to the door and opens it. The paparazzi are there, piled up from floor to ceiling]* Hang on, hang on, she'll be out in a minute.

The manager leaves, closing the door. No paparazzi get in. Once the place is silent, she sits back on her armchair and relaxes with a sigh. Stan and Kyle can only look on as somber piano music swells]

Stan: We have to get her away from all this, dude. People just aren't gonna let up. We have to take her somewhere to just be at peace.

Kyle: Dude, where in the world can Britney Spears go where nobody will bother her?

Stan: *[strokes his chin and takes a few steps forward]* I know where.

Stan and Kyle want to put Britney Spears on a train to the North Pole where she will be safe but the paparazzi are never far behind. Kyle and Stan create a diversion, as Kyle dresses up as Britney and even though he looks nothing like the pop star, the media instinctively follows her trying to get a photograph. This is a great commentary on how the media certainly misses the details of what is really occurring to Britney, caring only for the story with the photo op and not what is behind the story. At the same time, Britney and Stan have safely boarded the train to the North Pole. Eventually, Kyle gets trapped by the media, and decides to plead for Britney's life. During his pleas the audience finds out what is really going on in the episode, as revealed by one of the members of the horde. Play video:

Kyle: Now, wait a minute! Everyone stop for one minute! *[the group turns around. Kyle drops the sunglasses]* Look, you guys are gonna end up killing her. Can't you see that Britney isn't in any condition to handle this crap anymore? I know watching celebrities go down can be fun. Me and my friends are as guilty as all of you, but maybe, well just, maybe, … it's time to let this one go. Just this one time, let's, let's all stop before it's too late, huh?

Paparazzo 6: *[steps forward]* Son, you don't seem to understand. Britney Spears … has to die.

Kyle: *[quizzically]* Huh? *[Thunder starts rolling in the distance]*

Paparazzo 7: What do you think all this effort has been for?

Manager: *[a sinister smile crosses his face]* It cannot be stopped. The purpose is too great.

Officer: She must … die.

Background Singers: Hetus. Alte omnebus. *[The photographers begins to join in]* Virtu e poquebus. *[other adults join in this nonsensical Latin chant]*

It's as if Kyle is trying to stop the Harry Lime philosophy and at the same time undo the Roger Rabbit reality that we are a sadistic people and the works are created because of that aggression.

Kyle would prefer NOT to have the art if it caused harm against Britney but the press explains, this is necessary; this is who we are as citizens. As more people within the episode explain the philosophy: "We Americans like to think we're more civilized now but the truth is our lust for torture and death is no different than in gladiator times." The gladiator times could easily be substituted for the time of medieval kings and the Borgias as Harry Lime spoke about in *The Third Man*. Then back on the train, Stan thinks he's safe with Britney but the train comes to a screeching halt because the paparazzi have located them even though the train is in the middle of nowhere. The paparazzi's reach truly knows no limits or is bounded by isolation. Britney and Stan run out of the train, and this is where *South Park* takes the episode a step further by creating violence through imagery, music, close-ups, and a level unseen before on the show. In this scene, there is no real violence occurring—but it's incredibly unsettling—as the best violence is sometimes what you don't reveal, but simply create by using tension and anticipation. Britney and Stan run through the cornfield being chased by an unknown number of people and end up in an open field, alone, yet somehow are surrounded by hundreds of bloodthirsty people. *South Park* is tapping into basic humanity here. Everything is frightening, even if it is *South Park*, but this is a new level of violence for the show. As an audience member, you're transported back in time to when our most primitive instincts and murderous urges ran rampant as our species indulged in things other species do not: the murdering for pleasure or killing for sacrifice to a higher power. Humans are seemingly the only animals that kill for other reasons than simply survival.

Pay attention to the shots, notice the close-ups, and the music that was played as Matt and Trey use extreme long shots to create a feeling of being trapped, and in turn, a violent atmosphere of inevitable death. To create a deeper tension, they cut right to a close-up of unforgiving human faces ready to execute the pop star. The scene takes another turn as both Kyle and Stan's parents show up and reveal to them that this is who we are as a people and Britney had been built up since the beginning to be sacrificed "for good harvest." And everything is a remix, as *South Park*, which used Shakespeare and other stories as inspiration, now turns to the 1948 short story "The Lottery" by Shirley Jackson for their climax. In the story, a small town uses a lottery to select a winner who will be stoned to death as a traditional sacrifice. It's unexpected and incredibly brutal when the lottery winner's fate is revealed at the end of the story. The short story caused a huge controversy in America when in was published and *South Park* used the story's final sequence to set up their controversial and violent ending. Replacing the rocks for cameras and using lines from the story, as one of the elderly characters says, "You go ahead, I'll catch up" and a mother hands her son a camera, instead of a rock, and says, "Here Davey," just like in the story. *South Park* creates a fascinating work of art that comments on the sadistic society Lime spoke about and then murders a cartoon in a horrible way, like Judge Doom did with the cute Disney shoe. We see what all the drawn and animated works before this episode have led us to: we are a vicious culture documenting our art and that art gets to the soul of what we are as a people as the synergy is completed. Make no mistake, *South Park's* choice to replace the rocks for cameras, modern society's documenting tool that has now become a tool of death, is no accident. The scene is saying quite a lot about the things we use to destroy people and the things we idolize. Play video:

Stan: Kyle, what the fuck is going on now?

Kyle: She's been built up to be sacrificed, Stan!

Stan: Sacrificed? For what?

Randy: For harvest, Stanley. Same reason we've always done it.

Canadian Paparazzo: Sacrifice in March, corn have plenty starch.

Kyle: Corn harvest!?

Randy: We haven't told you about it, Stanley, because we, we like to wait until kids are a little older to talk to them about things like condoms and ritualistic human sacrifice for harvest.

Stan: All right, enough already! This has all gone on long enough!

Manager: The kid is right. This has gone on too long.

Paparazzo 12: Yeah. She was supposed to have killed herself a long time ago.

Farmer: And harvest is coming soon.

Bob Summers: All right, folks, let's finish this quickly. *[Everyone whips out a camera and starts taking pictures, closing in on Britney all the while]*

Stan: No wait. *[Britney groans. People get close, take pictures, then make way for more people]*

Woman 2: Come on, hurry up.

Obese Woman 3: I can't run. You go ahead, I'll catch up with ya. *[the barrage of picture-taking continues. The McCormicks come up to take pictures. Britney drops to the ground, sort of pleading to be left alone, the camera flashes creating a strobe light effect on screen]*

Mother: Here Davey. *[Hands a camera to her son. The barrage continues, with Randy, other familiar faces from the show ... Britney wilts under the lights and finally lies down completely]*

Bob Summers: *[throws out his arms]* Hold on. *[A doctor walks up and checks for vital signs]*

Doctor: She's dead.

Randy: Well, I think it's time for us to leave the poor girl alone. *[Everyone turns and goes off in different directions through the windy fields and under a thunderous sky. Stan is left alone staring at Britney's corpse. Kyle is a little further away, but he too looks at the corpse]*

The scene's final image of Stan standing over Britney's corpse is held for a second or two, allowing Stan and Kyle and hopefully us to reflect on what we have done to her. The media's fascination and obsession and humanity's fascination and obsession are captured perfectly in this scene. Viewing this, we see what we're willing to accept from our society but also what society has made us into. We haven't evolved as much as one would think; we are still fans of death and destruction, but now it's in the media arena and not in a physical one. The media and society are willing to sacrifice youth and glorify beauty, all leading to the seemingly inevitable fall from grace. All the horrible notions of what Harry Lime in *The Third Man* spoke about were true then and are true now—our society has relished the carnage we partake in. It fuels us. We want to view these people as they're put on display for us to acquire the role as the judge, jury, and in this episode, executioner. But if we were to be honest, seeing what happens to a cartoon doesn't move people, it doesn't get them to change their view, but within this extremely violent and brutal scene, it has to give you pause. And sometimes that's all a piece of art is supposed to do: give you pause and reflect. The audacity of the violence is meant to scare you and to make you think. Is our society sadistic towards anyone and everyone, famous or not? Are we that violent of a species by the way we treated Britney—whom Randy calls "the poor girl" after her death—or was this *South Park* situation just an exaggerated anomaly of celebrity sacrifice? The end of the episode certainly answers that as Matt and Trey have predicted Miley Cyrus to be the next celebrity sacrifice, as Miley will be built up and then ceremoniously destroyed in some brutal fashion.

As a country we've glamorized death because we've glamorized violence, and animation has allowed us to glamorize both in a way unseen before. This *South Park* episode, while probably not the most popular, is one of the most revealing of where we are as a species. But all of this, everything we've discussed and reviewed, adds up to something: Documentation. A cataloguing of our existence of the here and now, because as Beverly Sills said, "Art is the signature of civilizations." The current and future crop of animators, they are the signatories Sills spoke about leaving their marks all over the cultural landscape. The animators reveal what the twenty-first century is truly about and where we will end up. Future historians will study animation to investigate the zeitgeist of today's culture in the hopes of understanding more about why we acted in the manner we did. Because I truly believe that every piece of animation, every character, every plot, every color, black and white, every perfect circle and imperfect square leads us to more understanding. And whatever was created last and is created next will only add to the library. Everything that came before has been remixed and re-edited. There's no spontaneous creation, it's a timeless collection of all your ideas before coming together to create one nebulous experience. The art has been there the whole time, waiting to reveal itself, because everything that has been done has led to the next creative moment. It's fate that gets us to the door, and destiny decides whether it's opened or not. Controversial pieces of art once deemed too offensive, intense, or blasphemous are now considered docile or tame. What was once taboo is now commonplace; artists and animators have created new standards as we continue to break through to move the social metric of acceptability a little further away from where it was yesterday. The question to ask is: how did that happen? The answer never is simple but, just like Thomas Nast did, our most divided times can be explained through political cartoons; like Ralph Steadman did, the world you no longer recognize is made grotesque. Robert Zemeckis answered the question in his own way by changing the rules on the treatment of the cartoons in *Roger Rabbit* and the audience accepted that treatment because we had changed with the times. This seminal moment would break open the dam and send us down the river into the lives of a little mountain town, where four boys experience violence in a very real way in *South Park*. These artists made the world real by combining art and violence as animation has moved from pencils to styli, Claymation to CGI, paints to pixels, and paper to modern tablets. Everything that is put on paper, drawn, sketched, loaded, and deleted is a representation of our civilization. Those who contribute in production or criticism are the cataloguers now, and we are allowed to interpret the world we live in. As film icon Charlie Chaplin accurately noted: "There are more valid facts and details in works of art than there are in history books." Whether it happens today or a decade from now, all creators are advancing our society by focusing on the brutality involved within it by confronting the audience with imagery that is usually shied away from. A response will occur; violence always gets a response as it always moves to the top of everyone's list. The critics are only surveyors of the war after the battles have all been fought, walking through the wounded and the lost, wondering what could have been done differently to make the work survive. The artist's job is to inform about truth, or to paraphrase Picasso: The *animated* work is the lie of reality that helps us to realize the truth about reality. But for the work to be unforgettable, it has to be uneasy and violent. There has to be a cathartic release for the viewer to enable the emotional release that we so desperately need. But whatever is drawn or animated next, Harry Lime's philosophy and worldview will be followed as long as what is animated is more than just a cuckoo clock.

3

"I am not comfortable with this," I declare with confidence. I had my last cup of coffee about three hours ago and I'm feeling fine. "I am not comfortable with this" should be the mantra for the rest of my life, especially after what James and Declan just proposed. My apprehension comes from experiences we shared in our student days, because once the three of us get going, momentum is difficult to stop or even slow down. I am not comfortable with this but from first glance, it seems as if I'm the only one. One rarely utters those words when you're younger but now the narrative has changed. I'm responsible with responsibilities, or so I think. With friends like these, any thought towards what happens tomorrow is tossed off a skinny bridge into an Amsterdam canal below and swept into the sea. Professor Beckett Adler's old lesson of forthcoming events is not applicable here and I bet he would expect nothing less from three of his former students. This is not the time for application of that type of ideology or restraint. At the moment, we're having an excellently prepared cup of coffee in Bar Italia. Luckily, our paths have crossed and we're all able to get together for most of the week. Usually, there's more planning involved, especially with our schedules, but this

worked out as if it was years in the making. The animation and violence lecture is finished. The festival's organizers were very nice and understanding given the quick three-month turnaround from *The Daily Show* lecture. But now, I'm on vacation, so there's no pressure except the one James has bestowed upon me. Old friends obtain plenty of files of information over the years and know where to push, how to bend something unbendable, and are never hesitant to use it, especially given it's been a year since our last trip. We've been taking these trips since the three of  us graduated together. After missing the first year, we've been fortunate to meet up for seven straight years. Best of all, it has never gotten old. Declan stayed in Amsterdam but travels extensively and James moved down to Spain with Lucia, the woman he met while here in school. When we get together, James acts as if he's a prisoner on a weekend furlough holding nothing back, and anyone he comes into contact with pays the price.

James's perfectly combed dark haircut refuses to move even during his most demonstrative moments and his overweight body stands out in a crowd of the slimmer Dutch and no doubt, the Spanish. The amusing aspect to his body change was because Declan and I convinced him a year ago to gain weight. On our last trip to Iceland, all James ate were salads and grilled chicken every night. Declan and I ingested all kinds of Icelandic delicacies but with James, there was nothing ever creative or abnormal in his diet. Finally, it was Declan who pushed him over the edge by hounding him constantly, and I cut the rope, and from the incredible weight gain that is evident, James hanged himself with that rope. One year and thirty-two pounds later, James's dedication to our pestering is quite jaw dropping, Lucia is anything but thrilled with us, hence her absence from this trip. Even at this age two old friends can make you do idiotic and surprisingly detrimental things to your mind, body, and soul. However, now it's my turn to get the proverbial business.

Declan remains stoic as per usual. Maybe he'll say twenty sentences tonight. Declan's brown hair, eyes, and skin have malice surrounding his every move but his stoicism adds to the mystery: his glance says everything and nothing. The interpretation is each person's to analyze. The three of us sit in front of Bar Italia as a partly cloudy day has given way to a crisp evening and the big windows are open facing the Rokin. The bar side is packed and the crowd is starting to drift towards the corridor by the bathrooms. Eventually the dining room will be converted to a bar and food area, adding to the space and excitement. There are all types of professionals, college students, and tourists here, but the Dutch are the predominant group of patrons in the bar area. Declan sits on a stool and leans up against the wall, letting James do the heavy lifting of what has to be the one of the odder requests during one of our annual trips together.

"It's expensive but it's certainly not illegal. How bad can it possibly be?" James asks both of us.

Are those famous last words of a decade-plus of friendship? "I love you guys, I do. But this is not happening," I declare with as much believability I could muster.

James ignores my steadfast remark and continues with the plan, "So, Butch will meet us around 8:30, I just need about one fifty from each of you."

There's an understandable silence between the three of us. Finally, I speak up. "James, the money is not the issue, I mean it is—"

"If I recall correctly, you forced us to spend one hundred fifty euro on a one-way ticket from Prague to Amsterdam because you 'overslept.'"

"And I still maintain it was the best one fifty we ever spent. But with this, I'm conflicted on the act and that a guy named Butch is the mule."

"First of all, he's not a mule. He probably makes more money than all of us combined." James's Midwest accent is still there even though it's fading from not being around Minnesotans for over fifteen years. "And you know, this whole responsible thing was supposed to be left on the other side of the ocean. You're done with the lecture, you did all your work, and the expenses are all paid. We're here, we got the week ahead of us, we may as well start it right."

"Or burn ourselves out so we never recover. That's all we need is to be wired on this stuff all night." I'm doing my best to stay negative. Declan watches, listens, no doubt waiting for the precise moment to tip the scales for or against. "So, what's wrong with pacing yourself? And if you remember correctly, three years ago, we were out all night at that college party and then you slept for twenty hours straight."

"Yeah, that was a good party."

"We missed the cross-channel boat and were stuck in that old lady's house for two days until it came back."

"But she did make a really good cup of coffee." James gets in the final word. He was right, she did make a good cup of coffee.

James inhales three bites of his shawarma, a meat sandwich, he got from a neighborhood joint. Declan steals some of the bread and vegetables off his plate when James looks away or towards a Dutch girl he notices. With Declan's long reach it's like stealing candy from a baby who is distracted by the shiniest object in the room.

"I want to do this," James announces as he notices some food is missing. This is how our friendship has been for the past decade: one of us wants something, we argue about it passionately, and one of us falters or wins the battle.

"And I just want to pace myself."

"I just watched a tiny little Disney shoe get murdered on a big screen, reliving childhood nightmares and you're worried about pacing yourself? This from a guy who—"

"Don't bring that up unless you're willing to make good on the money you still owe me." I interrupt James hoping that bringing up past debts is a way to get out of it. I should hold him to that obligation—I'm sure with interest it's close to four figures by now. "There's something wrong about it."

James's obvious confusion is a good stall tactic for me. "Like morally? It's not like we're killing a celebrity with cameras and using their body for corn harvest."

"Interesting argument. You were paying attention to the lecture. Here I thought you would be dreaming about this crap," I say to James as Declan straightens up. This is it, this is my big sale. James's phone vibrates, he points down to it. There's the message. It's time. "Right, this is a different kind of harvest. But yeah, morally … and I guess ethically too. How does this not make us proprietors of repugnance? All those people we used to despise, and now, you want me to join their ranks?"

"It's just once, I want to see how the 1% live. Think of it as flying first class." Ah, first class. James knows me well enough to go for my weakness.

"NO. We're like funding those who are working in a circus or something. Except this circus provides entertainment for the super-wealthy. And how long can it last? It reeks of self-importance that you're paying someone to actually do this. Declan, aren't you a vegetarian anyway? How do you rationalize this one?"

Declan shrugs his shoulders. A person's hypocrisy knows no consistency or pattern and is easily malleable given the situation.

I continue with my closing argument, "You want a better analogy …" I stumble for one. "I don't have one." I can't help but laugh. I search for the analogy and nothing comes. "Occupy Wall Street would be so proud. But regardless, there's something wrong about it, something that just—no. This is wrong and—"

"It's not as if we're committing a crime. Everyone involved knows what's going on. Everyone is well compensated. Come to think of it part of the money goes to conservation!" James is still working on Declan, and his environmental ploy may work. He knows it's going to be a two-to-one decision. If Declan agrees, I'll agree to it as our rulebook states during these trips.

There was a time when James would be on the other side convincing me not to do something this abusive? How you don't hate yourself after this is beyond me. This dilemma is no different than James's last idea of eating chocolates sprinkled with gold flakes and four hundred Swarovski crystals adorning the box. Thankfully, that was vetoed by Declan because in his words: "Someone, somewhere died for that decadent piece of dessert." That idea and this one has to be on some kind of "unacceptable for normal human actions" list, and yet here I am, debating with one of my oldest friends on why I do not want to be part of that list.

I down the last bit of my drink as James finishes his food—another round? Sure. I would happily pick up this round but if I leave, James will have free time with Declan and no doubt convince him to say yes. James won't leave because he feels I'll attempt the same. Declan looks at both of us, shakes his head, obviously annoyed that this has continued for as long as it has. He's seen this before between the two of us, it happens every time. He also knows this is his decision but has yet to acknowledge the fact. Declan always is the tiebreaker, especially when James comes up with an idea. Or maybe Declan's already reached a verdict but refuses to let the two of us know his decision. Instead, Declan is allowing us to engage in some verbal gymnastics for his amusement. However, now, maybe his patience is wearing thin. That's happened before, too. James's phone vibrates again. No one moves.

Declan rolls his eyes and makes his way over to the bar to get another round. He towers over everyone in the place; it's usually why he sits wherever we go. It's a courtesy to the surrounding area. Even when we drove to the South of France for the Belfort festival, he made sure to stand off to the side, in the back, so no one would be blocked. We also asked him to stick his head out the sunroof and yell at the top of his lungs, hoping to scare all the people in the town. He happily obliged and the irony was that he became more and more of a celebrity because of that stunt during the festival. Though we both wanted him to use his newfound fame for backstage passes or even a hotel room, he refused—that's just the type of man he is, a gentleman through and through. Walking through the crowd to the bar, several Dutchmen turn around and gasp at Declan's height, a staggering six-foot seven. When the Dutch are impressed with a man's stature, that says a lot. Yet, he's unassuming and never causes any problems with anyone. Once in a while, I wish he would just so I can view the fireworks.

James leans in, "Declan's going to say yes. So, this is decided. It's done. Over. You lost. Take the defeat and quit stalling. So, just agree to it, throw down the money, and I'll respond to Butch's text. You can't run out the clock here. Butch is close."

"Brother, all I know is that we've done plenty of things in our day. Montreal. Chicago. Edinburgh." James smiles, oh he remembers. "But there was no exploitation going on there. And I still feel bad about that cat, no matter what you tell me—"

"Oh give me a break, exploitation?! It's not as if we're buying Fiji water or investing in farm-raised salmon. That's a step too far. That stuff is god awful—nothing is ever THAT pink. But regardless, it's not exploiting."

"It isn't?" I say with doubt. If the article didn't fascinate James as much as it did, maybe this wouldn't be happening right now. We'd be here at Bar Italia having a normal drink and that would be that.

"Granted it is over-indulgent." James pauses, he knows it's more.

"Over-indulgent was taking a helicopter ride to an erupting volcano in Iceland." I pause. "Eyjafjallajökull."

"Nice pronunciation." James smiles and we each take a drink to celebrate my nailing it to perfection. When the three of us decided to take a helicopter near the volcano, the pilot kept making us repeat the name over and over. After twenty minutes, he tested us and if we didn't pronounce "Eyjafjallajökull" correctly, he would do a loop and put us upside down. Nothing motivates someone to learn a language more than the risk of vomiting up his nose and into his hair. I've never heard a giant of a man scream before and even though he doesn't look it, Declan has the most high-pitched scream ever for a man that size. Add in that Declan was afraid of the helicopter ride to begin with and capitulated only because of the two-to-one rule.

James stares at me "Ok, fine, this is REALLY over-indulgent but 'exploitative'? You have an iPhone! So don't sell me your righteous attitude—we're westerners, we exploit, it's what we do. Now let's do this." He's got me there. Declan comes back and puts the drinks on the table. He stands there, we both look up towards him.

He slams his hand down—his hand covered half the table, it seemed. It's like five tree trunks on a plank of wood. How he handles tiny screws or the keypad on his phone, I'll never know.

"Pony up, old man. You're doing it because you've both exhausted my patience. This has been going on for an hour. Get your money out." Declan removes his hand and there's one hundred fifty euro on the table. James holds his hands up in victory. My revulsion is palpable yet I begrudgingly, without argument, reach into my pocket and count out the same, placing the money on the table.

Declan sits back down and I turn to him, "Explain to me how you, a vegetarian, are going along with this?"

"I'm not eating an animal or wearing a piece of its skin."

"No, just something else." People can rationalize anything especially in the company of non-judgmental friends. James sends the text message and then, two seconds later, a response.

"We're good to go. He'll be here any minute."

"How's he so close?" Before I finish the question, I know the answer—James knew he would win and planned it accordingly, down to the minute. He slides a piece of paper towards me and smiles victoriously. If it's within five minutes, I owe him five rounds in a row. I open up the paper and it reads: 8:30 PM. I look at my phone and it reads 8:34 PM. I never had a chance. Next five rounds on me.

"How good can it be … to go through all of this?" I ask. For a place that has legalized certain drugs and practices, this whole process seems a bit overdone.

James takes out a candy bar, "As if it matters. We'll do this." He opens the candy bar and takes a bite. He chews with his mouth open.

"You know this is exactly how it looks before you get it, they just clean it for you. I should take a photo so you can see and maybe then you'll change your mind." My last-ditch effort falls on deaf ears as James gorges himself in the rest of the chocolate, never offering to share. Animal. And James used to be such a sharer.

"Just don't say, 'you got the stuff?' to this guy."

"I promise."

At that moment, James waves to someone as Butch has walked into the bar. Butch is exactly what you would expect someone named Butch to look like. He has a completely shaved head, a full beard, average suit, but also tall. He carries a suitcase that has several stickers with Asian countries on them. Is he coming or going? He walks over to our table and shakes James's hand.

Butch and James are new friends; they met when James did a Pacific island holiday with Lucia. Declan nods to Butch, refusing to shake hands as his OCD continuously evolves. Then Butch and I shake hands and we get down to business.

"You got the stuff?" James asks. I hate him as I shoot him a look. He did that on purpose. Butch nods and puts his suitcase on the table.

Butch's pitch begins, "It is not stuff, James. Only available in areas in Thailand, Abu Dhabi, United Arab Emirates, and the Maldives, this is for high-end clients who take pride in what they do. There are no exploitations of workers, as the Mahouts are compensated for their work. Nor are the animals maltreated in any way. We work tirelessly to make sure. In fact, we've seen no evidence that says they are affected by the process. We have an on-site veterinarian monitoring the situation."

"Satisfied?" James asks me without any hint of regret or subtlety. I roll my eyes in disgust, hoping the story ends so we can get moving. If I'm going to do this, I'd like to just get it over with.

"Ecstatic," I say as I channel Jafar from *Aladdin*.

Butch continues, "You are part of an exclusive club … and through that, we hope to have more people join us over the coming months and years."

I have to ask, "Hey, Butchy-boy. Is it as good as they say?" cutting right to the chase.

"Better. All the flaws from what most people are used to are eradicated within the Thai—

"I like the flaws," I interject.

"—Thai-Arabica. All the imperfections in the shit you buy are removed during the process."

"Interesting phrasing."

Butch refuses to allow my asides or interjections knock him off his flow, "With that, we can produce only a few kilos at a time, hence the cost. But I promise you, it's not as good as advertised, it is better. But discussing it, my friends, does not do it justice, only the experience will." Butch ends his statement, ignoring me, and he turns to James. "Would you like a receipt?"

Declan finally leans in, "A receipt? You're joking."

Butch looks at Declan, and realizing his stature for the first time, he takes a step back. "Yes, this is not an illegal transaction. We're businessmen, I happen to know James, that's the only reason for this level of service. If a pound went missing, there are only a few of us to blame. I'm not making money off this—it goes right into the business. So, I ask again, would you like a receipt?"

"Sure, for the record books," James says. I hate him at this moment.

"Maybe you'll frame it," I sneer at James.

Butch's spiel convinced me about the exploitation aspect but I'm still unsold on the ingredients. James hands Butch the money as if he's trying out for a role on *The Wire*, buying illegal drugs on a Baltimore street corner—even Butch has become slightly exasperated. "James, just hand the money to me. If I had a credit card machine, I'd take it out of the suitcase and use it." He turns to Declan and me: "Is he always like this?"

"Yes," Declan and I say in unison with a healthy dose of annoyance.

Embarrassed and somewhat disappointed, James sulks for a moment but perks up when Butch hands him a black brick with a round peach-colored sticker with an elephant in the middle and the words "Black Ivory Coffee" stenciled in at the bottom. With that, Butch salutes us and leaves. The three of us stare at the one-pound $500 brick. James opens the pamphlet on the Black Ivory coffee and begins to read aloud, "Invented by Blake Dinkin. He spent $300,000 on the investment. Produced in Thailand's Golden Triangle jungles."

"Isn't that the drug trade capital?" Declan asks. He's speaking more and more as the night goes on.

"The Golden Triangle Asian Elephant Foundation was chosen by Dinkin after he researched thirty-five different elephant sanctuaries in Indonesia, Laos, and Thailand." James continues to read to himself, skipping to the parts he thinks are worthy. "Ah! A herd of twenty elephants are fed a mixture of coffee beans, rice, fruit, and water. Thai-Arabica coffee beans are used; they contain only one percent caffeine. Since the coffee beans are raw, they do not extract the caffeine, thus the animals are not at risk from it. Vets perform blood tests to ensure the elephants are safe. There is not much change to the elephants' diet since they have naturally been drawn to eat coffee plants before. Does this ease your precious apprehension towards the product?"

"I'm overwhelmed with confidence," I say with as much sarcasm as a single sentence can carry.

"Interesting. It says after ingestion the beans are ready to be harvested fifteen to seventy hours later. The animal's digestive system is supposed to break down the coffee's protein, acting as a living slow cooker to bring out an exotic flavor that is unachievable otherwise."

"I bought a slow-cooker from Crate and Barrel once," I say, with my sarcasm dripping over the conversation, and hoping it hangs over the rest of James's monologue.

James has now taken to ignoring me. "Whatever, protein is responsible for the bitterness of coffee, so since the enzymes of the elephants break it down, the resulting coffee is almost bitter-free. It takes around seventy-two pounds of coffee cherries to produce two pounds of Black Ivory Coffee since elephants sometimes defecate in places like rivers that make it impossible to recover the dung."

"If the flavor is described as nutty, I'm going to be very upset." James scans the pamphlet looking for something. A huge smile comes over his face. He's trying not to laugh.

"The flavor is described by those have tasted it to be rich, earthy, and nutty."

I turn to Declan who shrugs his shoulders, then to James. No one says anything for a moment then I speak up.

"We're going to drink coffee that an elephant ate, then digested it, then … yeah. Like I said, I'm not comfortable with this. And I don't have my press, it's at the hotel, and I have a feeling Bar Italia will not want this flowing through their machine for us to drink. I don't care how friendly they happen to be."

James opens the packaging with the utmost care and precision. It's like doing lines in public. Some things no one should see. James takes out nine beans and puts three in front of Declan, three in front of me, and three for himself. "Who said anything about drinking it?" James asks rhetorically.

I am not comfortable with this. "You think I'm going to crush these up and snort them?"

James and Declan look at one another and start laughing hysterically. Finally they stop and Declan says, "You'd have to be in a really dark place in your life to snort coffee beans, my man. Matter of fact, if and hopefully not when that does happen, stand up and declare yourself to be an addict because you officially are."

Declan picks up the beans. His giant palm makes them look like three small islands in the Pacific Ocean. I know there's some reference to Jack and the Beanstalk that needs to be made here, but I'm too distracted by the moment. The beans are regular-looking beans without any hint of being fermented in elephant dung. I sniff my three beans, nothing other than perfect-smelling coffee.

"I'm not going to count to three. Just eat them," James declares. I can't bring myself to do it, regardless of the cleanliness or the taste, the simple fact is: an elephant ate this, then excreted it, someone picked it out of their crap, cleaned it, put it in a box (which is quite nice by the way), and now a few thousand miles later—three beans sit in my hand. I stare at them. Wondering one thing: what's next for my coffee fascination? Olli should be here for a follow-up article.

Declan puts the beans in his mouth, my horror is evident, three chews and the beans are swallowed—god, even his mouth is huge. James, seeing Declan beat him to the punch, eats them as well, but instead of three chews, James works the beans from side to side, all around his mouth.

Watching him all I can think about is that this man wouldn't even eat meat now he's eating elephant dung–fermented coffee beans.

"Those are pretty good," Declan muses, he's about to take a drink, but stops himself and then says, "I'm not going to wash it down. Let it marinate—"

"Just like it did in the elephant's crap. Yeah, man, let it marinate."

"For a price this high, I'm going to savor the flavor because this will not happen again."

They both are waiting for me, like two teenagers who took acid for the first time, now waiting for their friend to partake. Not much more to do but to eat it. How awful could it be? Ignore the terrible reality of where it's been, rationalize, and be pragmatic. I can do this.

James gets serious for a moment, "First time we're all back in Amsterdam, brother. Time to pay his tribute." Like I said, friends know how to push each other, James goes for my weakness. "I don't even drink coffee but we all know you do, that's why I got this. I did all of this—for you, for him, for us."

"Cheap shot."

"Yeah, but it's working. Told you I would think of something good for him."

The three beans are nestled in the palm of my hand, and the beans are split down the middle looking perfect. The shape, texture, size, and everything—but for the fact that this has been in—

Out of nowhere, a Thai elephant seemingly possessed my mind and body, forcing me to experience his spoils (in this case soils). And I am eating them.

Chew. Ignore the reality. Ignore the strange tastes. Chew and chew some more.

"So, what do you think?" James asks, as he stares at the brick of coffee, and caresses it like a new food dish he has discovered.

Declan nods in approval and awaits my response.

"It's absolutely … " I want to say: disgusting, repulsive, vomit inducing but "this is really good. What the—oh man. That is good. Why does it have to be good?!" I finally say, giving in to everything that James fought for.

"I KNEW IT!" James yells, declaring victory to anyone in earshot. He checks the time, and I know what's next. "I know you have your press in your hotel room, if we leave now we can drink some to start the night."

Declan nods and is putting his jacket on before James finishes his sentence. James follows suit. Peer pressure and exotic coffee. I'm loath to admit it but I'm getting more comfortable with this.

James smells the coffee brick, "Welcome to the one percent."

"God, I hate you guys."

ORIGINS: SHADOWS OF FORTHCOMING EVENTS

1

The heat has been oppressive. There are daily reports throughout the summer of a rising death toll spreading across the continent. The panic hasn't stopped the Dutch, determined as ever, from biking through the streets, lounging outside perched above the canals, and enjoying the unusually hot summer. Despite the extreme temperatures, Professor Beckett Adler requested our weekly meeting to be moved to the Oude Leliestraat Bridge near the famous Multatuli statue over the Singel Canal. Professor Adler says the heat and humidity reminds him of home. I responded, "It reminds me of why I left." We're waiting for a waiter to come by and take our order. This could take a while. The impromptu venue change elevates my nerves, as Professor Adler wants to discuss my thesis project. Let the mental games and gymnastics begin. Deep breaths. Deep. Breaths. I can navigate through this.

Professor Adler, or Beckett or Beck, as he always reminds me to address him, was exactly what you would want an intellectual to look like. He has round thick glasses, long hair that is slightly graying, and facial hair indicating his passion for work foregoing other details. He's fit from biking for the last few years but is beginning to expand a bit in the stomach area. We usually meet after class or in the evening, but not today. Beckett smokes a cigar, and puffs out the smoke away from any of the patrons seated around us. He's very cognizant of smoke even if the Dutch do not seem to mind. I appreciate the effort. I hang on Beckett's every word. He knows it but doesn't acknowledge the information, nor would I disclose as much, because if I did, he'd have to answer the statement, and I'm not mentally capable of handling the possible negative reaction.

Even though the heat is intense, the numerous conversations with Beckett are as imposing as his name. The pressure to live up to a legendary writer and thinker turns my stomach. Every time we speak, I feel like it would be best if he were in my headphones so I can drown out the entire world. I am not prepared for the rigorous interrogation, especially after my latest adventure with Declan and James.

"You just returned from …?" Beckett's voice represents all he is—half Irish, half American, raised in the Northeast corridor right outside New York. His parents were obvious Samuel Beckett fans: talk about familial demands and expectations. My mother wanted to name me Lennon but she thought better of it. Beckett's cigar and alcohol abuse is just starting to affect his bass, vocal cords, and cadence. Over the subsequent years, one can only imagine how low his voice will go but right now, it's hypnotic and addicting. There are days when I wish he would just read a monologue standing in a square.

"Berlin, Prague, and Bratislava. I went with Declan and James—you know them," I answer, giving my travel itinerary and companions.

"Yes, the skinny one and the tall one from my US-EU relations course. Talented kids."

I laugh a bit because that's how everyone describes them—the skinny one and the tall one. I wonder how he describes me to others. "That bus ride was brutal," giving him my one-star review.

"Eventually, you will not have to partake in such mode of transportation. Nothing says accomplishment more than foregoing a bus schedule and never buying from IKEA again. That is the moment when you realize you are successful," he says with an air of well-earned superiority.

"Actually, we missed the bus home, totally my fault, but we caught a flight from Prague to here. Took an hour."

"And would have been over fifteen hours, I would guess, by bus."

"About that. Best use of one hundred fifty euro."

Beckett removes his notebook from his bag and nods. The pleasantries are over and he's ready to work. The notebook is a brown leather-bound book that looks incredibly worn and damaged. There are several dark red blotches on the cover, from what, I'm not too sure. Most people would toss out a notebook that old and stained, but Beckett continues to use it and refill the pages when needed. I counter with my own pathetic excuse for a notebook. A pen mark on the cover is all the wear mine bears. I quickly and discreetly bend the spiral a bit just to keep up the illusion of usage.

"Your growth is what I care about and the thesis will reveal to me how much you have evolved as a student. In a few weeks, you'll present some of your research and I'll approve if you're ready to write your thesis. I'm aiming for sixty pages. With that, the last we spoke, you discussed artists, yet you lacked any real art history foundation. With your time drawing to a close here … ."

"I'm never going back," I correct him, with a resolve that surprises even myself.

He takes another puff. "Yes, you've indicated as much. We all go back home, regardless of what's waiting for us, prodigal sons, disappointing daughters, or not. We all go home even knowing the memories that come with that return."

He wasn't joking. As a kid in the late 1960s, Beckett witnessed his gay younger brother be sent off to a mental hospital and die mysteriously weeks later. He was never shy about sharing the story, in fact, he told it to the class on the first day. This traumatic event would dictate Beckett's future experiences and his outlook towards intolerance, racism, and bigotry. He strived to understand why people do the things they do. He once told me, "If you're going to be tolerant, you must tolerate the intolerant. The advantage to knowing someone's outlook is you are aware of where they place on the spectrum. I'd rather know a racist than be surprised by a bigot."

Though somehow, Beckett didn't mind racism or any ugly bits of humanity, as long as no one was hurt or affected by them. Which never happened. While there's hint of idealism sure, it's quite functional given the times we live in. Considering his history, it's an astounding thought progression. But his fears, which influence his lectures and writing, are about power and what it does to people. To Beckett, just because people can, doesn't mean they should, especially when discussing society's upper classes. Beckett wanted to know why people did what they did, when they knew they probably shouldn't do it. During the age of terrorism, the words and ideas have flowed for him. Those tragic events were where we connected. Even though it's only been two years, the recovery for him while living abroad hasn't been any easier. The struggle of knowing someone who died hasn't faded; it just makes the two years seem a little more torturous. For me, the event was the impetus to leave the city and pursue an ex-pat existence. Some friends and family claimed I ran from dealing with the tragedy. I would counter that New York just wasn't fun anymore. Considering all the drawbacks in New York from the trains to the overcrowding to the smells or any other complaints New Yorkers rightfully have to list, most are still excited to live there. New Yorkers put up with the inconveniences because it is New York and the city is alive. However, if the city's carnival atmosphere were swapped for an interminable Irish wake, you'd want to leave as soon as possible, too. That was New York after 9/11.

Beckett's latest lecture on what he felt would be the inevitable civil war between the three factions in Iraq went over well here in Holland, however, the same cannot be said when he returned to the states. No country wants to hear that their pre-emptive invasion of another country is going to go horribly wrong, especially only a few months into the war of choice that a majority of the country's citizenry supports.

"After this you have what class?" he asks me without making any eye contact.

"A guest speaker in my Constitutional law course—something Mueller."

"Yes, Gerhard Mueller from Rutgers, he is an incredible lecturer. You'll enjoy his style."

For Beckett to praise someone is not necessarily rare but definitely surprising. His frustration with his current crop of students stemmed from professors being too soft on the next generation of thinkers. To him, if you didn't cry at least once in his class or during a meeting, that was his failing, not yours. He joked that it was his revenge for his Catholic upbringing.

"Your interests in power are obvious to everyone in the class. But what aspect of power? Your humor and political ideology lend to satire, given your philistine nature and lack of taste." He always manages to insult, like a sniper, where you're on the ground and bleeding before you even realize you've taken one to the chest. Worst of all, he smiles when he does it. "But that is what you need to articulate, this is what you need to explore further." Beckett leans back awaiting my answer.

I want to impress him, blow him away with something that excites him. Beckett has zero ability to hide his enthusiasm so when it does happen, there's an incredible satisfaction. "Influence. Power. Why one has it, how someone loses it or squanders it—"

"YES! Squanders it!" he perks up properly stimulated. "Apparently some leaders refuse to read the history books." He takes another puff of his cigar, cracks his neck left and then right, exhaling away from me. "Politicians, and people for that matter, myself included, rarely see the shadows of forthcoming events."

I write that down: Shadows. Of. Forthcoming. Events. The waitress finally comes over to take our order. "Coffee. Black. What would you like?"

"Tea."

Beckett puts his cigar down, "'*Tea*'? I swear tea parties will lead to society's end," he says contemptuously. "If you plan on studying under me during your time in this program, you have two choices and two choices only: coffee or whiskey. Being ten AM, it's too early for one of those choices."

I want to be a smart-ass and say, "whiskey" but I can sense he's being quite serious. "My girlfriend drinks tea. She makes me have teatime with her … three times a day. I've grown accustomed to it over the past few months."

"No need to lie to me, she's not around."

I put my head down in shame. "I hate it, I really do, it's painful but she's English, with a posh accent, difficult to say no—"

"Yes, Isabella. The girl who believes Marx is the answer to everything who also wears a thousand-dollar watch. Regardless, tea three times a day, huh? What an absolute waste of water. Coffee is the drink of the gods. Whiskey is that of the devil. Tea is a drink's version of waiting in limbo, passing the time before—eh, who bloody who cares! Coffee. Whiskey. Next." Beckett stops his inevitable rant and changes tone, hoping the next few sentences penetrate my psyche. "A good cup of coffee will propel you to wonderful things. The coffeehouse is still one of the oldest meeting places in the world. Our existence is predicated on the cup and sharing one with friends or the commencement of a new friendship."

He called me a friend. Don't acknowledge it, and just act like it's the most natural thing. "I've never really drunk coffee." I realize my mistake, and a flush of red covers every part of my face. "I mean—I mean I have but I never really got into it. I'd rather have a beer with friends."

"Ah, graduate students. We will just have to remedy that." He turns to the waiter, "Two coffees. Black. Rather, bring him some milk for his and make sure he receives two cookies." The waiter nods and walks back into the restaurant.

Maybe it was the cult of his personality that had me believe every word he said. He'd later profess he was just older and declare, "You'll get there too, and someone else will look at you the same way."

"You were saying something about the shadows of forthcoming events," attempting to get the train back on track, which is an absolute necessity considering our propensity to ramble. He finishes his cigar. Over the past eight months, we've gotten closer but still maintain the teacher–student relationship, even if he did just use the word "friend." Over the course of these meetings with him, I've realized that when Beckett finishes a cigar, he admits something from his past. Not that he ever smokes in class, but his class lectures are autobiographical and that is what draws you in. "My plan wasn't to end up here. After Bosnia, Somalia and Rwanda, I wandered into a self-imposed exile. I miss the work, especially now with what is happening in Iraq but …" His pause completes the sentence: he was burnt out and suffering from what he witnessed. "I relocated to Amsterdam with a beautiful Dutch journalist and I have been here ever since."

On the attacks' one-year anniversary, the University hosted a special lecture with Beckett, the lone American, taking part in the panel discussion with two guest speakers. I had no desire to go but felt obligated to do so. I hadn't watched any video clips or read any news about that infamous Tuesday. I just couldn't. A year later, finally having left the scene of the crime, it was the right time for me to deal with the catastrophe in my own way. Arriving in the lecture hall, Beckett and I were the only two Americans in attendance. I was seated next to a wonderfully polite Dutch-Indonesian girl whose ability to take dictation was absolutely top-notch. She'd make an incredible court reporter. She continuously underlined any terms that she felt were objectionable but she refused to speak up. It wasn't until one of the lecturers said that, "America is to blame for their own tragedy," that I felt compelled to defend my country even if a majority of the room stayed silent. Before Beckett could interject on behalf of the panel, I stood up and railed against what I thought was an unnecessary and heartless insult. Eventually, though, and quite tactfully, Beckett stopped the arguing between us and thanked me for my outbursts. After the lecture, he approached me and critiqued what I said but also what I didn't say. He told me he was impressed even when I "passionately yet probably foolhardily" yelled: "the only acceptable form of international racism is anti-Americanism." Beckett threw a few insult grenades at me for good measure and we've worked together ever since. The abuse and critique still occur on a daily basis. You should see his emails!

Beckett's stories were never linear, they are told as if he's trying to put his life puzzle together by recollecting out loud the major plot points. The tortuous logic sprinkled with the what-ifs can be heard in each reflection and pause. He continues, "If history had been the proper guide, I would have seen everything laid out before my feet. If these last two years are any indicator of where we reside as an evolved species—"The puzzle pieces are forming in his mind. "—I can bestow examples of how we're not superior to our parents, our ancestors or our forefathers. Whether it's war or love, our hopes and dreams will continue to cloud reality. Eventually, losses will stack up like a pyramid scheme built on defeat, regret, and expectations piling up, one above the other. And one of us will have to sacrifice for the other. In my case, I could either have gone to DC or stayed here; if her path took her anywhere else, we would move on from one another."

The waiter brings the coffee, and Beckett checks that I have been served two cookies. He nods in satisfaction. I watch him with his coffee. Should I emulate him or should I guess how to prepare this on my own? Beckett opens a pack of sugar, licks his pinky finger, and dips it into the packet and then into the cup of coffee. He licks his finger, looking at me, smiling. "Everyone has their things. It's an acceptable vice."

I debate whether to add sugar or the milk but decided against it. My first cup is black. We each take a sip. My facial expression cannot hide the disgust. Beckett smiles and does his ritual once again. "You'll find your way. Everyone likes their own cocktail, so, when you find yours, do not judge others. Unless they use 'non-dairy coffee whitener.' That has to be dangerous and without one iota of nutrition. In fact, judge those who use artificial coffee additives and judge harshly."

"You use sugar," I sarcastically remind him.

"Ah, yes, but sugar in the raw and never saccharin. Never. That and those god-awful non-dairy creamers. Even in a pinch."

His life lessons were never trite, or for me, they weren't. If I were to review them, I would have to say each one is drenched in failure with a small fault line of optimism. No amount of success or money could alleviate the pain inside or calm the nightmares he was still having even years removed from what he witnessed working in Eastern Europe and Africa. Some students shied away from him because of the violence and slaughter he documented while covering the atrocities. Add in Beckett's brashness, and only a few could survive his tough-love approach. He would say "honesty makes us better thinkers." Students would call him a prick after he'd steamrolled them in front of the class. And they'd both be right. When he revealed that he'd reported on a mass grave of Tutsis Rwandans, only days after hearing a radio broadcast calling them cockroaches and advocating their deaths, some students softened their feelings towards him. But most never understood how fundamentally changed a person is from witnessing such carnage. Or the bitterness that grew inside him that a majority of people he dealt with never would understand. His personal and professional circle consisted of mentally damaged journalists and humanitarians because they were the only people who understood each other's pain. This tight circle benefited me when trying to understand why military people stick so closely together. Only those who know and were there get the story, the pauses, the pain, and hence the camaraderie.

Beckett continues his story about where he came from and enjoying his coffee. I observe his facial expressions and nervous tics as he ponders his next thought.

"There's something to be said about proximity. While humdrum to humanity's romantic nature, the benefits in hindsight are rather inviting. Dealing with someone else is a challenge in and of itself, no use in adding to it," he says, resuming his story. "We, naively, believed that because we're in a time period of new kinds of technology and communication, we could defy the odds."

"But you couldn't," I interject, attempting to grasp where he's headed with today's lesson.

"Precisely right. I'm sure those who used the telegraph felt the same way. This time, it will not be like the others," he says with added oomph. "If you attain any knowledge in your time here outside of books, know that there is nothing new, just a slight evolution of presentation. As most stories go, we refuse with every fiber of our beings to see the shadows of forthcoming events—we honestly believe that THIS one will be different."

"You're not together anymore? You broke up?"

"She prefers to say that, 'we began to present our true nature.' And she was not inaccurate with her assessment. She wanted to continue working, and I found my niche at the University. She took a job in the Middle East. I remained." Beckett takes a packet of sugar and pours it into the cup. There's only a quarter cup of coffee left. He polishes off the last bit as I struggle with my black coffee. He motions to the waiter for another round. How can he drink hot coffee in this weather? He continues with his soliloquy, "When presented with a decision and we're fortunate enough to cosmically see all the variables—the sacrifice, the reality—that lay ahead, if we can channel that insight, our decisions will not be as agonizing as we all feared. In fact, we'll end up appreciating what we had before we decided to alter it."

"The shadows of forthcoming events."

Every conversation is this intense and filled with pearls of hard-won wisdom. I should buy a recorder so I don't have to write everything down and soak my hand in warm water afterwards.

Maybe because Beckett and I grew up in the same region, had the same hatred towards superficial and regional things, or were similarly affected by events no one saw coming, I never succeeded in seeing how others saw him. Maybe he saw something in me that let his misanthropic nature dissipate with each meeting. However, today, this is by far the most he's ever revealed and I can't help wondering why.

"And that leads up to your research. Your love of animation, violence, satire, power, cartoons, and history made this an easy decision."

The coffee's bitterness rushes down my throat but I am able to reach the bottom of the cup. Beckett takes out a large book, faded and ruffled. A Jabba the Hutt–type cartoon is on the cover. He hands the book over to me, and I read the title out loud, "The Art and Politics of Thomas Nast."

"You can read, surprising me still, even after a year together. Eventually, you'll be reading paragraphs." An unnecessary sniper shot. "Turn to the page with the post-it."

I open the book almost dead smack in the middle. On the page is a rendering of Thomas Nast's drawing from June 4, 1870 titled: "Shadows of Forthcoming Events." I was enthralled by the details even if it was split down the middle because the image adorns both pages. There were three rows of boxes all telling a story about what will happen when the Democratic Party wins power in 1870. Nast's signature in the middle box on the bottom row, the TH with a period and Nast with a "T" that was swooshed under the "S." it was like his signature was running into the future to come back and report on what will happen to New York City.

Beckett clears his throat to put more bass into his voice, "Thomas Nast, the father of American political cartoons, prophesied what would transpire if Boss Tweed and Tammany Hall won their elections. He saw the future. He could see the suffering, the pillaging, the cronyism, and the brutality. His prophetic eye was put on paper for everyone in New York to see …. Why would an image be more powerful than the written word?" He is always testing me but I am too stunned at Nast's work, having never before seen anything like this, to muster a response. I want to see more and flip through the pages; I want to see every piece he's ever drawn.

The answer comes to me, "Because … in the nineteenth century, literacy rates were low due to the influx of immigrants, especially the Irish, even with the universal education laws of the 1820s."

"They couldn't read but they could see those damn pictures." The waiter brings over our refills but I'm too transfixed on the images before me to acknowledge the new cup. "Thomas Nast kinged presidents and then used his influence and power to go to war with the most corrupt American political party possibly ever—and won."

"How did he … "

"That's your task. My charge is to introduce you to things—yours is to find your place within the story." I continue perusing the book with each image giving me more and more ideas on what to discuss. Beckett sits across from me in silence and lets me work. He lights up another cigar and puffs away, basking in the warmth of the day. He then motions to my coffee by tapping his index finger on the table. I venture a guess on what would appeal to my taste buds: milk and sugar in the second cup. That's how James took his coffee and his taste isn't horrendous. I finish pouring and begin stirring, trying to formulate ideas. But Beckett continues with his lesson of the day, "What makes history so fascinating is that we are aware of the outcome. Being a student of history, you have the knowledge of the mistakes of Gettysburg and the correct decisions of Normandy but that can only go so far for this new Battle of Baghdad." Beckett looks out towards the canal. "So, why are those who pushed for invasion so convinced they're right in this war and some are so convinced it's the greatest blunder in our country's history, maybe worse than Vietnam?"

Overwhelmed is the only word that comes to mind. I want him to slow down, it's all going too fast but if I do, he will only speed up. I stop and realize the book is not arranged in sequentially but by subject. Nast was around during the rise of Communism, the Civil War, Lincoln's assassination, and the Republican North and Democratic South. I notice several images of the Republican Elephant. I turn to Beckett, "Nast seems quite influential towards the Republican party."

"He did create their mascot. And not a mascot for just the Republican Party: it represented a majority of America. Especially, as you read, during war time—and why would that be? Why would people turn to a cartoonist in a time of war?"

"Because humans turn to those in influential positions in times of crisis, and in the nineteenth century, Thomas Nast was one of those men." Beckett nods but wants more, I'm beginning to understand, "And in today's crisis, Americans have their influences and not just those in power but those in media. The commentators, the pundits, even the propaganda to win public opinion." I get it. "There is nothing new, just a slight evolution of presentation."

Beckett's satisfaction is as evident as his joy in dipping his finger into the sugar. "Excellent. Now drink your coffee, you have class soon. Give my best to Professor Mueller."

2

There's nothing worse than seeing a fallen idol revealing who they truly are. It's on par with the first time you witness your father showing physical pain: the varnish of invincibility begins to wear, and mortality takes shape. The superhero's cape, tattered and torn, reveals weakness. But because he's shown so much strength through the years, you'd rather not focus on the flaws. Human nature forces us to move past the minor (or major) imperfections. Beckett's pain is evident as he continued to grapple with the decisions he's made and his inability to foresee the shadows of forthcoming events. Over the next six weeks we met frequently, drinking coffee (though I observed he drank more whiskey than coffee), sitting outside by a canal, suffering through the severe heat and humidity while discussing Thomas Nast and more current events. Our meetings were usually in the afternoon because classes were over; mornings were out because Beckett preferred to sleep in. Within those discussions, the teacher–student relationship started to move towards friendship and a form of mutual respect. I will always adore him, no matter what success I achieve (or lack), but

Beckett reciprocated by removing any veil of secrecy he had left. It's an interesting contract that neither of us signed but both followed nonetheless.

He was alone but not lonely—maybe I was his outlet? And his recovery from losing his woman was not going as planned. The way Beckett described the aftermath of his relationship was "I live in a cemetery and I am petrified of ghosts." It's a statement anyone who has suffered yet-feared memories of the past could understand. That's what Amsterdam had become for him. He longed to leave but complacency and comfort overtook any notion of movement. Even the most driven tend to lose focus when they've been spun off their axis for too long. Beckett accepted his path of grief but the silver lining was that he knew there was an end game, even if he couldn't envision it at the moment.

Our meeting on the Spuistraat at Café Schuim was going to be the last meeting of the summer before he went on vacation. Usually meeting outside, today it's finally raining so we will meet inside. I arrived early to finish some of my notes, and observed the décor of the café. The waitress comes over and I order a coffee and apple pie with whipped cream. I eat dessert only when I'm nervous.

The bar is to the left of the entrance and has several stools and a chalkboard of food options. Scattered throughout are round and rectangular tables with colorful low chairs with high-rise backs. Most of the chairs' backs look like different colored bananas, making almost a glove or hand to sit in. They're surprisingly comfortable. The art on the wall is always changing. This month's collection looks like a Jackson Pollock rip-off with no discernible rhyme or reason. Who chooses this artwork?

I'm still affected by Professor Mueller's lecture from six weeks ago and Beckett seemed rather fine with the influence. Mueller was able to tie together the beginning of time and civilization and relate it to what George W. Bush did to the United Nations. At the end, I shook Professor Mueller's hand but couldn't say anything more—I was that anxious and immediately left and got some dessert.

But now, my work is ready to present for formal permission to proceed to thesis writing. Beckett walks in the door, carrying a large plastic bag about two feet by two feet. He's more sober than usual, and almost giddy. His normally surly attitude can be observed by anyone with better than 20/40 vision. He scans the room quickly and sees me in the corner and walks over.

"Who in bloody hell chooses this artwork?" he rhetorically asks anyone in earshot, looking at the paintings on the wall. He sits down and nods to the waitress placing his usual order. "Every time the artwork gets more and more unbearable."

"It's part of the charm."

"It's part of something, all right—not sure if 'charm' is the word I'd utilize for this abomination."

Beckett reaches into his bag, taking out his favorite notebook filled with pages, and is ready to write. I can't help always looking at the red blotches, which I found out were blood spatter from friends he lost while working in war zones. This is his shrine to them and he takes the book wherever he goes. When he caught me staring at the stains one day, he told me, "Tragic events need constant reminders" and proceeded to tell me about his friends and what happened in those last moments. The details of the story harkened back to when he told us the story of his younger brother's mysterious death; his memory was like a curse he couldn't break.

"Everything all right after the blackout? Everyone check in?" His concern for everyone was evident. Being so far away from home during events like a blackout, you wish you were there to help but are so glad you aren't there suffering with them.

"Yeah, pretty crazy stuff. We were in a bar when we found out. I turned to James and said, 'That looks rough,' and we ordered another round. Being away from home, I've come to accept distance makes you powerless. How about you and yours?"

"Yes, all is well. Though some places are still without power and, of course, the inevitable rush to assume the worst. Understandable after everything that has happened, but disappointing that we even have to entertain the thought."

Beckett stops mid-thought. "Are you ready?" he asks, throwing me completely off guard.

"Um, I think so. Got my coffee, apple pie for the nerves."

"If I was worried about your project you'd be well informed of it by this time," Beckett says, immediately calming any anxiety I had. I push the pie towards the middle of the table. "You're prepared. Now present."

I take out a digital recorder and hit the play button, then reach down to the floor and pick up a large bounded book. "It's amazing what an old library's basement has." I hand the book to Beckett and pick up a binder and put it on the table, ready to open when needed. "Albert Bigelow Paine wrote Nast's biography and it's quite expansive, seemingly covering all the events of the man's life. I didn't want to do that with you. But I have to start somewhere and when Nast, a German immigrant, moved to New York City at seven years of age, he would wander down to the Five Points area. Major fires would often engulf apartment buildings, businesses, sometimes entire streets and neighborhoods. Nast had never seen a neighborhood fire before and he watched with wonder as the inferno raged through the Five Points, lighting up the hell the people lived in. Crowds could gather not to simply observe the blaze torching their block but the battle royale that was certain to come. Warring fire companies would fight one another, instead of the fire itself—"

"That's the one thing Scorsese seemed to get right in *Gangs of New York*," Beckett remarks, loud enough for me to hear but not emphatic enough to warrant a reaction. He is smiling as he drinks his coffee, intently paying attention, waiting for the precise moment to interrupt, pounce, and knock me off balance.

I continue before giving Beckett a real opening, "The fires and the fighting companies didn't matter. The only element that mattered was William M. Tweed, the man running the show. Over the next two decades, Tweed would amass great power and eventually be known as Boss Tweed. The seven-year-old Nast, in awe of a burning building, would meet Tweed during the fire riots, twenty years before their epic fight over New York's soul, its government, and its treasury. It's quite cinematic and dramatic. I sit there and imagine a short boy looking at this giant of man, as Tweed

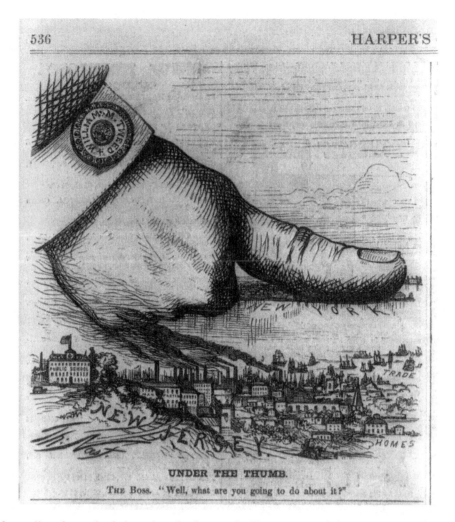

536   HARPER'S

UNDER THE THUMB.

THE BOSS. "Well, what are you going to do about it?"

was six feet tall and weighed three hundred pounds. Even to an adult, six-two is tall; visually, you had to wonder what that means to a seven-year-old. When Nast would eventually battle Tweed and his corrupt political machine, Tammany Hall, Nast would treat Tweed as an oversized bully who was overwhelming everyone around him. Nast viewed Tweed as a man so powerful he had the entire city of New York under his thumb."

I open the binder to show him the first image: "Under the Thumb."

I break down the print as best I can, "I'm amazed at this political cartoon. Even though I have no 'art history' background, it's easy to see why Nast was able to reach everyone who viewed his sketches. They're simple, bold, and unmistakable in their intent. Even me, with my philistine nature, can understand what Nast is attempting to portray by having Tweed's thumb cover all of New York City. The imagery needed to be this way, as the bulk of Tweed's supporters were immigrants and in all probability illiterate, too. Another image is 'Can the Law Reach Him?' with a policeman attempting to handcuff the massive Tweed while a petty criminal is in jailhouse clothing. Tweed truly was a gargantuan figure towering over the law."

Beckett observes the two pieces and makes a notation in his book with the red stains. He motions for me to continue.

"It's as if Nast would forever draw Tweed as Nast the child remembered him: an ogre of a man standing over the fray of riots and fires. Tweed, as Nast would immortalize him, was a man who surveyed the carnage from high above as the fires burned and engulfed his people. No matter the how high the flames got, Tweed was always unscathed. Tweed was a vulture, a predatory emperor perched above our democratic system, destroying it from within and picking off every last bit he could. But Nast's journey and Tweed's reign wouldn't intersect with one another for some time. For two heavyweights to meet, they have to overcome or dispatch several obstacles, and Paine as Nast's biographer does an excellent job at taking us through Nast's life step by step. Nast would have to survive and take part in tragedies and victories. But in every good story, there's a similarity as the rise between two players leads to the eventual showdown. This story is no different. Comparable to Tweed, Nast's power was not in the ballot box but with the hearts and minds of the people.

Beckett finally interrupts, "Something every army needs to win to survive, especially against an embedded foe with a huge following."

"And it's needed to conquer. Tweed accomplished this by catering to the Irish as well as the poor. Giving them food and aid but stealing from the city in a way unseen before and probably since. It's a classic sleight of hand, respectability out in the public forum but behind closed doors, robbing the people blind."

"Good."

I inhale deeply and exhale slowly, knowing the next words will either make this meeting a success or a disaster. If Beckett insults me, it's a disaster; if it's a success, he will go along with the statement and help me expand.

"Relating Nast to today, Fox News has captured the hearts and minds of the American people over the past few years," I declare, hoping the definitive statement convinces him to play along.

Beckett thinks for a moment. "Even if the mind is clearly traumatized—"

"And the heart is broken with only time able to properly heal it," I remark, finishing his sentence.

"Are you comparing Nast to Fox News?" Beckett says with a smile that can mean only one thing: He's enjoying himself and where this is going.

"Well, Nast was a Republican, but the original version of the term that stems from President Lincoln, and not the one that has been on the news today or even the last several years—"

"You think this is bad? It's only going to get worse," Beckett says, prophesying to everyone and no one in particular. He should sell stock on his prognostications. I'd buy a few shares.

"Nast's meteoric rise can mirror that of Fox News. Then again, I don't necessarily agree, but yes, both dealt with national tragedies 9/11, the Civil War, Lincoln's assassination, and gained support for their causes—"

"Say 'ginned up' when speaking about the South. I love the play on words."

"All right, ginned up support for their causes by portraying the enemy in a less-than-flattering light." He's right, definitely a nice pun and fun to say. "Nast's ascendancy and eventually being coined 'the father of American political cartooning' and 'a king-maker' would commence with his coverage of the American Civil War."

Beckett holds up his finger, indicating a pause. He sips his coffee, catches a quick glimpse of the pie and takes a bite, chews slowly. This is Beckett in all his glory—you wait for him and he builds up the suspense. As I've said before: Some like it, others love it, and many are frustrated by it. I'm all three at the moment.

"Good, keep going. You researched Fox News, and then you radically changed direction to study a 19th century political cartoonist. Merge the two and don't waste my time." I'm officially the latter at the moment. I gather my thoughts, hoping for no more interruptions.

"During the Civil War the country was split in two. Over the past few years, this country has experienced the same and we're only becoming more and more divided. Nast had the events leading up to the Civil War and" I pause, hoping the abstract train leaves the station with Beckett on board, "contemporary America had the Clinton Presidency, his impeachment, the Bush–Gore election debacle, the year 2000 with the Y2K scare, and then of course, September 11th. Fox News represents a voice of a bewildered and frustrated people as the network is yelling and screaming at a foreign entity, blaming others for the struggles of our country, refusing to look inward for the flaws."

"It's quite the challenge to comment on the flaws of your own relationships," Beckett adds, and writes down a few things in his book.

"So I am learning. The network's ascension was aided by their viewers' unflinching support and fear of the other. Due to the events of the past few years, Fox News has become a powerful media entity because they had the perfect narrative—fear of the future. The reason for the cable station's success was a series of unfortunate incidents that played into their conservative hands. In fact, Fox News was hemorrhaging money during its first few years of existence and probably headed for full cancellation—"

"Are you saying that if the 2000 election was a normal election, Fox News wouldn't exist in its current form?"

I struggle with a declarative statement of that magnitude. I'm doing my best to keep up with his interrogation. "I think it being their first election, they were primed for some success, but not this level of success. After the Clinton Presidency and all the disappointments of his last two years from both sides of the aisle, frustration was bound to boil over. But it is never just one occurrence or scandal, no matter how badly we want it to be, it's these few in succession that would give Fox News its power. Just like Nast, one Nast drawing or cartoon didn't change the tide or give him the power he would eventually wield. It was a series of drawings that would lead him there. Nast would use emotional collateral from his Civil War pieces to the Abraham Lincoln pieces to take on even more prominent issues in the future."

Beckett makes a note in his book, reciting the words, "Emotional collateral." He motions using his pen for me to continue.

"Everyone from businesses to governments wants to move the populace to its causes and needs, and all the while attempting to stock up on the emotional collateral they'll cash in on later. Just continuously putting it in the proverbial bank of unchecked emotion until you decide to use it."

"Emotional collateral allows for a cartoonist to affect a nation's feelings towards a political party or politicians?" Beckett asks, seeing where this conversation is headed but he seems skeptical. "The truth and the human emotion of 'I've been with you through thick and thin.' Trauma makes for wonderful yet distorted friendships. The hope is the person who obtains this collateral uses it wisely."

"Then again, who decides what is 'wisely,'" Beckett chimes in, interrupting my flow.

"Nast would use his emotional collateral to take on Tammany Hall and Boss Tweed, a corrupt organization and politician to save the city and maybe the country."

"Yes, but right now, what is Nast's advantage? Why does his story seem to work and the others do not?"

"Because we know the answers to the Nast questions. The present has no final answer because the story isn't finished. George W. Bush may be right that Iraqi freedom will lead to an awakening in the Middle East, but the answers aren't there yet."

"Correct. History is the great equalizer because it takes the past and the present and we get the answers to our questions. We have the information but can we apply that knowledge and answer what is transpiring today? Regardless of all of that, it's quite a task to impose freedom through the barrel of the gun. The awakening will coincide with what sparks any revolt—information and a media event that stirs the people to openly question the status quo."

I start to think of a media event and information , the Boston Massacre and the clandestine pamphlets published by Paine and others. I'm about to speak up but there's a loud popping sound near the bar. Everyone is jolted from their conversations because the TV was just turned on with the volume at full blast. Both Beckett and I are jarred from our discussion and turn to see what happened. On the TV is a news story about the rising death toll in Iraq of American soldiers. No matter how hard we work, nothing stops you cold like the presence of death. We watch as images of war, riots, Osama bin Laden, George W. Bush, protestors, supporters populate the screen. There's not much to comment on even as the talking heads continue to do so. Beckett and I watch in silence, as the rest of the café patrons have long grown weary of the story.

"All I think about is what if we're wrong?" I say to Beckett, breaking the momentary silence. Beckett is transfixed and unable to take his eyes off the TV screen.

"We're not. Fear, anger, hatemongering, loathing of the other will always lose out. Eventually, the public will tire of war, hate, scandal, and recklessness on all ends," he responds without turning around. There's Beckett's hope for humanity that it will appear after the darkness. He rubs his hair, trying to witness the shadows of forthcoming events.

"We have a year to find out."

Beckett whips his head around and stares at me. "No, we're still too scared. Anything short of a scandal of epic proportions will not sink this ship and honestly, even then I have my doubts. This administration for all its flaws understands the American corporate media better than the previous one. There truly is no need to take on every battle because the media will forget about it tomorrow, as will the American people. But come election time, everything that occurred will be renewed, and fresh, and believe me, we will be reminded of all the pain we endured."

I don't want to have this discussion. I can't have this discussion, my faith is in the people seeing what's right, and Beckett's faith is in history and the inevitable repeating of events. Even if there is a glimmer of hope, I think it's closer, and Beckett thinks there's more to put on our shoulders. I get us back on track. "But Thomas Nast was different, and he was right."

"The great equalizer. We know he was right … now. But did they then?" he says with an extra bit of pause to prove his point.

"But even if some of his methods were questionable, at best, he didn't trade in fear or hate."

"Then explain his 'Shadows of Forthcoming Events'—how is that drawing any different than a president painting a picture of what would happen if we didn't engage in the War on Terror?"

"Nast challenged people with his imagery and yes, some of it was scary, and some instilled fear, especially the images depicting what would happen if Tweed gained control of the city. But Nast's methods were necessary because Tweed and his crew were corrupt and robbing the city."

"You see it as fear, I view it as a harsh reality necessarily bestowed upon an uneducated public," Beckett says, growing a bit agitated at having to entertain even the slightest dissent. Did he expect me to just agree with him or to continuously challenge the notion that history has written the future? "That is what's happening now."

I pause. "Every story needs a boogeyman, a mythical creature hell-bent on destroying everyone and everything we've come to know and love. It's how emotion is inspired in a population lacking political savvy and the learned skill of comprehending nuanced arguments and issues."

"You need to give power to get power. An all-powerful singular entity does not last but an equally powerful foe, that's how you usurp and remain firmly entrenched in power."

Think about power, counter him, and use what you've learned. "In George Orwell's *Animal Farm*, where Napoleon used Snowball as that powerful boogeyman. Even though Snowball was chased off the farm and never seen again, Napoleon always used him whenever something went wrong or whenever anyone questioned Napoleon's intentions. Blame Snowball, blame Snowball, and remind them of Snowball. As we've studied, every leader rises from the ashes of destruction, even that self-inflicted disintegration or unfortunate decimation of that society, and then the capturing of the imagination of the emotionally damaged people. Whether they remain influential or in power or not is contingent on the message."

"So, FDR's New Deal from the Great Depression," Beckett interjects, starting the rapid fire.

"Hitler. The Treaty of Versailles leads to World War Two."

"Rudimentary. Go further."

"Senator Joseph McCarthy. The Red Scare, blacklisting. JFK, RFK, and MLK's assassinations and the 60s counter-culture?"

"Good. Ronald Reagan. The Carter Administration. Trickle-down and voodoo economics." I can't help but laugh that Beckett believes the Carter Administration is on par with the Great Depression. I refocus.

"Any despot in recent memory and UN sanctions." Beckett waits for more. "The despot then has a villain to blame no matter their fault. The people don't have enough food, it's not the dictator's fault, the sanctions imposed by the UN or the US are the reason they're starving. Not enough medicine—it's the sanctions not allowing medicine to arrive in time. Having a villain or an outside body to blame is the key to maintaining power."

"So, a dictator wants sanctions?" Beckett asks, ending the brief rapid-fire exchange.

"Of course not but it helps to maintain a level of victimization and hence some sympathy from your subjects. From my vantage point, you can oppress your people all you want but if you're the lone oppressor, it's possible the people will be more apt to revolt against your regime. However, if you consistently show an outsider oppressing your people via sanctions or bombings, the citizens may be more willing to follow you for fear of the other."

"Interesting theory. Not sure if I agree."

Speaking of sanctions and dictators, over Beckett's shoulder I see that the BBC is showing a video of Saddam Hussein firing a rifle amongst his military guards. I must have watched that three-second video a hundred times by now and it means absolutely nothing. If Saddam had been throwing a chemical weapon or a nuclear bomb at his people, I can understand the repetition. But how is this video dissimilar from President Bush or Vice President Cheney quail hunting with rifles? Is that the best the administration's got?

"Every battle and war needs a villain. Capitalism had Communism, United States had the Soviets, and vice versa. This time is no different and no matter what happens in Afghanistan or Iraq, if it goes any less than perfectly flawless, they have their enemy. Everything old is new again." Beckett gives the floor back to me.

"Nast had his villains. First in the Civil War, where he would have to rally the Northerners to not fight for the cause but to understand what we're fighting for and against. One way was to appeal to the atrocity of slavery. He draws a beautiful double-page piece with the simple title: 'Emancipation.' Each section on the right side relates to the current situation of a slave-holding nation and the

other side reveals what the country will be like in the future, when the newly freed slaves will assimilate into society. Nast drew the positive shadows of forthcoming events in 'Emancipation' and his audience responded. The most important aspect is this image here." I point to show Beckett where Nast has drawn two former slaves showing respect to their boss. "A huge Southern fear was the violent retribution they might endure from the slaves after they were set free especially after all the atrocities they suffered through. But to show the slaves as being cordial, respectful, it's difficult to make an argument for anything other than emancipation and support."

"Smart man, like Harriet Beecher Stowe creating Uncle Tom in *Uncle Tom's Cabin*, it's better to portray your side as benevolent to win over your audiences than as standoffish or angry, even if that anger is justified."

"But before this, Nast would have to convince the Northerners who they were fighting and he did this brutal piece of work titled 'Southern Chivalry,' dedicated to the Confederacy's president, Jefferson Davis. Nast had to design a Southerners' persona that went counter to what we knew of the South. Here, his center cartoon is a rebel soldier decapitating Union soldiers and other horrible war crimes the South was perpetuating during the war. Whether it is true or not is irrelevant. Nast, and in turn, Lincoln and the North had their villains. Lincoln would use Nast as well, calling him the best recruiting sergeant (for the war) and saying his cartoons have never failed to rouse enthusiasm and patriotism, and have always seem to come just when those articles were getting scarce. Lincoln would also utilize Nast's power, influence, and imagery especially in the 'Compromise with the South' from September of 1864. There's so much going on here. First, we have the upside-down American flag, depicting a country under distress and within the stripes are battles the Union fought. But the other elements work, too. Notice the Union solider and Columbia—the historical and poetic name for the USA, which Nast would consistently draw—the solider is mutilated and Columbia is weeping over the grave, which is marked: 'In Memory of Union Heroes Who Died in a Useless War.' Behind them are just horrible images of the war's effect on the American people; juxtapose that with the Southern fighter. The soldier is standing upright, one foot on the grave, his Southern pride evident, and he is breaking a sword in half that once read, 'Northern Power.' Even someone lacking in any form of education can certainly understand Nast's intent and be moved by the sentiment. Lincoln would use this political cartoon to garner support for his reelection campaign. This is from Morton Keller's *The Art and Politics of Thomas Nast* with regards to his Civil War drawings." I open the Keller book to a page I have saved, ready to use and read to Beckett. "Thomas Nast's first opportunity to influence American sentiment came with the Civil War. His commentary on that struggle is an evocative record of its development into a contest between opposing ideologies. At the same time his work contributed largely to the appearance of a Northern sentiment that made the preservation of the Union and the end of slavery inseparable causes. ... But as the war dragged on, and deepened in ferocity, changes began to occur in the way in which it was perceived. And *Harper's Weekly* was the most important organ of information and opinion in the wartime North. Never before had a great event been conveyed pictorially as well as verbally to so vast an audience. The war as seen through the eyes of the *Harper's* artists became the closest approximation of the sight and sense of the conflict for hundreds of thousands of Northerners."

Beckett gets my attention and gives me his you-are-getting-it-now face, which I have seen a hundred times in the last month. I nod, I get it. I continue, "Lincoln's tragic death elevated Nast even further, like 9/11 and the War on Terror do for Fox News." I stop myself. I don't want this comparison, nor do I like it, but I know it will make for a hell of a thesis. "Even so, we're not as uneducated and isolationist as they were one hundred fifty years ago. We've evolved. We're better prepared than they were. Nast is better than that."

"You created this comparison and it's quite logical."

For the first time I wanted Beckett to attack my thought process and statements. Where are the insults? Why is he not ripping me to shreds? "I am not suggesting Nast or *Harper's Weekly* is Bill O'Reilly and Fox News. I'm simply implying that 'everything is old and new again.'"

Beckett pounces, "Precisely. You researched and found a connection, so do not shy away from it. And here, my friend, is your proof and with that proof maybe you can see the chess game in front of you. That's all politics is, that's all media is. Some understand the chess game and others are playing Connect Four, a simple child's game connecting four pieces in a row and then restarting again similar to the media cycle. Disregarding the facts that each game is connected and a short victory may only seem to indicate success or righteousness, there are more moves to be made, the long game is tedious, the short game is exhilarating for all to take part in." Beckett's explanations always sound rational even if I want to yell and scream and lose my own rationality.

"It's always been this way; making small and incremental gains is the new political strategy. The faster the reaction, the more scandal and controversy—"

"And hence viewers for media outlets and money from advertisers. It's all a game, a rigged sport that only a select few partake in. Nast played it too but only week to week, not minute to minute."

"But Nast was right."

"History's outcome can be quite convenient to proving your point. Let me ask you, what if Nast went against slavery's abolishment?"

"Nast wasn't against—"

"I understand but what if he was, would you defend him then?"

"No, because he would be wrong."

"Did he have any negative feelings towards other groups?"

"He was born a Catholic, but took on his wife's Protestantism. However, he hated the Irish Catholics."

"As did everyone," Beckett quips, reliving the pain of our ancestors for a moment.

"He was just going through the motions and would eventually capitulate. He was not an absolutist."

"Precisely. An absolutist, no matter the situation, is wrong because there are no absolutes. Absolutely. Everything changes with a situation and absolutists are always left behind as progress moves us forward. You should always talk about Nast. I can tell you've come to admire him."

"I admire everything Nast did but also I love the fact that he was a flawed man and thinker. Even though he was progressive on so many issues, he still had his racist and stereotypical tendencies. Nast made me realize that anyone who expects perfection from opinion makers and leaders is bound to be disappointed. All we can hope for is those who influence thought are willing to realize that eventually progress will be made and the future is coming regardless of the past. Yes, Nast hated the Irish and felt such animosity towards them, but he drew 'Uncle Sam's Thanksgiving' in November 1869 where he placed an Irishman at the table. He may have despised the group but he knew eventually they would be welcomed into the fold." I flip through the binder of Nast images, and present 'Uncle Sam's Thanksgiving' to Beckett. Beckett scans the piece observing the ethnicities sitting at the table with Uncle Sam carving up a turkey.

"Nast certainly is hopeful."

"He certainly is. Everyone is there from black to white and Chinese to German and best of all, a few seats away from Uncle Sam sits an Irishman. That is what stands out for me, that Nast will evolve, just like everything does. What seemed so unacceptable today will eventually erode and progress will be made for tomorrow. It just takes a bit of time. Everyone, every new idea, every new acceptance goes through the wringer."

"Winston Churchill once said, 'You can always count on Americans to do the right thing—after they've tried everything else.' So, you, like he did, think it's a ritual or some sort of fraternity hazing to get into the club?"

"Look at the evidence. In Nast's time, it was Catholicism and the Irish, today it is Islam, Muslims, and Arabs."

Beckett's nod seems like he's satisfied. He makes a few marks in his notebook, then removes the page from his journal and places it in his bag. That's a first and has me concerned. By now, I've picked up on each of Beckett's tics and rituals but he never removed pages from his journal before. "All right. Tell me more about Nast."

"Nast was a Republican through and through, creating the Republican Elephant as well as other iconic imagery. This would be his calling card. An indelible mark on history; if history does not remember his name, it is our fault, not his."

Beckett nods in agreement, making a few more notes in his book, and then removing the page again. This is very bizarre behavior for him.

I continue with the presentation, "The correlation between Nast's rise and Fox News's rise continues with the first Electoral College failure in 1876. Republican Rutherford B. Hayes won the electoral vote by one but lost the popular election by 300,000 votes to Democrat Samuel Tilden. And Thomas Nast was right in the thick of it. Nast would follow each development with a drawing as the events unfolded. I actually found a website called Harp Week that shows each cartoon. The presidency was eventually awarded to Hayes but the deal was known as The Compromise of 1877. Basically, it was a deal that awarded the presidency to the Republican Hayes even though he lost the popular vote. The Democrats would give up the fight for a Tilden presidency in exchange for the removal of all federal troops from the former confederate states. This deal ended any chance we would have of full reconstruction after the Civil War. Relating it to today, the 2000 presidential election between George W. Bush and Al Gore there was another Electoral College failure and it took a Supreme Court decision to—"

"Forget the Court's decision. Al Gore lost his home state of Tennessee. His campaign was run so poorly and is truly summed up in that one simple and obvious fact. Forget the other faux scandals and real ones. That defeat was his defeat. Mondale won Wisconsin even during Reagan's 1984 landslide victory."

"Nast sketched several pieces but the one that really just—it's perfect—is his March 24, 1877 cartoon titled, 'Another Such Victory, and I Am Undone.' This saying refers to the ancient King Pyrrhus of Epirus, after whom the term 'Pyrrhic victory'—or a devastatingly costly win—was named. While King Pyrrhus may have won the battle, he did such damage to his people and army that he would eventually lose the war. Nast saw what The Compromise of 1877 meant for the Republicans and the problems that would occur when enacted—"

"He saw the shadows of forthcoming events."

"As a man who believed in equal suffrage for newly freed slaves and the Chinese. He knew what this compromise meant for the future of reconstruction in the post-war South. The deal struck by Republicans and Democrats to award Hayes the presidency and move the occupying Northern troops out of the South was also known to many African American historians as 'The Great Betrayal' and rightfully so."

Beckett looks at the piece. The Republican Elephant mutters at the graveside of the Democratic Tiger that he cannot endure "another such victory." He is battered and bruised, with a severed tail, yet wears the laurel wreath of champions. The waitress comes over and asks if we would like anything else. Beckett orders another coffee, I follow suit.

"Was he engaging with Tweed during this time?" Beckett asks, still focused on the political cartoon.

"The dramatic image of Tweed leading the Americus Big Six Fire Company and a seven-year-old Nast meeting twenty years before is so powerful. Nast's first formal attack against Tammany Hall came on February 9, 1867, a few years after the end of the Civil War, which had well established his credentials. The piece, titled 'The Government of the City of New York'—" I find the image in the binder and show Beckett, and we both scan the cartoon. "—Propaganda at its finest. Only a full dramatic step-by-step retelling would do it justice."

"You freely admit this is propaganda."

"Promoting a doctrine or a cause to fight for, all Nast pieces were propaganda—the 'Gallant Color Bearer' a piece for the North against the South, 'The American River Ganges' a piece against the evils of Catholicism. I have no issue calling what Nast did propaganda. Tweed stole between $30 million and $200 million—that's close to 4 billion in today's dollars! With that in mind, this cartoon created the pervasive image of Tammany Hall recklessly running the New York government."

Beckett is scrutinizing the cartoon. He writes in his book and motions for me to continue.

"Within the Government of New York piece, I kept thinking about the Wild West's lawlessness, as Nast made it seem this is what was occurring. Even the way Nast drew the Irish, the ape-like beast, it's almost as if Nast doesn't believe the Irish have evolved to Homo sapiens. It's a powerful first shot but this was not the only piece, more work would be needed to change the public's opinion."

"One cartoon doth not a rebellion or riot make," Beckett adds to the conversation.

"Tweed understood that he would be doomed by a cartoon if he didn't stop the ink from flowing. Apparently, Tweed said, 'Let's stop them damned pictures. I don't care so much what the papers write about me—my constituents can't read; but damn it, they can see pictures.' Tweed attempted to purchase as many newspapers as possible to counter any allegations in *Harper's Weekly* where Nast was featured. When parts of that failed, Tweed through an associate attempted to bribe Nast!"

"How much was the bribe?"

I smile, "Half a million to leave New York and travel to Europe, not to return home until after the 1871 election. Nast, of course, said no. But $500,000 in the 1870s, that's an incredible amount of money."

"Not when you're stealing millions. It's a worthy investment. Nast certainly was a man of principle."

Principles are necessary to tell the truth and to be as clean as possible, especially if you're going to take on the most corrupt and powerful political party in the country. Nast did not need to be perfect, but the moment he takes the bribe from Tweed's people, any cartoon that would follow would have to be questioned. No one would attack the message, just the messenger. It's easier to destroy the person pontificating than halting the influence from the sermon. Nast's enemies and targets would have the ammunition to destroy his reputation. Nast would never be able to draw again."

Beckett makes some more notes and drinks his coffee, and I make a few notes to pretend I'm countering and thinking along with him.

"There are so many political cartoons that Nast created to take down Tammany Hall and Boss Tweed. Each one did a little bit of damage, each shot across the Hall took the shine off the veneer, and led to eventual revolt by the people."

"And relating this to today … ."

"There are certainly parallels, but as per usual, point of view will ultimately judge who plays what role. Those who support the Iraq invasion and Saddam's forceful removal from power can turn to Nast to compare 9/11 to the horrors of the Civil War, then his attacks on Tammany Hall and any corruption. Nast can be seen from whatever point of view in that sense—"

"Especially considering he was a Republican. A term I feel will become more and more misused as we become more and more embedded in this war. The press is a powerful ally and an influential enemy."

"And Nast was both. Presidents Lincoln and Grant both valued his support and benefited from his allegiance. Nast's enemies were eventually defeated and their careers were destroyed by his 'two-fisted' attacks. George W. Bush values Fox News's support because they take on his enemies for him, either destroying them in their own manner or weakening their case where they have to capitulate."

"Is a partisan press nothing more than a professional hitman targeting an adversary so the beneficiary of the execution can claim innocence? I love the notion of comparing a legend and hero like Nast to Fox News."

I want to tell him how much I despise the comparison, but it'll make for an interesting read—and a PhD!—and fascinating research. Beckett has pushed that exact thinking: Do your best to compare things you're passionate about but not necessarily agree with. And here I am comparing Nast, a man who is a God in so many ways, to a devil in Fox News.

As we sit in momentary silence, panic sets in and the questions have to be asked: Will linking Nast and Fox News work? Can I finish this in five months? Beckett makes a notation in his book again. Without looking up, he says, "I do not see any hurdles that cannot be overcome. You should check out the cartoons by Herblock, Mauldin, and Dr. Seuss."

No need to take notes, the digital recorder has plenty of space left. "Dr. Seuss?" I ask.

"You'll see. Oh, and Garry Trudeau's work with his cartoon, *Doonesbury*. This will expand your work and your base."

"I know Trudeau but did he have as much influence as Nast?"

"Influence is a complicated word. Only cartoonists and scholars know of Nast, and maybe some others, yet he was incredibly influential. Study the rise in power and the contrast of the work with Trudeau in the 80s, and Herblock and the others in the 1950s, 60s, and 70s. Could be a fascinating comparison and a nice modern-day primer for what you plan to accomplish."

I forego the digital recorder and take some notes of my own. Beckett takes the opportunity to rummage through his bag and peruse other comments he jotted down.

He finds something, and clears his throat. "You said something about emotional collateral. Do you have other examples?"

"Absolutely. Newsmen like Edward R. Murrow and Walter Cronkite, but also JFK and Ronald Reagan—"

"Right, because of President Carter's disastrous administration." Any chance Beckett gets to attack Carter's administration's failures he will take it. "I think you should investigate more into emotional collateral and expand on that term. Would you say emotional collateral is reserved for media pundits or politicians? How about comedians? Painters?"

I furiously scribble Beckett's ideas and start to think of my own. Who in recent times has created enough emotional collateral to have an influence on the population? How did they obtain emotional collateral? Was there an event? A tragedy? Or perhaps, positive examples will do.

"George W. Bush certainly fits the bill here, especially considering the parameters you have created," Beckett remarks, interrupting my train of thought. I shake my head in disagreement. "Whether you agree with his policies or not, this pre-emptive war of choice was possible only because of emotional collateral—"

"You mean emotional trauma."

Beckett enjoys the back and forth and nods to me, "Yes. But conflating the two I think is dangerous. Trauma doesn't ALWAYS get you your way; it certainly helps, but receiving and then ultimately using collateral will. If it were peacetime with no media event such as 9/11 to spur us along, Bush does not invade or have any support for war. But Bush was allowed to pursue his war by the majority because in times of trouble and desperation—"

"We turn to our leaders regardless of political affiliation," I finish his sentence, resigning in defeat.

"You have to remove your own emotions from the situation even though the people who are attempting to obtain emotional collateral trade on exactly that part of you. That's the game and you're now aware of it." Beckett observes the café's patrons, and he focuses in on a couple then turns back to me. "So, take your emotion out of it and give me an example."

"Joseph McCarthy and his rise to power through the Red Scare."

"Exactly. Ah, but there is a rub, YOU continue to think is a negative use of emotional collateral but it is possibly a positive for someone with a divergent point of view. Even you mentioned

earlier about Nast and his fight against Tammany Hall. Your charge is to accept that ALL emotional collateral is positive—"

"But engage with history as a guide to determine whether the collateral was exploited or not."

Beckett smiles, "You got it. Any other Nast examples?"

The ideas are flowing now, so many ways to approach this but at least the foundation is laid. Did he create the blueprints of the foundation or pour the cement? Would I have come upon this on my own? I cannot wait to get started with Beckett looming over my shoulder like an animal ready to pounce.

"Nast would bombard Tweed and the Tammany Ring every opportunity he had. He drew cartoons depicting Tweed's gang as vultures, or as a Roman emperor presiding over democracy's destruction with the tagline, 'So, what are you going to do about it?' The political cartoon was called 'The Tammany Tiger Loose.' The ravenous tiger, evolved or better yet adopted from Tweed's fire company, is tearing apart Columbia, the representation of American democracy. The political cartoon was released only a few weeks before the 1871 November election. Nast's next Tweed cartoon followed a similar theme to the 'Tammany Tiger Loose': the Roman emperor, except this time, Tweed and his Tammany Hall brethren are broken. Nast was victorious though more work was needed. Someone from the Ring had to go to jail.

"Did someone?"

I can't stop grinning. Researching the Nast–Tweed story and what happened at the end was absolutely thrilling. My confidence at the moment is sky-high. "Beckett, you're just going to have to wait for that!"

Beckett nods and agrees, he puts his hand on my shoulder, "It better be good."

"Tweedledee and Tildendum," I mumble.

"What?"

"You'll see."

Nast and Tweed's final act would play out over several more years with court proceedings, arrests, Tammany's members fleeing to Canada and other countries, leaving only Tweed at battle's end to take the fall. Eventually, yet with no sense of irony, Tweed was done in by Nast's cartoon in the most fascinating way. The cartoon named "Tweed-le-dee and Tilden-dum" from *Harper's Weekly's* July 1, 1876 cover would be Tweed's end. Having been incarcerated numerous times but always managing to find a way out, it was the civil trial that did Tweed in. Tweed was forced to pay over six million dollars in fines and restitution. Tweed was broke from all his other trials and his opulent lifestyle, but he escapes from prison, makes

it to Cuba under the alias John Secor, and somehow barters passage to Spain. The government was hot on Tweed's heels. US authorities did not send photos to the Spanish cities where Tweed might disembark, but instead sent the Tweed-le-dee and Tilden-dum cartoon. While in Vigo, Spain, authorities arrested Tweed—not for fleeing but because of Nast's cartoon, they mistakenly believed Tweed was a "child-stealer." Tweed was held in custody for three weeks and then returned to America in late November. He was sent back to Ludlow jail where after numerous attempts at obtaining his freedom failed, he died on April 12, 1878.

Beckett has just checked his watch—I know what that means, time to go. I want to tell him every single detail of Tweed's escape and capture but I'm sure Nast biographer Draper Hill, or someone who has archived and indexed every *Harper's Weekly*, can do a better job than I. My job was to create a thesis and a statement. I clear my throat to get Beckett's attention, and he readies his pen.

"And with that, my thesis statement is 'Thomas Nast utilized his emotional collateral gained during the Civil War and President Lincoln's assassination in a positive manner to destroy Tammany Hall and Boss Tweed; Fox News, and others, employed their own brand of emotional collateral obtained over the span from the 2000 election to 9/11 to divide the country and lead us to war with Iraq.' I will compare the two stories and investigate in full how Nast and Fox News achieved their stated goals using emotional collateral." I wait for a moment as Beckett scribbles in his book. "That covers your concerns because regardless of the 'War on Terror's' outcome, Fox News did contribute to the country's division and it did push for the conflict."

"As did others."

"Yes, as did others." Beckett leans back and scans the room again, shaking his head in disgust at the artwork. His eyes wander and he turns towards the TV. He hasn't said anything for about two minutes. Should I have said "thank you" to let him know that was what I had? My nerves lead me back to the apple pie, but right as I reach for the delicious dessert, Beckett clears his throat.

"You seem to idolize him. I thought you would take to his work," he says, without turning to face me.

My enthusiasm was evident throughout so I know he's not just mocking me. "That one person can do so much yet no one really knows about him. Inventing the modern-day version of Santa Claus, Uncle Sam, the Skeleton Army, the Republican Elephant, popularizing the Democratic Donkey—how someone could have had so much influence on a culture and be so unknown within a hundred fifty years is riveting."

He finally turns around. "Tying together today's situation with Nast's situation: that is an ingenious approach and hook. There will be plenty who disagree with you but just stand firm and stay the course. Excellent work. Now start writing it. You have my approval for your thesis." Beckett smiles while reaching down to the floor to pick up the plastic bag by his feet. He places the plastic bag gently on the table in front of me. "However, I do have something for you before you begin your odyssey."

A gift? Friends get each other gifts—is this the moment when Beckett calls me a friend? He puts his hand on the plastic bag and holds it there for several seconds. It's like Christmas. The anticipation is killing me.

"I'm not going to be around this coming semester. Van de Bilt will be your secondary reader and assist you when necessary." Beckett's voice lowers as he finishes the sentence. My face asks all the questions in my head: What? Why? What is happening?

I'm able to speak but barely, "Um, what? Why?" I can't even formulate a full sentence from the shock. I don't know what to do. Is this a test? Beckett isn't cruel nor is he a man who gets a rise out of you just for its own sake. Everything he does has a reason but I passed his test, and I did the work. What is this?

"I need a break from this city. I'm going to get back to work and cover the inevitable civil war in Iraq. Though I did hear someone float the term 'sectarian violence.' An amusing euphemism, to say the least."

Did his ex-girlfriend contact him? Is he going after her? There are a thousand questions to ask yet I'm stunned into silence. I don't want to pry but I have to. I'm about to speak up but Beckett continues, "I'll still advise you even with the second professor's contributions."

I want to ask how but my disbelief has turned to disappointment with a hint of anger. When I need him most, when I feel like I'm finally forming, he is leaving. I could imagine the work and research communicating through email without any face-to-face interaction being incredibly ineffective. "There's this new technology called Skype. As long as you have a microphone for your computer, we can speak as often as you want."

"Skype." I write down the name, wondering if it will be a success or a bust like the other dot-coms of the end of the twentieth century. I look at the plastic bag as Beckett runs his hand over it. "If you think this is for the best." I'm seventeen again in Elizabeth's bedroom being dumped and trying to put on a brave face to not give the dumper the satisfaction or revealing pain.

"You'll be fine and we'll schedule enough meetings that you're not alone. I promise. It will work out." He smiles at me again. "So, as my parting gift to you and a small apology … ." His voice trails off as he opens the plastic bag and hands over the gift.

It's rectangular and poorly wrapped in newspaper. The gift has some weight to it. I tear into the wrapping and a black frame is revealed and then a green border, and I almost drop it in disbelief. In front of me, in my hands, is a framed color print of Thomas Nast's "Shadows of Forthcoming Events." I am in absolute astonishment, never having seen a Nast drawing up close before. The details are richer than I thought and the drawing more impressive than any paper reproduction or Internet jpeg could offer.

"I'm blown away. I'm speechless," I say after a few moments. I really was, I couldn't believe he did this. "Where did—I mean, how did you find a piece like this?"

Beckett smiles at me and for the first time, I felt like his protégé and him my mentor. This is how someone treats another person, and he did this because he wanted to, without asking anything in return. I suffered through his sniper-like insults and took the hits only to be rewarded like this. "There's a place online called Prints Old and Rare based in California. They have a nice collection of Nast prints for sale."

"You mean I could buy more of these?"

"Plenty more, my friend. Just direct your requests to Kathleen. She's expecting you and I set up a credit line of $1,000 to start you off."

I write down Prints Old and Rare. I wonder which they have. I wonder how much they cost! For the moment I forget that Beckett is leaving to head to the middle of a warzone and that he said "my friend." "Thank you. For everything. I'll never forget this."

Beckett nods. A comfortable silence between us as I continue to stare at Nast's piece. It's absolutely gorgeous. Each detail is beautifully colored, though I do wish it were black and white like the original. But who cares! The color work is incredible.

"Time to go," Beckett says, standing up and finishing his coffee. He puts some money on the table to pay for his coffee. We shake hands. Beckett reaches in for a brief hug and then pulls away. "I'll see you soon. Good luck with the thesis."

"Yeah, I'll see you soon."

Beckett gathers his things, "I truly hope you see the shadows of forthcoming events." Without waiting for a response, Beckett walks towards the exit of the café. Somehow, we neglected to notice that we had been there for hours. I also failed to realize that since we sat down, the café filled with people who now occupy every chair and stool. I watch Beckett as he opens the door, but suddenly he stops and stands at the threshold for a moment. He turns around, half in the café, half out, and gives me one final nod. I nod back at him and Beckett leaves the café. I sit back down at the table. I stare at the framed Nast piece, my reflection over his signature, oblivious to everyone in the bar. I run my hands over the glass. Then something catches my attention. On the table is Beckett's notebook. He forgot it! I debate going after him, but my opportunistic streak kicks in and I have to sneak a quick peek inside. What's a little larceny between friends? I pick up the journal, touching the front cover, running my fingers over the dried red spots. I open the notebook and on the first page is a message that reads: "Tragic events do not need constant reminders. Always, Your Friend, Beckett." I have it in writing: he called me his friend.

I flip through the book; it's been restocked with blank sheets all waiting to be filled. I put the journal down next to the framed Nast piece. It's official: I'm ready to write my thesis and order another cup of coffee.

LECTURE THREE: SOUTH PARK AND THE AMERICAN EXPERIENCE

1

The seatbelt's ping alerts the passengers that we have permission to stand and exit the airplane. First, the most important aspect, as every traveler checks their phones to see what they missed. It's a sea of iPhones—some old versions and some new ones—after the brief flight from Germany to Sweden. We make our way out of the aircraft as I follow Samuel, my new best friend of two hours. If the flight were any longer, I'd fake an illness and spend the rest of the time in the bathroom. I'm immediately reminded of Black Ivory coffee, Amsterdam, and the twenty-hour binge drink I promised I wouldn't partake in. So much for promises to oneself.

I gave a lecture earlier this morning in Germany, and had all my bags packed and waiting in the car. Boarded the 2:30 PM flight to Sweden and arrived a few hours later. The next lecture is my first in Scandinavia. No pressure. The tour started well, the organizers hired an incredibly efficient PR team (I wonder if this is standard operating procedure), and they asked what I would like. I was tempted to ask for a rider of three hundred green M&Ms with a single blue pretzel M&M on top, but being a Yankee I thought better of it. Europeans have so many stereotypes of the typical American, why add to it? It's also why I say, "I'm from New York," as opposed to the States. I find survival of judgment is easier that way. I do regret not requesting the M&Ms now: the image of all those M&Ms would have been amusing. All I asked for was water and a Swedish roasted coffee ready for me while I am being escorted from the airport to the lecture. The contact over at the PR firm even asked what size, how I take it, and what type of cup I prefer as if he was making the cup himself—like I said, efficient.

As is customary before leaving for a city or country, I check out what coffee they have or what kind of coffee to expect and the rituals that come along with drinking. Searching for the perfect cup so I can crave it beforehand and then spend way too much money on it once I get there. In New York there were two places, and that was enough research. The first was a chain of about five stores called Fika, which translates into English as "a coffee break with a sweet pastry." A word after my own heart, for sure. The word has morphed further in the Swedish where they apparently Fika three times a day as an institutionalized work break. I suppose that is better than a government-mandated cigarette break. Fika uses coffee as an alibi to leave work for a little while. We should Fika more often in America. Looking forward to having one—a Swedish siesta as I am going to think of it.

The other coffee shop is called Konditori (translates to "café" or "cake shop") and they have four locations, with three in Brooklyn and one in the city. It seems as if New Yorkers and Swedes have a connection in our love for coffee and sweets. I tried some pastries and coffee from each place and probably Fika'd at Konditori too much over the past few weeks, but I was preparing—call it research! That's tax deductible, right?—for this trip.

Making my way to the baggage claim now with Samuel close on my heels. It was futile to under-pace him as he waited for me and impossible to outpace him because of his insistence on escorting me to the baggage area.

"The Arlanda train leaves in ten minutes," Samuel lets me know as if the huge countdown clock in front of us displaying the next departure and the one fifteen minutes after that is visible only to him.

"Thanks. Sadly, I have a car service. Gotta make that lecture on time."

"You're missing out. The train is fast, clean, and has wifi."

I turn to him. I've heard the stories (or propaganda if I'm feeling snarky) but being from New York City, this is something not easily believed and has to be seen. A public, albeit expensive, train system that's clean and overly efficient that's been in service for the past decade and change. Right. And I'll start drinking Earl Grey instead of coffee.

"So I've heard." Both my suitcases arrive together—definitely a good feeling. We walk together through customs without incident. Can't wish his bags were delayed, never want to jinx that.

"The train is faster than a car to the city center. Cleaner for the environment, too," Samuel proudly tells me about Sweden's transportation marvel.

"Yes, I know, but the organizers thought it would be best to get an escorted ride to the lecture." At the end of the arrival hall and I see a man in a suit holding a placard with my name on it. I say good-bye to Samuel, thank him for his help, and walk towards the man. The one detail that surprised me as I got closer was that it was a small dry-erase board, not a piece of paper with my name scribbled on it. The company's name, Taxi Stockholm, at the top, my name below. One step below having my name in lights, right? I identify myself and the driver takes my bags to the parking garage adjacent to the terminal.

Nice car, a basic sedan, all black, leather—not cheap, for sure. The driver enters and turns around giving me the details of the trip, how long it will take, and all the basics. At the end, he says, "From the firm" and hands me a thermos. "It's filled with Swedish coffee and prepared as you requested."

The driver reminds me of the specificity of my request, I can't help but laugh that the PR team actually went along with it. I was half-joking! I should have asked for the M&Ms. I'm going to like Stockholm. Is this Fika? The first sip. I like what I am drinking. It's the taste of socialized medicine, an aroma of pensions for all, and an aftertaste of paid maternity leave.

"Your lecture starts just after seven, yes? With no traffic, we should be there in about twenty minutes," the driver tells me. That will leave me little time to get dressed, and get the audio levels and the presentation tested. It's going to be close. Looking out the window, I see it's all highways. I haven't been to many cities, but there's something similarly drab about the span from an airport to a city center. It's always the same. If someone kidnapped me and took me from the airport, I wouldn't be able to guess which city I was in—Amsterdam, Stockholm, Reykjavik, Oslo, even Newark International and others are the same. Even New York's JFK is built within a major city but the airport has a "you're on the outskirts traveling far outside the city" aspect to the drive, too.

The second sip. Solid. I have to get the name of this. I'd be surprised if it was Gevalia, but not shocked, and remember, I'm no coffee snob. The driver, on the other hand, is fascinatingly friendly, cordial, and inquisitive. He's asking about America, New York, and the president. Thankfully the president is one the Swedes kind of like, making it easier to navigate the interrogation. Imagine the difficulty of answering these questions when George W.—oh, I do like this coffee. The caffeine isn't THAT pronounced, yet I can feel it. Each sip has smoothness to it, almost as if the liquid evolves with my taste buds. Wouldn't put that past the Swedish, considering their accomplishments. Definitely reminds me of the Swedish roast from Konditori. Actually, I think it is. No time to look over my notes, but the lecture is fresh in my mind and this will be the twentieth presentation, counting this morning. This lecture is the one that started all this madness. Somehow from an innocuous email from a wonderful student who was part of an organization called Studium Generale in Groningen, Netherlands, to an escorted car to Stockholm, I'm looking out the window and thinking: "How did I get here?" I take another sip and remark to the driver how Obama's challenges stem from—eh, who cares! I don't even know what I'm saying to him. I'm enjoying the view as the city closes in. Forty minutes left. The driver is giving me a primer on Stockholm's history but stops abruptly mid-sentence and says:

"Have you read the millennium series?" The title doesn't register. "*The Girl with the Dragon Tattoo.*"

Ah yes. Filmed in Stockholm. Got the reference. The driver clears his throat and begins his review of the book and the two film versions—the Swedish and American. I nod in agreement as he complains about the American version.

"Why have it in Sweden with people speaking English? You know that our English is better than most Europeans because we have subtitles—not like the French or Germans who dub their movies and TV shows."

The classic northern Europe insult, The Netherlands does the same thing. "It's a valid complaint. But it was done to entice American audiences and other countries around the world to see it. The box office and investment, et cetera," I tell him.

My only Swedish culture references are Ingmar Bergman, Lasse Hallstrom, *Insomnia* (though it's part Norwegian), and a bunch of actors and actresses. The idea crossed my mind to mention ABBA but then thought better of it. Don't want to confirm the stereotype for the guy that all Americans are culturally inferior. Stockholm is gorgeous; add in the coffee, and this is heaven. We dip under a tunnel and take a highway loop of the city. The loop seems to be designed to show off the city's sprawling architecture and roadways. Even the tunnel has personality.

The driver returns to his abbreviated history lesson. "The area has the largest archipelago in Sweden with 30,000 islands. It's the second largest in the Baltic Sea and Finland has the largest," he says, with a hint of unrealized jealousy. "There's very good food places near good transportation in the center. Do not neglect to visit Old Town during your visit."

"I have every intention to see it. I'm looking forward to it." I keep focused on the breathtaking skyline and topography. From the way the driver speaks, he understands what he has in the city. Stockholm still impresses him and he's been here his entire life. The way he describes the city, the colors of the buildings, the bridges, the feel of summer, the brutality of the winters, no wonder Stockholm consistently ranks in the top ten of best cities in the world. The city and the people seem to have an enduring affection for each other. A mutual love affair between the citizens and city is evident and illuminates the town. Though I do wonder if this love is reserved only for spring, summer, and fall, as he conveniently leaves out the scant six hours of daylight in winter. Thirty minutes before the lecture begins, and the traffic gets a bit heavier as we edge closer to the center of town.

"We should be fine, unless there's an accident," he remarks with diminishing confidence. My eyes are fixated on a cliff of buildings; not sure I care about standing still at the moment. The yellow color is hypnotic and the dome cathedral behind it adds to the seduction. I've never been so glad to be in traffic as I am right now. This must be how tourists feel coming to New York for the first time. But here the water, the cliffs, the islands, everything works. I can't wait to see what it looks like at night. The traffic eases up a bit and Talking Heads' "This Must Be the Place" comes on the radio and the driver turns the volume up. Realizing this may be rude, he motions to me, "Is this a problem?"

"Not in the least bit," I say. The song's title seems fitting at the moment, even if the lyrics are anything but. Another sip, I lean back and relax while staring out the window. The song ends—wish I could hear it again—the flutes and the city make an exceptional music video. Another Talking Heads song comes on, "Once in a Lifetime"—couldn't ask for anything more. The coffee hits the perfect uphill stride, I'm not yet at the zenith; that'll come soon enough. From the steady escalation, the rush will probably hit right when the lecture starts.

"Today, the sun will set around ten o'clock and rise at three in the morning. If you go north you'll get a full day of sunlight. We call it midsummer, everything will be closed that day except for bars," the driver informs me, lowering the volume on the final part of the song.

"Yeah, I planned to be here then. There's nothing going to stop me from doing that. I have to see it." As the last gulp goes down, the taxi makes a right and pulls over to park in one motion with no regard for pedestrians.

"Here we are, yes, Berghs School of Communication."

I check the time: twenty-four minutes till the lecture begins. I'm anxious about the time because the lecture is live-streamed. A prompt start time is essential for any audience, especially an on-line one. I wonder if it'll be just me or if there will be an audience. I exit the cab and see a line of people waiting outside either for the lecture (hey, one can dream) or maybe this is Fika because of the weather. Not a cloud in the sky, perfect temperature, the sun is out for another eight hours or so. Summer in Sweden. Nothing like it … or so I'm about to experience. So pleased that I extended my stay for three days to explore the city, right in time for the solstice. Why not? It's my last lecture for a while, and these cross-Atlantic flights have gotten brutal, may as well take advantage of it.

This lecture in Stockholm is unique because I rarely do two in a day and then one more the following night. Of course, some press is included as well. Hopefully, I won't get too worked up on the details and attempt to change things tonight. Too many problems can come from that for sure, as we have seen. Three people are waiting by the car to greet me.

"Oh! Good, you made it! We were worried with the traffic. I'm Jonas Herring. We corresponded via email. Welcome to Berghs. This is Peter and Anna, they're part of the organizing team. Sofia had to take an important phone call, so she'll meet you after the lecture. How was the ride over? Better yet, how was the coffee?"

"Very nice all around, thank you. A coffee was just what I needed."

Jonas is wearing a fitted charcoal gray suit; he's tall with pale skin and speaks perfect English with a touch of an upper-class accent. His pride in his language ability is obvious especially in front of an American. Everyone, or almost everyone, has the same reserved vanity with English proficiency—proud-yet-humble-yet-proud. Peter, Jonas's right-hand man, has a meticulously grown beard. I wouldn't be surprised if he trimmed it five minutes ago and will comb it several times before the day's end. I study the beard for the moment—it's flawless and Andrew Sullivan-worthy. He's wearing a t-shirt and jeans, I wonder if he's American or at least half American. Anna has dark hair, dark eyes, and dark skin. Not what you would expect from a Swedish woman or at least my stereotypical thought of Swedes. We exchange further pleasantries and head inside the building. A very old yet very cool-looking elevator is situated inside a spiral staircase, giving a nice juxtaposition with the modern décor and media subjects on the wall. Twenty minutes left.

Jonas looks towards me, "We have a full audience today and tomorrow is the same. I'll arrange for your bags to go to your hotel. After the lecture, we'll be joined by Peter, Sofia, and my very demanding younger sister, Cici, for dinner."

"That would be great, something to look forward to. Everything good with the live-stream?"

Jonas nods, "I also have water for you—I made sure it's 'still,' not sparkling, as you requested. Anything else I can get for you?" His tone seems sarcastic but it's not. I didn't ask for much of anything except the water and the cup of coffee, which surprised him. Though the details of the coffee were exact and creative, but that was it. He must deal with people way more important and demanding.

"The coffee concoction will have to do. I was thinking of some complicated M&Ms request too, but didn't want to be that guy. ..." I smile at the thought of being someone who can demand something that trivial.

Jonas laughs at me, "Well, it's too late now. Had I known earlier. ..."

I check my phone; time seems to be moving faster as the four of us get to the top of the staircase. We walk through the glass doors and make a left and then a right into the lecture room.

"What do you think?" Jonas asks with a tone of "you should be impressed by this."

Everyone asks that question as if I'm some arbiter of taste and would highlight flaws like the room here has too much light on the left and not enough on the right. Or, the screens are too big and probably block the line of sight for anyone in the back. I examine the room. "I like that the stage is raised. About two hundred seats, right?"

"One hundred ninety." He says as he takes a seat in the right-hand section near the podium in the corner away from the first two sections. I'm handed a wireless head mic by the audio engineer and start the sound test—everything is in order. I open my computer and confirm all the visual and audio aspects are good to go. No problems at all. In fact, everything is going way too well. Something has to go wrong. I can feel the coffee working its magic but also the adrenaline rush from getting from the airport to here in such a short amount of time. I'm introduced to several other people but for the life of me, I do not remember their names, though one of the guys could be Steve Martin's doppelganger. A Swedish Steve Martin. My mind wanders a bit, thinking about the possibilities. Where was that *Saturday Night Live* character from? No, he was a wild and crazy guy from the Czech Republic; well, he was from Czechoslovakia, but in 1993 the two countries split peacefully and now we have the Czech Republic and Slovakia. How do I know that? Focus and don't let the coffee overwhelm you. Six minutes left. I want to change into a different suit, but there's time only for a new shirt. Three shirt options: A dark blue, a black, and a white. I go with my favorite, the dark blue. The shirt's been good luck and everything seems to be going so smoothly, so why mess with a streak? I'm ready to go.

Back inside the room I grab a water bottle and walk over to Anna and Jonas who are chatting in Swedish but immediately switch to English as I sit down. I look at Peter who is combing his beard. I knew it! I smile and look at my notes. Peter puts on a gray-and-white-checkered blazer, definitely a Swede, and goes on stage to start the show. He introduces me but pronounces my name awkwardly. Maybe he isn't half American. He definitely isn't half Irish. While debating Peter's background, a small panic comes over me—or is it the coffee reaching its apex? Had an extra jolt of caffeine secretly been added? That must be it. I know the lecture by heart—it's my first one, the original, and the most personal influenced by death, loss, life, laughter, disappointment, and success. Even if I decided to improvise, I can do it and no one would ever know. So, why is there a sudden panic? I survey the audience and the crowd is split fifty-fifty between men and women. Some older Swedes, adults, and the rest are students. Then the reason for the panic dawns on me—it's live and recorded. Never have had this before. Don't say "fuck" too often. Nerves or not, there's no choice but to do the lecture—I'm not going to not do it; might as well not be nervous. The lights dim, the standard polite applause, the lecture begins, and the coffee hits its peak. I love Sweden.

2

What makes television unique or modern day television shows, for that matter, is there is no end day, even when a TV series ends. The show ends but the characters continue experiencing life, loss, society, and America. In all likelihood, a series' conclusion isn't the finality of a character, a family, or relationship, just the ending of the audience spending time with them. We develop a relationship with the show as their characters visit us once a week for years. Sometimes we spend more time with these characters than with our actual friends. Which isn't the case with film, yet the two have similarities, as do other mass media. In film, we have our two hours with the story and characters, and if we're lucky there's a sequel a few years later. Isn't that all sequels are but the studios responding to an audience's desire to spend more time with the characters? If film and television are friends, then film is the overseas long-distance friend who visits every few years. When the visit happens you reminisce about the great times you had together and try to re-create the fun and excitement of the times you previously experienced. Hence why sequels try to recycle themes from the original—just like old friends waxing nostalgic about the earlier encounters. Television, on the other hand, is the friend who lives in the neighborhood who you see on a fairly consistent basis. New television shows can change and evolve because they're constantly reacting to events and evolving with the times. The audience and the show progress together as the visit is always reserved for Sunday nights at 9:00 pm. This "visit" allows TV to best reflect experiencing America and American society, and the avatar to represent all of this is the hit animated television show, *South Park*.

However, before our discussion delves into the show, we have to think about what makes America and how television reflects our generational shifts as it evolves with us. A major thread through the last two decades—and of course, before that—is our need for and our love of controversy. Controversy or scandal is at the top of the list, and considering a top-rated show is called *Scandal*, it's easy to understand why. Over the past several years, more controversies and scandals have dominated the headlines with emergence of cable news, social media, and immediate-response mentality. Americans are borderline obsessed with the next gossip, rumor, or embarrassing gaffe, smelling the blood in the water. Due to the polarizing nature of controversy—what is controversial to you may be completely acceptable to your neighbor—we have become divided in a way unseen before and this divide has given rise to a huge split in the electorate, pulverizing any hope of progress and hope. America is torn between left and right, red state and blue state, with a dwindling middle ground. If anything, the red states, the conservative states, have become REDDER and the blue states have become BLUER. Unfortunately, there's no consistency anymore, it's just us or it's just them. But what is controversy to us? What is controversy to you? For Americans, it's what gets us riled up. It's what pits brother against brother and mother against daughter. Controversy divides the people, gets the blood boiling, and feeds the media, garnering them ratings and advertisers' dollars. And when advertisers are happy, they spend money, and media conglomerates get rich, and the people are left itching for their next controversial fix. The mainstream media wants and needs the next big controversy but controversy varies everywhere. In America right now, we have huge controversies continuously debated with one of the biggest ones being gay marriage. In some states there are bills banning gay marriage and civil unions while others states have done the exact opposite by accepting the culture regardless of public opinion on the matter. Though as the polls are indicating, the millennials are becoming more and more accepting and it's only a matter of time before gay marriage is a nationally accepted reality. And in 2012, Barack Obama became the first president in American history to openly support gay marriage. Another current controversy in America is women's rights, as some Republican-led states have attempted to curtail women's reproductive rights in a bizarre courting of the female vote. There is the sex education controversy and when and how children should begin receiving an education about sexual activity. There are arguments for abstinence-only, even if those programs have shown to be ineffective, misguided, and costly. There are other consistent controversies such as the banning of seemingly objectionable books like *The Catcher in the Rye* for language and for corruption of the young. *Harry Potter* was actually banned in a Catholic school in the Northeast, because the religious school leaders believed the books are promoting witchcraft and devilry. The controversy list is extensive; rather than cataloguing every single one in the US, for brevity's sake, we'll stop here. But the reason these controversies are listed is that *South Park* has explored each of them in their episodes. Over the years, *South Park* has reacted to the controversy du jour like no other show has. We will explore how the show has accomplished this, but also accept the reality: Things have changed and over the years *South Park* has changed along with it.

In today's media environment consumers are absorbing more information than ever before, but not attaining the knowledge necessary for proper engagement with one another. More Americans are choosing to seek out information on the ideas they agree with rather than challenging their own opinions. We have become an America blinded by our selective exposure, a process where people seek out messages that are consistent with their belief system, ideology, preferences, and attitudes. Those who prefer Obama choose to receive their news and other information from those putting a positive spin on him and his administration. Those who have a negative view towards Obama flock to Fox News and other conservative outlets. The network has successfully convinced their viewers to blame Obama for everything that is happening because the executives and hosts want their audience to stay tuned in. Why would anyone continue watching a channel that reveals everything they believe in is wrong? Instead, it is a philosophy of "facts be damned if the facts hurt the ratings and the viewers' fragile psyche." There is less effort required to blame Obama for the surge in gas prices than debate the nuances involved with the price gouging and the issues surrounding America's fossil fuel consumption. Fox News holds President Obama to account because they believe their audience needs a villain and Fox News gives the audience their antagonist. This is what the media does to us: it confuses the people and we are left out in the cold, not knowing whom to trust or invest in outside our respective ideological bubble. If we were honest, we're not exactly sure what's going on in mainstream America, as the media continues the farce through this left-versus-right prism. Sometimes the mainstream media covers only stories that they know are only valid for them—one where there is the proverbial and sometimes the literal blood in the water, such as the Trayvon Martin case in Florida, where a man shot a black teenager and claimed a Wild West–type law called "stand your ground." The media, CNN and MSNBC, originally dedicated forty-one segments to Trayvon Martin versus only one from Fox News within the first two months. The major issue here is those who watch CNN and MSNBC have become hyper-aware of the situation and have made their conclusions—justified or not—while those who are Fox News viewers may not be aware the shooting occurred. How can two sides speak when they are not privy to the same information, or worse, the facts in a given debate?

At this moment, Americans can't see the entire forest for the trees obstructing our view. While it is effortless for those outside or hovering above the forest to see where it ends, when you're stuck in the labyrinth, the exit is far from visible. Europeans turn towards American and ask themselves: "What on Earth are you doing over there in America?" While the question is valid, it's simple to comment on a relationship that you're not intimately involved in. It's effortless to comment on what someone else is doing right and wrong. But is it that easy to comment on your own relationship with your own situation? Stealing blogger extraordinaire Andrew Sullivan's masthead's famous quote from George Orwell: "To see what is in front of one's nose needs a constant struggle." This is the struggle in American media and people are currently engaged in as the media catalogues the American experience through news, information, entertainment, and infotainment. Sadly, a majority of the media are more agitators than facilitators for our education and progress into the 21st century. The mainstream corporate media rarely guides the people who are sifting through the detritus that is the American experience. We are mostly on our own if we want to understand those who are the other side of the debate and those who are similar to our sensibilities. If we want to understand the Bible-toting, gun-waving, Glenn Beck–watching citizens as much as we want to understand the atheists, pacifists, and vegans, the media needs to guide us. However, the media does not help us grasp the degrees in which we are distinct; there is too much effort involved for the rapid reaction of the 24-hour news cycle. What ends up occurring is the chasm today and nuance has all but disappeared from our vernacular in the battle for ideas between left and right.

In the 1995 film *The American President* written by Aaron Sorkin of *West Wing*, *Social Network*, and *Moneyball* fame, President Andrew Shepherd played by Michael Douglas talks about America during an impromptu press conference to address a possible challenger to his presidency:

> America isn't easy, America is advanced citizenship. You gotta want it bad 'cause it's gonna put up a fight. It's gonna say, you want free speech, let's see you acknowledge a man whose words make your blood boil, who is standing center stage and advocating at the top of his lungs, that which you would spend a lifetime opposing at the top of yours. You want to claim this land as the land of the free? Then the symbol of your country can't just be a flag; the symbol also has to be one of its citizens exercising his right to burn that flag in protest. Show me that, defend that, celebrate that in your classrooms. Then you can stand up and sing about the "land of the free."

This is what America should strive towards and Sorkin has attempted in his utopian fantasy HBO show *The Newsroom*. Regardless of this failure, this is the ideal we based this grand experiment called America on. To our detriment, there is no middle anymore in America, whether class, ideology, or balance. Rarely do we witness the sides working together unless war is involved, but even that is steeped in political positioning, cover, and hypocrisy. There are two ideologies that dominate America: the haves and the have-nots, Republican versus Democrat, the rich versus the poor. Or applying this to *South Park* characters: Cartman versus Butters, Cartman versus Kyle, basically Cartman versus everybody.

So who are we to trust? Returning to Aaron Sorkin once more explains the current state of America during the opening scene of *The Newsroom* using protagonist Will McAvoy:

> We stood up for what was right. We fought for moral reasons. We passed laws, struck down laws, for moral reasons. We waged wars on poverty, not poor people. We sacrificed. We cared about our neighbors. We put our money where our mouths were. And we never beat our chest. We built great big things, made ungodly technological advances, explored the universe, cured diseases, and we cultivated the world's greatest artists and the world's greatest economy. We reached for the stars. Acted like men. We aspired to intelligence. We didn't belittle it—it didn't make us feel inferior. We didn't identify ourselves by who we voted for in the last election, and we didn't, oh, we didn't scare so easy. (*He chuckles.*) We were able to be all these things and do all these things because we were informed. By great men. Men who were revered.

Gone are the days of the revered like Edward R. Murrow, who rose to fame broadcasting from Britain during World War II. Every night he would come on the air and people in America would tune in to listen to his broadcast. Murrow would end every show with his signature "Good night and good luck." That good night and good luck wasn't just "good night and good luck," it was "good night and good luck, and I hope you survive the German Blitzkrieg" that was bound to come or "good night, and good luck and I hope your boys are safe." Immediately a connection was established between broadcaster and audience. Once the war ends, Murrow becomes one of the most trusted newscasters in America and he uses that moniker, moving his radio show *Hear It Now* to TV and renaming it *See It Now*. Murrow and his men used the platform to expose the abuses of migrant farm workers and then battled Senator Joseph McCarthy during the 1950s Communist witch-hunts. The Murrow broadcast contributed to the downfall of Senator McCarthy and initiated the beginning of the end of the mounting hysteria in America. No longer would people have to sign waivers pledging to be only American and for America. After Murrow leaves television for a myriad of reasons, Walter Cronkite takes up the mantle as the one to revere. His moment was on November 22, 1963 when he announced President John F. Kennedy's assassination live on TV. Right there, he becomes a trusted voice for America. The audience, whether rightly or wrongly, believed in him because he showed emotion and humanity during a traumatic event. He almost started crying during the broadcast, but ever the consummate professional, Cronkite held his emotions in check. Cronkite was there on television also during the assassination of Martin Luther King on April 4, 1968, connecting deeper to an out-of-control and troubled nation. Cronkite used this connection to repudiate President Johnson and American's foreign policy in Vietnam. Cronkite actually stands up from behind his desk, walks over to a map of Vietnam, and says to the camera: "Mr. President, this is not working." He would dedicate numerous news shows revealing why the Vietnam War is a massive foreign policy mistake. What ends up happening because of this critique? Lyndon Baines Johnson, who watched Cronkite every night said, "Shit, if I lost Cronkite, I lost America." That's how ingrained Cronkite was in the American psyche and that's how trusted he was as a broadcaster and a newsman.

However, if we were to expand on this notion of trust, the philosophy makes sense when people turned to and began to trust Fox News after the September 11 attacks or after Barack Obama's election to the presidency. The world they knew was not just altered, but now "their America" had radically changed and this was the network that attempted to stem the tide from flowing. The same happened to those on the left when MSNBC's Keith Olbermann went all Murrow on the left, taking on the Bush Administration with his occasional "special comment" segment that ended his show. A Cornell graduate at the age of twenty, Olbermann's rise in cable news corresponded directly with the fall of Bush's approval numbers and the several disasters the administration failed to respond to or directly presided over. In times of crisis we turn to those we feel best comfort us, it's why *Friends* jumped significantly in the ratings after the 9/11 tragedy: the audience wanted to stick with those who were, in essence, their friends. But what happens when the crises and controversies are geared towards a narrative of separation and agitation? Who do we trust after all of this? Bill O'Reilly from Fox News? Regardless of the feelings towards the man, he is quite educated, holding two master's degrees, one in politics and the other in government, from John F. Kennedy School of Government at Harvard University. Or MSNBC's Rachel Maddow: she has a Ph.D. in politics from Oxford University and was a Rhodes scholar. Maddow knows politics and attempts to explain complicated political issues using the vast knowledge she has acquired over the years. Yet, a large portion of the country does not watch her nor do they want to watch her. Why do you think that is? What do you think it is? Is it because she's a woman? That would be too easy. Maddow is a lesbian, a progressive, and stands up to those on the left, so there are a majority of viewers who will not watch her program on principle, which of course is their right. She might say the most intelligent things on television, but if the viewers refuse to watch her, does it matter?

The fourth estate or the media was designed as the unofficial fourth branch of government envisioned by Ben Franklin and Thomas Jefferson. The estate has failed over the last several years. The fourth estate is supposed to be a balance representing the people, and due to media consolidation, it is failing. We have all of these choices, or at least we think we do, but in essence, we have less clarity and fewer options. In fact, we don't have as much as we think because the media industry has been deregulated over the past twenty years as we've gone from a healthy amount of media outlets options to an oligopoly. There are significantly fewer media outlets broadcasting news to the American mainstream than ever before. It's natural for those who disagree to say: "well, just go to someplace else and find the information." Most people don't have the time, especially since we have the least amount of free/vacation time in the industrialized world to actively search for information. A typical viewer would prefer the passive experience and let the information come to them with minimal effort, so they tune in to the most popular and visible source, whether it's ABC, NBC, FOX, CBS, or CNN. Less choice leads to less effort by the players involved and the zero-sum game takes hold as the networks fight each other to steal the audience's attention. How do you do that? Controversy and scare tactics, as it's easier to mirror the success of the other and play to your audience than to take chances by breaking the mold. A small piece of evidence revealing how badly the corporate mainstream media has failed the American people is held by CNN's Anderson Cooper—who's actually considered one of the most trusted newscasters because of his coverage of Hurricane Katrina—has a segment called "Keeping Them Honest." Cooper has to have a special segment to keep people or politicians honest. Wasn't that the original intent of media to keep those in power honest? So what's happened with this? Trust and confidence in media, other than their own, has all but disappeared.

The fourth estate has let down the people and a new fifth estate has emerged. This is where satirists, bloggers, comedians, and We the People have found a new home reacting to the disappointing fourth estate. Anyone can be part of the fifth estate because it's all-inclusive and a direct repudiation of the fourth estate's exclusivity, though they have to earn their keep by contributing with impeccable credibility. And when a member of the fifth estate breaks a story that the fourth didn't, there is usually resistance and childish name-calling; the story of Glenn Greenwald's NSA and Edward Snowden is a prime example. These are the new watchdogs for the people, and they are the new check on those in power. This new balance is more representative of the people and there's a connection between consumer and fifth estate member. Leading the way are Jon Stewart and Stephen Colbert, Andrew Sullivan and his subscriber-supported website "The Dish" as well as *The Onion* newspaper. *The Onion* released a story—one week after a poll was taken showing a large percentage of Republicans believe that Obama is a Kenyan, socialist, Muslim terrorist—that a poll found, "1 in 5 Americans believe Obama Is a Cactus." The piece was created to highlight what Americans believe because of their blind hatred towards the 44th president. But of course they'll believe it 'cause the information outlets they're tuning into are telling them so! Can we blame them for their stupidity? Besides those, there is the most financially successful of the fifth estate, *South Park* and its creators Matt Stone and Trey Parker. The animators have managed to catalogue the American experience through animation and weigh in on controversies of the day in a way no other has. Their show is what Aaron Sorkin was talking about with regards to advanced citizenship when he wrote the Shepherd speech in *The American President*. This is what Sorkin wanted and *South Park* has managed to provide from episode to episode and season to season.

Owing much of their success to the revolutionary animated show *The Simpsons*, and Matt Groening, *South Park* launched in 1997 with their pilot episode "Cartman Gets an Anal Probe." The episode and the show were an immediate hit for the struggling network Comedy Central and the network became known as "The House That *South Park* Built." The show's genesis came in the early 90s with a video Christmas card known as *The Spirit of Christmas*, animated with construction paper by the two college friends. The video made the rounds in Hollywood pre-viral/internet days and a few lucky turns landed it in the right hands and *South Park* was born. In the beginning, each scene had to be changed by hand if a character had to move or speak. This type of animation was a painfully arduous task and had to be done over and over within each and every scene. After the show's successful first few seasons, the computer technology finally caught up to the creators and now every single show is done via computer. The computer technology allows for more immediate social commentary because the animation is ready to go. Matt and Trey can sit in their writer's room and figure what story they want to tell, knowing that they don't have to worry about the basic animated parts of the show, though occasionally an episode forces them to create completely new characters and sets. Since *South Park*'s first airing, the show has fascinated its audiences with their philosophy and ideology ranging from libertarian to liberal to conservative and everything in between. They've insulted all and left no one in their good graces. No topic or celebrity is safe in the *South Park* world. They've been called Equal Opportunity Offenders, taking on the Transporation Security Administration or the TSA, but instead they're the Toilet Security Administration as the comment on how "shitty" and ridiculous both toilets and airport securities are. In a perverse way *South Park* is exactly what Edward R. Murrow wanted when he said for TV to teach, illuminate, and entertain. Obviously, Murrow did not have this type of education in mind when he said television should do this, but wasn't that his fault for not being specific?

Murrow's weapon of choice to get his message across: radio, then TV; *South Park*'s weapon is computer animation. The technology has enabled the show to do things no other fictional show has been capable of accomplishing. The technology allows Matt and Trey to produce an episode in just six days beginning on Thursday and delivering an episode to air Wednesday. Their six-day struggle has been profiled in the incredibly revealing documentary *Six Days to Air*, as the viewer is given front-row seats to the struggles and advantages of working in such a limited time frame. As a comparison: *The Simpsons* takes six months to animate a show, *Family Guy* and *American Dad* nine to ten months, and FX's *Archer*—which is slowly becoming one of the best animated shows on TV—takes six months to animate. The *South Park* seasons were until recently structured in two seven-week blocks where they air seven episodes in a row, take months off to recover, and then return for another seven episodes to finish a season. This quick turnaround makes commentary on current events possible and when they do weigh in on such controversies, they become the middle voice in the cacophony of left versus right. This middle ground is what makes the show unique as they tackle any issue they feel is worthy. The social, political, and world issues they've confronted range from euthanasia, climate change, immigration, gay rights, women's rights, sexual identity, religious cults, and religious pluralism to the War on Terror, 9/11, politics, and most importantly family, gender, love, loss, and friendship. Make no mistake, the creators still manage to offend plenty with carnivalesque grotesquery and fart jokes that would make Aristophanes, Shakespeare, and Jonathan Swift proud. They are satirists holding up a mirror to society in the hopes of improving it. The show captures the zeitgeist but they also have to understand the people and what's happening in the world and portray those events accurately. Matt and Trey were able to accomplish this once the technology caught up to their preferred method of thinking and understanding complicated topics.

One of the first forays into "immediate response" episodes was in Season Five airing an episode only weeks after September 11th titled "Osama bin Laden Has Farty Pants." While *Friends* still had Ross pining for Rachel and *The West Wing* aired an "after-school special episode" to process the tragedy, *South Park* dealt with their grief differently. In this episode, the four boys, Kyle, Stan, Kenny, and Eric Cartman are, as per usual, at the bus stop waiting for the bus but in this "new world," the boys are wearing gas masks in case of a chemical attack. As the boys get on the bus, Officer Barbrady searches their backpacks, even though he has known them for years. The commentary is obvious: After 9/11 no one, not even people you've known your entire life, can be trusted. The boys get to school and have hooks for their gas masks instead of their jackets. And the door has a huge lock on it just in case a terrorist tries to infiltrate the classroom. They're all scared, and Matt and Trey are satirizing our fear shortly after one of the most traumatic events in American history. The episode also spoofs the adult reaction as Stan's mom Sharon has refused to leave the couch as she's glued to watching CNN non-stop since the tragedy. The episode is a departure for the show, as they animate Afghanistan during the American bombing and invasion. They also create four similar-looking and -sounding boys as a not-so-subtle reminder of the other victims of the war. Their presence is vital because it humanizes the Afghan people, something that was missing from the media's coverage, and it separates the civilians from the murderous Taliban and Osama bin Laden. Of course, in typical South Parkean fashion, the boys end up in Afghanistan and are taken hostage by Osama bin Laden and the Taliban. The four Afghan boys who mirror our South Park boys decide to help them escape from Osama bin Laden. As the eight children are sneaking out of the Taliban's hideout, Cartman decides to stay behind.

Cartman: I'm gonna go take care of this prick.

Kyle: Cartman, he's crazy!

Cartman: He's not crazy, he's an idiot. I know how to deal with these people.

The episode then morphs into a classic Looney Tunes skit, as Cartman becomes Bugs Bunny and bin Laden is thrust into the Elmer Fudd role. Cartman proceeds to torture bin Laden for the next five minutes of the episode and towards the episode's end, Cartman pulls down Osama's pants. Nine magnifying glasses appear one on top of the other to find bin Laden's minuscule penis. Cartman figures it out and remarks: "So this is what this is all about." By the end of the episode, the American government and military have killed Osama bin Laden and the war against the Taliban is over. But within the episode, while definitely pro-American, there were honest critiques about America and its foreign policy as US fighter jets destroy the Afghan houses, playgrounds, and buildings. Within the episode, one of the Afghan boys saying, "America did start this war when they put the military bases on Muslim holy lands" or another remarking that a third of the world hates America because Americans don't know that a third of the world hates them. At a moment of unbridled patriotism, this critique was as surprising as it was true. Less than two months after 9/11, Matt and Trey are criticizing US foreign policy and their fellow citizens; it would not be the last time.

Spinning off that episode a few years later, "Cartoon Wars Parts I and II" has *South Park* entering the debate on whether or not to follow the laws, rules, and regulations of another religion even if the person does not follow that religion. The episode revolved around events in Denmark when *The Jyllands-Posten* newspaper printed political cartoons depicting the prophet Muhammad and other Islamic images. The debate that was sparked was whether or not anyone can show or draw a picture of the prophet. The Danish cartoons ignited Muslim riots in Europe and even today, one of the cartoonists is still under special protection for fear of retribution. In the *South Park* episode, no one in America wanted to deal with the riot possibility when *South Park's Family Guy* version wanted to illustrate the prophet Muhammad in one of its episodes. Most people remember the episode for Matt and Trey's takedown of *Family Guy* as formulaic and interchangeable jokes that are not integral to the plot. However, the real "immediate response" aspect of the show is what be discussed long after *Family Guy* is off the air. Reacting to *Family Guy,* the South Park citizens did not want to incur the Muslims' wrath so instead of fighting for free speech, they decide to bury their heads in the sand. This is done so that when the riots come, they'll be safe because they could claim they never saw the images because their heads were in the sand. While this is being debated, Stephen, a little-known and little-used adult character, stands up and addresses the citizens in one last-ditch effort to convince the people this is a mistake:

> Stephen: No, no, wait a minute, [Mrs. Garrison looks at him] it's ridiculous. [Gerald looks at him] What we need to do is just the opposite. Freedom of speech is at stake here, don't you all see? [makes his way to the board] If anything, we should ALL make cartoons of Mohammed, and show the terrorists and the extremists that we are all united in the belief that every person has a right to say what they want! Look, people, it's … been real easy for us to stand up for free speech lately. For the past few decades we haven't had to risk anything to defend it. But those times are going to come! And one of those times is right now. And if WE … aren't willing to RISK … what we have, then we just believe in free speech, but we don't defend it. [the other people there mull this speech over …]

> Randy: I like the sand idea.

> Mr. Mackey: Yeah, me too.

> Gerald: Yeah. The sand thing sounds a lot simpler. [everyone else agrees]

South Park is calling out those Americans who profess that free speech is the most important thing in the world but the moment they're challenged, they bury their heads in the sand. The sand idea IS a lot simpler, as the townspeople say, but that's the whole point! As President Shepherd said about free speech in *The American President,* you got to want it bad and the citizens of South Park would prefer the easier way out. The South Park citizens and much of the world do not want it "bad" because they refuse to fight for their rights when challenged by an outside force. The debate throughout the episode was whether or not a cartoon can be shown that will knowingly offend a religion. The reason the episode was in two parts is that the creators and Comedy Central continued to fight about whether or not they should be allowed to broadcast the Muslim images.

On the side of not broadcasting the images is Cartman, but not because of his sensitivity towards Muslims: he wants the hated *Family Guy* off the air. He knows once an episode is "pulled," the show will eventually have to be taken off the air completely because their creative freedom is gone. This is Cartman's master plan under the guise of respecting religion to hide his true agenda. Cartman heads to Fox Studios and convinces the network to not air the episode. Kyle, originally believing Cartman wants the episode off the air so it won't offend anyone, now stands in opposition to Cartman and wants the episode to air. The episode's climax is in Fox's president's office with the president having to make the final decision on whether to air the episode or not, and Cartman and Kyle representing each side of the debate. And of course, here is *South Park*'s contribution to an issue that has pervaded the American media.

Kyle: No! You have to show Mohammed, Mr. President!

Woman: Mr. President, we're awaiting your orders!

Kyle: Sir, just think about what you're doing to free speech!

Cartman: No! Think about the people who could get hurt!

FOX President: Ah … I don't know who to listen to!

Cartman: Okay, I'll make it easy for you. [pulls out a gun and aims it at the president] Pull the Mohammed episode, now!

FOX President: Okay, I'll listen to you. [gets back to the phone] Julie?

Kyle: Noo! Wait! You can't listen to him! He's a lying deceitful monster who only wants *Family Guy* off the air!

FOX President: But he has a gun.

Kyle: You can't do what he wants just because he's the one threatening you with violence!

Cartman: Shut up, Kyle!

FOX President: I can't be responsible for people getting hurt. Especially me.

Kyle: Yes, people can get hurt. That's how terrorism works. But if you give into that, Doug, you're allowing terrorism to work. Do the right thing here.

Cartman: Give the orders to pull the episode, Mr. President!

FOX President: I shouldn't even be in the office still. It's supposed to be half-day Friday.

Woman: Mr. President, thirty seconds to airtime. What do you want us to do?!

Kyle: Do the right thing, Mr. President.

FOX President: How about I allow the episode to air but just censor out the image of Mohammed again.

Kyle: I wish that was good enough, but if you censor out Mohammed, then soon you'll have to censor out more.

Cartman: No gay speeches, Kyle!

Kyle: If you don't show Mohammed, then you've made a distinction what is okay to poke fun at, and what isn't. Either it's all okay, or none of it is.

Woman: Five seconds, Mr. President! [the programmer J. Walker has his finger hovering on the button]

Kyle: [softly] Do the right thing. Show Mohammed. [Cartman still has his gun on the president] Do. The right. Thing.

Woman: Mr. President, we need a decision now!

FOX President: *Family Guy* goes on air as planned. Uncensored.

The episode is aired except right when the Muhammad image is about to be shown, a title card comes on screen that reads:

In this shot, Mohammed hands a football helmet to *Family Guy*. Comedy Central has refused to broadcast an image of Mohammed on their network.

With this title card, we get the episode's true meaning! This was an actual fight between the show's creators and the Comedy Central executives who were generally concerned about what would happen if the images were shown. Remember, a network's job is to offend the least and protect their product in any way. Kyle, usually representing Matt Stone's personality, represents both Matt and Trey in this episode as their argument for "all is ok or none is" fell on deaf ears. Ironically, the image that was censored can be found online but what is even more confusing, the prophet Muhammad was shown in an earlier episode called "Super Best Friends," but that was before the 9/11 attacks. If you visit southparkstudios.com, the "Super Best Friends" episode is currently unavailable for streaming.

Matt and Trey would broach the Muhammad controversy again in their episodes, "200" and "201," commemorating their 200th episode, which aired during Season Fifteen. Like "Super Best Friends," both episodes are currently unavailable on the *South Park* website. The only way to view the episodes is to buy the DVD or find an illegal stream. The episode was a celebration of all the characters *South Park* had satirized over the years. Celebrities are tired of being mocked, especially Tom Cruise. With the actor in the lead, the celebrities devise a plan to sue the town of South Park unless they can meet the prophet. Of course, if the prophet is shown, the town will be attacked, so the people debate what to do about this catch-22. But back in Tom Cruise's mansion, the real motive behind Cruise's plan is explained:

> Tom Cruise: Muhammad has a power that makes him impervious to being made fun of. What if we … could harness that power. [walks up to Jimmy Buffett] Jimmy Buffett, how would you like it if nobody could call your music drunken fratboy monkeygarbage?

> Jimmy Buffett: I'd, I'd love it.

> Tom Cruise: By taking what Muhammad had, we would all be safe from ridicule. Like Tim Burton here. Imagine this, Tim: nobody could rip on you for all the rehashed movies you've made lately. There'd never be a TV show that pointed out you haven't had an original thought since *Beetlejuice*. And you put Johnny Depp and the same crappy music in every film. And if you're that in love with Johnny Depp you should just have sex with him already. A TV show could never say that!

> Tim Burton: Gee, that'd be swell.

> Tom Cruise: Well it can be a reality. Once we have Muhammad, we can take his power from him!

Then the episode cuts to Kyle and Stan going to visit the Super Best Friends where Jesus, Buddha, Joseph Smith, Lao Tse, Krishna, Sea-Man, and Muhammad all work together "to right that which is wrong and to serve all mankind." Jesus explains that times have changed and Muhammad cannot make public appearances because "we simply cannot risk any violence from the Muslim people." Kyle can't believe it and yells: "Jesus fuckin' Christ!" To which there were no riots or protests even though it technically is blasphemy. Then sometime later at the Hall of the Super Best Friends, the negotiations begin as Kyle and Stan struggle to find a way that Muhammad can meet Tom Cruise and the town will not be sued. The finest element about this scene is once again this is representative of a real debate between *South Park*'s creators and Comedy Central's lawyers. How would the creators be given permission to show Muhammad without getting in trouble, having a title card censoring the image, or worrying Comedy Central (and their parent company Viacom) with the threat of violence towards the animators?

Kyle: Okay, will you let Muhammad come to South Park if we dress him up like a pirate?

Joseph Smith: Nooo, Muslims would still be angry if you showed his face.

Kyle: 'Kay, w-what if we cover his face with a paper bag?

Lao Tse: Nnno, because-a you still be showin' him-a walkin' around. That could be-a the trouble.

Stan: Okay, a suit of armor. We just have Muhammad in a suit of armor so you can't see anything.

Jesus: But it's still Muhammad walking around in human form.

Kyle: Aw, come on! This is ridiculous!

Joseph Smith: Boys, you need to understand that people get very offended when Muhammad is mocked because he's a religious figure. [snorting noises are heard, and the camera shows Buddha …]

Jesus: Buddha, don't do coke in front of kids!

To clear up any confusion: the prophet Muhammad dressed up as a pirate or in a suit of armor is unacceptable, but having Buddha snort cocaine in front of kids or in episode "201" revealing that Jesus watches porn is one hundred percent acceptable. The hypocrisy from Comedy Central knows no bounds! As Kyle argued in "Cartoon Wars," it's either all ok or none of it is. However, this scene is also a statement to what other religions are willing to accept and how they react when offended. Regardless, it is a fascinating deliberation on how certain tiny factions of a religion are willing to accept and react to, and what others will not. Back to the episode: The Super Best Friends and the boys come to a compromise by putting Muhammad in a bear costume and the episode ends leaving the drama for another week. The next day, a Muslim fanatic group responded by threatening Matt and Trey that if the prophet Muhammad is shown during the next episode, they will kill the two animators.

Both episodes sparked a huge debate on both the right and the left, but most supported the show's right to free speech: *The Simpsons* paid homage in their opening title sequence with Bart writing on the chalkboard "*South Park*—We'd stand beside you if we weren't so scared" and *The*

Daily Show with Jon Stewart responded with a ten-minute segment with Stewart discussing the threats, their numerous religious satirical sketches, and how well the other religions handled the jokes aimed at them. Stewart ended the segment by separating the enemies from those whom he simply disagrees with, such as Fox News and absolutists. Then, piano music starts, Stewart runs to a different part of the set, and the curtain opens, revealing a five-person choir telling the Muslim extremists or any extremists, for that matter to "Go fuck yourself!" Stewart sings and dances the show into commercial but the highlight of the controversy came from the most unexpected source when Fox News host Bill O'Reilly on the right and MSNBC's Keith Olbermann on the left defended *South Park*. Two commentators who never agreed on anything finally found an issue where their interests align, and it turned out to be the rude and vulgar *South Park*. With six days to air, the clock ticking, the question of what Comedy Central will do now that their stars' lives have been threatened was hanging over the episode. A decision was made out of an understandable fear, and it was determined it would be better to censor not only the image of the prophet Muhammad but also the name itself. The bear costume with Muhammad supposedly hiding inside at the end of "200" turned out to be Santa Claus. As Stan says, "If we were gonna have someone in a bear costume, why would we actually have it be Muhammad, you fucking idiot?!" an obvious swipe at the fanatics who threatened them.

The tribute episode celebrating the show's 200th episode has numerous elements and returning characters adding to the complicated plot. Finally, everything comes together with all the past and present characters from the show fighting, and Kyle makes a speech with the classic beginning of "You know, I learned something today …" Instead, of learning the all-important lesson, the entire speech is bleeped out by Comedy Central! Then Jesus continues Kyle's lesson but his sermon is bleeped out, as well. Lastly, Santa Claus starts to speak and the same thing happens. The speeches finish and everyone in the town agrees saying "yeah" but sadly, the audience never hears what the oration was really about. On the show's website, the episode is unavailable for streaming as a text appears on the screen:

> We apologize that South Park Studios cannot stream episode 201 at this time. After we delivered the show, and prior to broadcast, Comedy Central placed numerous additional audio bleeps throughout the episode. We do not have network approval to stream our original version of the show. We will bring you a version of 201 as soon as we can.

Even years later, the episode's original version without the censoring has yet to be viewed. But this is what *South Park* continues to do: they enter the debate and present theories most would stay away from or have never broached before. By evolving with their audience, the technology, and utilizing the advantage of never-aging characters, *South Park* answers the controversial questions the mainstream media outlets have struggled with. And with that they have managed to capture the American zeitgeist on a consistent basis.

3

In 2008, *South Park* aired an episode the day after Barack Obama won the presidency titled, "About Last Night." It is by far one of the most frighteningly accurate episodes in the show's history. With the normal prep time of six days and some alterations coming the night before, the show accurately predicted America's reaction to Obama winning the presidency and the McCain supporters' response in defeat. Matt and Trey also prophesied that the adoration and love felt towards Obama is misplaced and will eventually sour. The show delivers all the Obama prognostications using Stan's father, Randy as their vessel.

[Chicago, night. Barack Obama stands behind a podium facing two TelePrompTers, two glass walls, and a crowd of supporters. He has just won the presidency.]

Obama: If there is anyone out there tonight who still doubts that America is a place where all things are possible, who still wonders if the dream of our founders is alive in our time, who still questions the power of our democracy, tonight is your answer. [a cheer goes up in the audience]

[The Marsh house. Randy jumps for joy while his family, including Grandpa Marsh, sits on the sofa behind him. Another couple stands behind the sofa. Gerald and Sheila sit on a second sofa. Randy and Gerald wear Obama shirts]

Randy: YYEEAAHH!!!! [pumps his beer can up and down a couple of times] Obama! [runs around] WOOOOO! We did it! We F'in' did it!

Gerald: [stands up] YYEEAAHH!!!!

Obama: It's been a long time coming, but tonight, because of what we did on this date in this election at this defining moment, change has come to America.

Randy: [running around] YYEEAAHH!!!! Yeah Obama! CHAAANGE! It's, it's CHAAANGE!

Obama: Sasha and Malia, I love you both more than you can imagine, and you have earned the new puppy that's coming with us to the White House. We will name him "Sparkles."

Randy: [kneels before the TV] He's so awesome! [runs his hand over the screen a few times] He's so perfect and awesome!

Obama: Where we are met with cynicism, and doubt, and those who tell us that we can't, we will respond with that timeless creed that sums up the spirit of a people: Yes We Can.

Supporters: [in Chicago] Yes we can!

Randy: Yes I can! Yes I can! [the others watch him run out of the house]

[Outside the Marsh house. Randy opens the door and proclaims]

Randy: Here comes the CHANGE everybody! WOOO! [people nearby gather around the front steps]

South Park's tightrope in this episode was not only their accurate predictions but also their lack of alternate episode in case McCain had won the election. Either way, this was the episode that would have aired the day after the election. Also, to emphasize *South Park*'s ability of uniqueness, Obama's speech and McCain's were the actual victory and concession speeches the night before. All *South Park* did was insert the speeches early Wednesday morning and shipped the episode off to Comedy Central to air that night. Back in the episode, Obama is victorious and the supporters know what to do now. For them, the answer is simple, besides calling McCain supporters "losers," it's time to celebrate and party in the streets. Matt and Trey knew that if Obama won, there would be spontaneous celebration because those who voted for Obama had to suffer through the last eight years under the incompetent and divisive George W. Bush Administration. The carnival-like atmosphere was an emotional release and the hope that things maybe can start to turn around for the country.

[The streets of South Park. Two men set up an "Obama for President 2008" banner over the roof of a house. Down below are posters and banners for Obama plastered all over the houses and the crowd is partying to "Celebration." Randy rallies them on by blowing through a paper horn]

Reveler 1: [gulps down a beer] Yoohoo!

Reveler 2: Obama yeah, I can't believe it!

Randy: O ba ma! O ba ma!

Revelers: O ba ma! O ba ma!

Randy: Cehhh-lebrate good Obama come on! [reaches a keg of beer and serves himself some into a mug] It's Obamobama! [someone walks by and just throws up]

[Stan's house. He and Kyle look at the partying going on outside. Stan is on the phone]

Stan: Yes, I'd like to make a noise complaint. [outside the music changes to "Who Let the Dogs Out?" Someone swings from a traffic light and falls. A truck full of young adults rolls by]

Crowd: Obama!

Randy: Who let the Obama out? [moments later a police car rolls down the street, slowly going through the crowd] Ohoh, police are here. OooooOOOOooo!

Crowd: OooooOOOOooo! [Officer Barbrady stops the cruiser and hops out of it]

Barbrady: Okay people, time to disperse. Party's over!

Randy: BOOOO!! [other people join in the booing]

Reveler: … party Obama!

Barbrady: Come on, time to go home.

Randy: What are you? A McCain voter?

Crowd: Yeah!

Randy: Sorry pal, but Obama's president now! [walks towards Barbrady, and his pants begin to fall to his ankles] Obama! Obama! [walks past him and towards the police car]

Crowd: Obama! Obama!

Randy: Yeah yeah, flip the … Flip the cop car! Flip the cop car! [other revelers walk up and help out]

Barbrady: Hey, put down my car! [Randy and the revelers succeed in flipping the car over]

Revelers: Yes we can! [they move in and keep rocking the car as the music switches to "Mickey."]

Barbrady: No! No! Hey, stop it!

Stan: Jesus Christ …

Randy: O-bama you're so fine, you're so fine you blow my mind. Hey Obama! Hey Obama!

On a personal note, I was living in Brooklyn's Park Slope and I was watching the election results with friends. We drank copious amounts of coffee, a Kenyan blend I believe, preparing for a long and gut-wrenching night ahead but around 11:00 PM Eastern standard time, the major networks began announcing one by one that Obama was the president-elect. Immediately, we heard people in the streets celebrating on the main avenue exactly the way *South Park* would predict a day later. Everyone was so happy, relieved, and the music was blasting in celebration. People brought out beers, cheering, hugging one another, just like on the streets of South Park. While it wasn't as blatant as Randy flipping a cop car over, the question has to be asked: How did the show know? How did Matt and Trey know this was how Obama supporters were going to react? There's no way they could have animated the scene in that short amount of time. Matt and Trey knew how America would feel after the election because they have their finger on the pulse of the nation. In the episode, they used Randy to represent the collective sigh of relief of America when Obama won. Randy, of course, is their go-to character when an adult is needed because the episode wouldn't work if Kyle or Stan were celebrating this way. The episode highlights the other side to the festivities as some McCain voters panic and head into an underground cave anticipating the coming apocalypse. However, the commentary on the risk of deifying a politician and the insanity of an Obama supporter that will eventually lead to disappointment for the people is the episode's real gem. The show also accurately ridicules those who thought that after they voted, all the work was done and everything will be different now. Randy certainly feels this way:

[South Park, early early morning. The Obama supporters are still partying on the neighborhood streets. The music this time is "Whoomp! (There It Is)"]

Reveler 3: Yehhheheah!

Randy: [even more drunk than before, serves himself more beer] Wooo, change.

Reveler 4: Change.

Reveler 5: Change.

Stan: [running up to him with Kyle] Dad, Dad, we have a problem.

Randy: Not anymore we don't; everything's different now.

Stan: No, Dad, we gotta take Kyle's brother to the hospital.

Randy: We don't have to take … crap … from the fit- rich, fat cats anymore.

Stan: Dude, he's wasted.

Randy: Hey, it's my boss. Hey boss! [walks over]

Randy's Boss: Oh, hello Marsh.

Randy: Yeah, you know what? Fuck you! [Stan and Kyle are stunned]

Randy's Boss: Huh?

Randy: You heard me, you fuckin' piece of shit! I can finally tell you what I think o' you, fuckin' asshole!

Stan: [quite concerned] Dad, what are you doing?!

Randy: It's okay, Stan, everything's changed. I don't need this stupid fuckin' job anymore! You lil fucking assfuck, piece of shit [gives him the finger again] You know what Obama said? Yes we can!

Randy's Boss: Hey, I voted for Obama.

Randy: Obama's not talkin' about you!

Kyle: [looks around] Can someone help us? My little brother fell out of a window. [Randy punches his boss in the face and his boss just leaves, holding his hands over his nose]

This blind belief that "everything is different now" is classic South Parkean satire, revealing humanity's ridiculousness with the intent of improving it. First, by mocking Obama supporters but also the fact they believed everything will be fine even though the US had so many issues to deal with and one man's election was not going to miraculously change that. When Randy yells, "Obama's not talkin' about you!" he felt that he owned Obama personally and he decides if Obama likes or doesn't like a person, and that is all dependent on the follower's devotion. Of course, in typical

South Park fashion, Randy wakes up the next morning, Stan tells him he was fired, he looks and sees that the TV is missing—Cartman stole it—and has no pants. Randy throws a mini-tantrum, ending the episode by saying, "God damn it, Obama said things would be different—that son of a bitch lied to us—I knew I should have voted for McCain!" The show was already predicting the end of the Obama-voter honeymoon phase. For Randy, the love affair ends the next morning, and like clockwork a few months later, the American public began to lose faith in Obama. They feel like they've been kind of abandoned by Obama-the-candidate for Obama-the-president. Regardless of the results in the 2012 presidential election, some are disappointed by the president's performance.

Even *South Park* creates an alternate Obama, not an inspiring one who captured the world's attention, but a George Clooney *Ocean's Eleven*-style thief whose only reason to run for president was to steal the priceless "Hope Diamond." The only way Obama could steal the jewel was if he won the presidency and the country was distracted by his victory. This would allow him enough time to steal the diamond before anyone realized it was missing. And for good measure, everyone involved in the election is in on the heist: McCain, Michelle Obama, and there is even a reference that Obama's recently deceased grandmother is in on the charade. And when there's a problem, the gang calls the genius of the group: Sarah Palin, who trades in her fake good ol' American accent for a posh British one. Is *South Park* not telling us that this game is rigged? That there's something wrong here? While Matt and Trey do it for comedic effect, there is an underhanded scheme subverting a flawed system. They're warning us about Obama and during his second term with regards to certain policy choices and missteps, they may have been right!

Matt and Trey are acting as the new type of teachers in today's media world, using their satiric program to educate, inform, and entertain just like Murrow wanted and requested television to do. And like Murrow, they've been justly rewarded for their efforts with an Emmy and a Peabody award for excellence. They're on the air, whether they know it or not, to be a trusted voice and bring a divided nation back together. In essence, how *South Park* became this way was by knowing that what they say at the end of every episode: "You know, I learned something today" summarized exactly what Edward R. Murrow asked for television to accomplish in 1958:

> We are to a large extent an imitative society. If one or two or three corporations would undertake to devote just a small fraction of their advertising appropriation along the lines that I have suggested, the procedure would grow by contagion; the economic burden would be bearable, and there might ensue a most exciting adventure—exposure to ideas and the bringing of reality into the homes of the nation. To those who say people wouldn't look; they wouldn't be interested; they're too complacent, indifferent and insulated, I can only reply: There is, in one reporter's opinion, considerable evidence against that contention. But even if they are right, what have they got to lose? Because if they are right, and this instrument is good for nothing but to entertain, amuse and insulate, then the tube is flickering now and we will soon see that the whole struggle is lost. This instrument can teach, it can illuminate; yes,

and it can even inspire. But it can do so only to the extent that humans are determined to use it to those ends. Otherwise it is merely wires and lights in a box. There is a great and perhaps decisive battle to be fought against ignorance, intolerance and indifference. This weapon of television could be useful.

FIKA!

Fika. Well, not quite. Apparently dinner is NOT at Fika. Regardless, Lecture One in Sweden done, and one left for tomorrow. Jonas made reservations for dinner at Pelikan in Soder, which is the Swedish word for "south." The place is hopping with every type of person you could imagine—artists, businesspeople, politicians, families, couples—and not one of them looks out of place. Pelikan reminds me of Café Schuim, where Beckett and I used to meet for our talks. Seems like so long ago … wish he could see even one of my lectures. Pelikan is precisely the place you'd want to be: not too imposing, yet there's a hint of monarchy in the air, and of course, the good kind of socialism. The building looks and is old, with the wood columns exuding a feeling of being in a time warp. While this is typical for a European city—except for Rotterdam, which was bombed out in World War II, which they apologize for at every opportunity—the restaurant is warm and inviting. Observing the place, everyone is well dressed, engaged with one another, and phones out, face up, with the occasional glance during a break in conversation. Some patrons have their phones face down, signaling their level of interest, the intent of breaking free of outside communication, or just good manners. We're situated in the middle of the room; the high ceilings allow the various conversations to hang over the room like the chandeliers. There's a beautiful gigantic window in the large main room, giving life and light to the old place. I've positioned myself to be able both to look out the window and observe the dining hall. I glance around at my table of Swedes; seated next to each other at the end of the table are Peter and Anna. If they are trying to hide their office romance, they're doing the worst job in history. I'm seated between Jonas and the organizer of the event, Sofia.

She's very sweet, explaining each dish from dinner mixed in with questions about the lecture, and of course, questions about America. "But once again, I apologize for not greeting you downstairs and for the lengthy question-and-answer session. Usually, we allow only twenty minutes."

"Twenty, fifty, it's totally fine. I enjoyed it. They had some excellent comments and questions—hopefully, after dinner I can resist the temptation to rewrite tomorrow's lecture. At least, as long as Jonas and company keep me entertained, I'll have no choice," I tell her.

Sofia's short reddish-blonde hair stands out from the majority of Swedes I've seen today. Her style is definitely unique as well—a bit of a punk rock girl mixed with business savvy. A fantastic mix of old and new. The look works for her as she commands the table, flowing effortlessly from conversation to conversation. She turns to Anna, getting her attention.

"No, that lecture was two years ago." Anna looks at her, nods. It's a fascinating display of acute awareness for the surroundings and ability to retain several levels of dialogue.

"I must say, before we contacted you to come here, we had seen this lecture online. I watched them all and would I be wrong to say this was your best?"

"It is my favorite because it was my first and most about me—but best? Best is too subjective. But I don't think you're wrong at all. Everything was perfect." I hope I can keep the momentum for the next night.

Sofia motions to the waiter and I glimpse around the table. One detail I notice is that everyone at the table is speaking English. They must be aware of my lack of proficiency in Swedish or are proudly displaying their dual language abilities. Regardless, their attempts at making me feel at ease are appreciated.

Scanning the table, I see that next to Jonas is his sister, Cecilia. She has long, straight, extremely blonde hair, green eyes, and porcelain-colored skin, and is dressed in an all-black pantsuit with a summer-green blouse. She's quiet and extremely jittery, fumbling around with her utensils, unsure of what to order, and peruses the menu for the sixth time. Finally, she caves in to the waiter's pressure and orders. The waiter continues to make his rounds as another waiter sets down everyone's drinks. Beer and wine only. No hard liquor. It is too expensive to drink liquor in this city. Even though I'm not paying for dinner, I usually keep with the customs. Though this is Sweden, I would assume Absolut Vodka would be acceptable, but no, stick with tradition. When a server is taking drink orders, I usually order last to get a feel for what the customs are, and it seems to work. Note to all: Beer and wine in Europe.

"I ordered some smor, ost, and sill for the table," Jonas tells us.

Sofia immediately translates, "Butter, cheese, and herring." I keep my eye on Cecilia who is back to her menu, possibly regretting her dinner choice. Several people at the bar who were at the lecture wave to me. I humbly wave back, nod, and then turn my attention to Cecilia.

"I went with the shrimp and fish."

Cecilia doesn't look up from her menu. "Wonderful. Thought you would have gone with the meatballs."

"No, the lox though I think it's salmon. If we'd gone to an IKEA for dinner, though, probably. But I don't see any IKEA furniture around." I turn my head, pretending to search for IKEA furniture, hoping the additional gesture sells the joke. Cecilia hasn't lifted her head up just yet.

"Shame. The meatballs are quite excellent here. Jonas says the place is famous for them." The joke falls flat; no crickets, though, just a small silence between us as Cecilia peeks up from the menu to observe my reaction. She smiles. "Though a Swedish meatball and IKEA joke—at least you're trying. You're failing, but trying. We're not all about IKEA, you know. I bet you think we have a

Swedish bikini team, too." There's another pause as I smile back at her, because I did think that. She continues, "Typical American. I believe it's an advertising campaign from Wisconsin."

She looks at me and can see the disappointment on my face. "Sorry to shatter your dreams, but not sorry." She means it.

"Could be worse, you could tell me that the Swedish meatballs I've been eating are not really Swedish. And there really is no such thing as Swedish massage." She looks at me. Oh, no. They're not. "Are you trying to destroy my reality?" I ask her, hoping she takes mercy on me.

Cecilia takes a sip of her wine, and says, "I'm trying to destroy your fantasy. The Swedish meatballs you eat are more from the US Midwest where Swedish people settled a few generations ago. Similar climate and topography, so technically, you're getting a Swedish-American meatball hybrid. Ours are made with milk, onions finely chopped and fried, some broth, and cream. I prefer it with white pepper; yours probably have corn syrup in them. You put corn syrup in everything. And a Swedish massage, you'd think that means it was funded by a health care system but I believe it's all marketing to get Americans to believe they're getting a massage from a European country. Make sense but at the same time, would anyone buy a Romanian massage?" She immediately returns to her menu as an image of a Romanian woman from Transylvania pops into my head.

My reality is crashing down around me. "Mission accomplished, everything I thought about Sweden has come to a tragic end."

"You're welcome. It was bound to happen. You built a world based on zero facts. Time to grow up and stop watching cartoons." There's a moment of silence between us as Cecilia looks like she regrets what she just said, but she changes course and peeks over her menu again. "I wanted to tell you I was fascinated by your lecture, and that I always thought *South Park* was vulgar kid-stuff, cheap laughs. No offense, but something about the show is very American and not very refined at all; not offensive per se, but lacking depth."

"It is. Don't let the talk fool you, I've been known to reach. Oh and I like cartoons and always will." I give her a smile. She finally puts down her menu and she's up for the conversation. She examines me. Feeling her emerald gaze, I add, "Most dismiss the show, but people forget that Shakespeare in his day was considered popular culture. Equate that to today—if the work produced is considered or called Shakespearean, it's the highest honor."

She perks up, fully engaged in the banter. "A confident statement. So, to that end, would I be remiss to say you are prognosticating here today, right now, that *South Park* and their creators will be the 25th-century equivalent of Shakespeare?" Her smile is effective as she moves closer to the candle on the table. The angle of the light reflecting off her skin creates a tint that produces an unmistakable glow to the left side of her face. She's probing me, seeing how far she can take things, and how much I can dish back. She's tough, no mistaking that. The cold and dark winters do that to people. I choose my words carefully.

"I'd be hard-pressed to imagine that level of ascendancy for an animated television show, but if a prediction is what you want, I'd gladly prognosticate here and now; yes, *South Park* will be remembered thusly. However, kind of a challenge to collect on a bet of that nature."

Cecilia thinks, continuing to fiddle with the utensils. There's a movement to her hands that seems premeditated. It can't be nerves or anything of the sort, and then it dawns on me—it's the coffee jitters. Has to be, this is how I am in the morning. The rhythm, the cadence, and the jitters; it's simple: she wants dinner to end so she can get a cup of coffee. Or am I projecting my own desires now?

She finally breaks the silence, "Collecting on a wager of this magnitude would require contracts signed, deals made, and escrow accounts created. It's not worth the investment unless you're willing to barter your lineage." She's probably a lawyer. Her voice has a raspy hint to it and her English is unblemished. It's a soft mix of proper British English with too many American sitcoms influencing the inflections. Not that I'm complaining.

Cecilia has an incredible ability to toy with you but at the same time put you at ease, or so I am learning during this trial by fire. The second she makes one emotion come through, she'll counter with the other. I can tell by her approach.

"I suppose I would have to see the offer sheet before committing." She taps her brother on the shoulder and motions for them to switch seats. She smiles at me and continues. "Though the thought of having your future family owe my future family money appeals to me. I have to think of my offspring."

"Enticing."

"Very much so. I will need to inspect your ancestry to see all successes and failures. And of course, which one outweighs the other. Don't want to invest in a failing line."

"How do you know there will be failures?"

"Because every family has one or several. Even those who think they're successes are failures in some way or another. Look at my brother here." Sibling rivalry knows no age nor ocean nor culture; it's always there. I laugh as she elbows Jonas, who is completely oblivious to the insult.

The wine is delicious and I continue to look around The Pelikan. Still exciting and full of life, the ambient light has dimmed, even though it's still bright outside. The artificial light inside mixes with the sun's light as it radiates throughout the room, creating a glow almost like a halo surrounding the dining room. I make my way back towards Cecilia, trying to read her, but she's revealing scant clues to her thought process. My stare forces her to acknowledge my turn to talk.

"I wouldn't say anyone in my family is a failure."

"You'd be wrong." She stops the conversation cold. I have no deciphering skills to use on her. Is she kidding? Is she just having fun? She's already insulted Americans, her family, and mine, but she said it with a smile. She moves a bit closer.

"I'm sure your family is full of success." Another smile. She's good. "Now, that the lecture's question and answer session is over, can I ask you one?" Without letting me answer, she jumps right in, "It feels like you meant what you said during the lecture, all of it. Seemed very much about you."

"I meant most of what I said and some is very much me, some not."

"When the crowd applauded after the scene with the blond kid, Butters."

I nod, knowing exactly what she's talking about. "Yeah, of course. Couldn't make that part up or research that. That was real and the applause from the audience was unexpected—"

"So was the realization for everyone in the room. The reaction was genuine. I do not believe anyone thought they'd have a cathartic experience."

"Especially from, what did you call it—'something unrefined and lacking depth'?"

"Exactly. But you paused there and allowed for everyone to reminisce about his or her own loss. It's why so many people asked you about it afterwards. I don't think anyone anticipated reflecting on life and losses tonight. We all thought it would be curse words and fart jokes."

"I edited those out on the afternoon flight over. Thought the Swedes were too refined for that considering my fantasy towards your country."

"Another joke. That was better than the IKEA one." She tells me it's a joke but hasn't laughed. I wonder why. Is it a horrible laugh that you makes you pray for someone to call, announcing the death of a relative, or is she holding back? We study each other and her jitters subside. She moves the candle. "There's this word, 'onsra,' in the Boro language of India—"

"Onsra."

"Nice pronunciation. And quick too."

"Well, I've been in a helicopter."

"What?" Cecilia is confused but I know it's too detailed to explain so maybe later or possibly another time.

"Nothing. So, onsra."

Without missing a beat she continues, "It means a bittersweet feeling that occurs in those who know their love won't last. I couldn't help but think of that word during the lecture."

Onsra. Well I guess I'm not going to be able to resist inserting that into that lecture for tomorrow night. What a perfect word to define a life. If only I'd known that word years ago.

Cecilia searches for her wine, reaching around Jonas to grab her glass. "Cannot forget the most important part of dinner." Her guard is lowering.

"But I thought coffee comes at the end of the meal."

She looks at me. "Well now that's certainly true. Speaking of which, heard you liked the coffee."

How'd she know about the coffee? Right, Jonas, he probably told her. I reach to the floor and pick up the gift bag that Sofia gave me at the end of the lecture. Inside the bag are three one-kilogram bags of the kind of Swedish coffee the driver had for me for the ride from the airport. I figure six and a half pounds of coffee should last for a few. I show her the bags.

"How am I getting these through customs and on the plane—"

"Just pack them, no one cares here," she says, interrupting me.

"It's not here I'm worried about. But I really enjoyed them. I sampled some Swedish coffee places in New York before I left for the tour. Fika and—"

Cecilia nods, "Yeah, Fika and Konditori are excellent clients, and you live in Brooklyn so I thought you should try those brands, on the off chance you hadn't yet. They're familiar enough for those American taste buds or lack thereof."

I ignore the insult as if I've become used to them. "'Clients'? You mean 'cafés.'"

She laughs at my assumption that *she'd* made a mistake, and she shakes her head. "No, I know the difference between the words 'client' and 'café.' I am their representative here and I deal with their coffee buyers in New York. In fact, I just got back from my yearly trip. Though, I think I'm being transferred to Africa soon."

Now, I'm not exactly sure if it was all the voices in the dining hall that made an angelic sound or it was a band tuning a harp in the other room, but I think she just said she buys and sells coffee. "So when Jonas said you requested a cup of coffee for the car service, I gave him my best Swedish brand." She finishes speaking and takes a sip of wine. "And anyone who has an opportunity to make ridiculous requests and asks only for coffee is someone worth meeting. At least get some chocolate out of it or something."

I'm at a loss for words at the moment. I'm transfixed by a) her beauty, not much of a debate there, b) the way she delicately holds the wine glass, or c) that she is a coffee buyer. Remain calm. There is always an option d: all of the above.

"The worst part of selling coffee to—"

"Hard to believe there's a worst part," I interject trying to maintain cool and collected, and failing miserably. She smiles and takes another sip of wine, finishing her glass, and motions to the waiter for a refill for both our glasses.

"My brother's paying for it, so why not another? Yeah, there is a worst part due to the fact that the best part of my day is going to sleep knowing I'm less than eight hours away from the first cup of the day."

I'm still waiting for the negative aspect of this profession. Cecilia continues, "Choosing what brand to drink will dictate the day, maybe even the week. Especially considering that I have about twenty half-kilo samples stored away in sealed jars—it becomes a momentary panic every morning. Thankfully, I wrote out each description, and take my time before making my selection. Jonas is convinced I am suffering from some form of obsessive compulsive disorder. I prefer to think of it as a dedication to the craft."

A huge and probably idiotic grin crosses my face. I hope this dinner never ends, but there's one lecture to go.

4

What traits has *South Park* acquired enabling it to become a trusted voice in a media landscape littered with yellers, screamers, drama queens, and Chicken Littles claiming the sky is falling? Matt and Trey's primary goal is to understand humanity and the people they represent. Once they do that, they can establish a connection with their audience. This will, in turn, develop a trust with the viewers as they are shown a consistent, worthwhile, and balanced opinion. From there, they can educate the audience in a way no mainstream animated show has done before. So how does a show do this? A relationship needs to be established between viewer and creator. One of the ways to accomplish this is reacting to current events and introducing a third option for how to think about it. This works because the audience tunes in weekly to see if *South Park* will tackle the newest controversy. Sometimes they do, sometimes they don't, but when the show does deliver, it always makes for an interesting debate. The other way to establish the relationship is to figure out what the most important thing is to humanity and use that as the foundation of every episode. For the show, the single most important concept in our society is the relationship between people; their mission: creating the relationships, making them believable even if they are animated characters.

Murrow achieved this relationship with his audience during World War II and Cronkite did the same with the political assassinations in the 1960s. Besides trauma or shocking events, there are other ways to establish relationships: laughter, longevity, and consistency. Making us laugh for a long time and doing it on a consistent basis without too much disappointment will endear you to an audience. Everyone loves the clown who continues to amuse. It's why Jim Carrey can do no wrong in my eyes even after *Mr. Poppers Penguins*. And remember that a satirist wants to heal the world. They want to make us feel, help us relate to forces we may not entirely understand. *South Park* is a show about friends and family and each episode revolves around these in one way or another. It is the norm for all forms of entertainment to do this, and *South Park* is no different. But there's one relationship that immediately connects to an audience: the girlfriend–boyfriend relationship or the first love.

The first love has been experienced by most and unless you're lucky, we've all had the trauma of losing that first love. Heartbreak is not an exclusive emotion. We all have been in relationships we believed would last forever but something happened, ending the affair. After that happens we're never quite the same, never as perfect as we once were. In fact, if anything, that bright shining star we call the heart is just a little duller, but as a silver lining, we're a little wiser too. Those who attempt to console you stating that, "It's not the end of the world!" If only they could understand by responding stating, "Yes! It's not the end of the Earth as we know it, but it's the end of the little world I created and now, I have to start over because it got annihilated in the most painful and unexpected way."

On a personal note, I was in a relationship, and one day, before I knew what happened, it was over and I was miserable. Nothing is correcting my axis because it is now spinning out of control.

My friends visited, telling me all kinds of things to make me feel better, saying all sorts of horrible things about her, which was nice of them—and true about her—but sadly, none of it worked. They took me out to bars, restaurants, and other places I'm not going to divulge, but they did it to make me feel better. That's why they are your friends. But their efforts were to no avail, nothing worked. Until late one night, the *South Park* episode "Raisins" from Season Seven came on the air. In this episode, Stan's long-time "girlfriend" Wendy Testaburger dumps him, except Wendy doesn't officially break up with him. In typical elementary school fashion, she sends her best friend Bebe to do the deed in the middle of recess in front of all his friends, with all the harshness and coldness only a mercenary can achieve. At first, Stan doesn't understand what is happening, but as Bebe walks away, things sink in for Stan. The heartbreak montage begins as cheesy 80s music blasts over the soundtrack with Stan leaving the playground. He's walking around town in the rain, absolutely depressed, seeing Wendy in the rain. But seeing her turns out to be a mirage: he's crying while sitting on a desolate street, and again while lying in bed looking at his one photo of Wendy. Stan is floored and forever changed by the events that will shape his existence maybe for the rest of his life. To counteract his descent into misery, Stan enlists his friends to help us understand what happened with Wendy. To Stan, and anyone who attempted this ploy, all that was desired was an understanding and maybe things can be fixed like nothing happened.

Stan: Kyle, will you talk to Wendy for me?

Kyle: [not looking up] Why?

Stan: 'Cause I need to know why she broke up.

Kyle: Aw, dude, come on. I gotta do my science homework.

Stan: [pleading] Dude, please. I might still have a chance to make things work. Please, just go talk to her?

Kyle: [puts his book down and sighs] God dammit! [walks over to Wendy, but avoids eye contact] Wendy, Stan wants to know why you broke up. [Wendy turns around]

Wendy: Look, Stan is really nice. I just don't wanna be boyfriend and girlfriend anymore. I've been wanting to break up for a while, but it's, it's nothing against him.

Kyle: 'K. [walks back to Stan, but avoids looking at him, as well] She says she's been wantin' to break up for a while, and it's nothing against you.

Stan: What? That's no answer! [nudges him a bit] Go tell her to be more direct with me.

Kyle: [goes for his books and picks them up] No dude, I'm out. Go talk to her yourself. Be poetic. [walks off. Jimmy appears]

Stan: Kyle, this is my life. [points at Jimmy] Jimmy!

Jimmy (who has crutches and stutters): Hey Stan.

Stan: Jimmy, will you go talk to Wendy for me?

Jimmy: For- Forw- Forw-w-w what?

Stan: Just go talk to her an-, and be poetic. Tell her she's my Muse—no! Tell her, [thinks] tell her … [gestures] she's a continuing source of inspiration to me.

Jimmy: She's what?

Stan: She's a continuing source of inspiration to me.

Jimmy: … Okay. [walks over to Wendy] Hey uh-Wen, hey wu-Wendy. [she turns around with her books]

Wendy: Yeah?

Jimmy: Stan says you're a cunt … you're a- cunt- S-Stan says you're a cunt- cunt-

Wendy: Well tell Stan to fuck off!! [closes her locker and runs away]

Jimmy: -cunt- You're a cont-tinuing source of inspiration to him. [his mission done, he returns to Stan]

Stan: Well?

Jimmy: She just- w-walked away, Stan. You're gonna have to face facts. It's over. [hangs his head for emphasis, then walks off]

Suffice to say, that was the first and possibly only time that word has ever been uttered on American television. How did *South Park* get away with using the word? It wasn't really the word, it was "continuing" but because he's a stutterer, they were able to get away with it. After that colossal failure, Stan asks Wendy's friends what he can do, and that fails too. Stan falls deeper and deeper into his depression and his friends come over his house and witness the downward spiral their friend is currently in.

Butters: We came over to cheer you up, Stan!

Stan: [softly, creaking] … Go away.

Kyle: Stan, you can't keep doing this to yourself. You have to go live.

Stan: Why? What's the point of living when the only girl I ever loved is gone?

Cartman: God, what a fag!

Kyle: Dude, not now! [Cartman looks down, embarrassed]

Stan: You guys have no idea how this feels. It's like, you always hear songs about a broken heart and you think it's just a figure of speech? But it's true. My chest hurts. I feel this like, sinking feeling where my heart is. It's broken …

Kyle: Jeez, he's worse than I thought.

So what do they do? What all friends do! They try to cheer him up and they take him to Raisins, which is the fourth-grade version of a restaurant called Hooters. It's a restaurant where the girls are very young, and dressed in barely there shorts and white tops. The girls flirt with all the boys to make them feel good, in the hope that their tips will increase. Even though flirtatious and scantily dressed girls surround Stan, his depression has yet to dissipate. But there's one boy in the group who feels way better, besides Cartman who ate an entire plate of chicken wings, and that is Butters. A somewhat new character, not in the original foursome, but still one of the show's best characters. Butters truly represents the innocence and goodhearted nature in everyone. At Raisins, Butters falls immediately in love with Lexus the waitress for no other reason than she called him "sweetie" and touched his arm and hugged him. This is the first time a girl showed affection for him and now he is in love. Over the course of the episode, Butters does all those things that we're supposed to do when we're in love. He calls her up, asks her how her day was, and he is willing to do things for her to show her his affection. He sends her flowers, sends her chocolate, and generally cares and wants to make her happy. Lexus, on the other hand, doesn't even recognize him when he brings her a gift after work. Instead, she calls over a bouncer/security guard to walk her to her bike because she thinks Butters is a dangerous stalker. Butters is so blinded by love that he doesn't realize what Lexus is doing and feeling. Just like how some don't realize the relationship they're in is with someone unworthy of their affection. We refuse to see what is right in front of our eyes. As Butters falls more and more in love, Stan falls further and further into depression. He joins the Goth Kids and starts dressing in all black, including an Edgar Allan Poe t-shirt, writing poetry about love, pain, and how terrible life is. Juxtaposing Stan's Robert Smith of The Cure-like disintegration, Butters believes Lexus is the girl for him and brings his parents to Raisins to introduce them to Lexus. In that scene, the audience is treated to one of *South Park*'s greatest moments in the show's history. What Butters says at the end of this sequence is so poignant, so important, that it's—granted it's an animated character—but it's something worth noting. It's worth believing in and living life by. First, Butters' parents Stephen and Linda experience Raisins for the first time.

Stephen: Oh boy, I think I know what's happened. Our son hasn't learned yet that girls will pretend to like him for money.

Linda: [holds her hands together] This place is horrible. To objectify girls like this.

Porsche: [arrives] Hi guys. Can I take your order?

Linda: Little girl, you shouldn't be working here.

Porsche: I shouldn't? Where am I supposed to be working?

Linda: No, I mean you shouldn't work somewhere where you're paid for how you look. You should be learning a skill so you can grow up to be a businesswoman or even a doctor. Who knows? You could cure cancer.

Porsche: I could cure cancer? Omigod! That would be sooo cool! I had a cancer sore on my lip once and it hurt sooo bad.

Linda: … Oh. Never mind, I think Raisins might be the perfect place for you.

Porsche: Cool! [grins and hops off the stool, then carries it off. Butters arrives with Lexus, who carries a plate of chips]

As per usual, Matt and Trey throw in tiny bits of social commentary when you least expect it. According to the *South Park* guys, Porsche is exactly where she belongs and will never cure cancer, so why even bother with building Porsche up for anything other than a Raisins waitress? It's obviously a joke but there is something behind it. Back to the scene and Butters' inevitable crash from the clouds.

Butters: Mom? Dad? This is Lexus.

Lexus: Hi. Welcome to Raisins.

Stephen: Uh, Butters, can we have a little talk with you? Outside?

Butters: Huh? Oh anything you have to say to me [holds on to Lexus] you can say in front of Lexus.

Linda: Butters, these girls pretend to be interested in you because they know you'll give them tips.

Butters: Huh?

Stephen: You see, Butters, women know that they can make men do anything by flirting. And some girls, like these, turn that into a profession.

Butters: Oh, I see. [gets angry] You don't approve of my girlfriend! [Lexus looks off and smiles at somebody] Well let me tell you somethin', Mom and Dad, our love is as pure as a mountain spring! The odds may be stacked against us, but we're gonna give it our best shot! And so, if you can't be happy for us, y-you can just go to heck, Mom and Dad! [walks away from the table with Lexus] Come on, Lexus. I'm movin' out of my parents' house and I'm movin' in with you. Uh let's blow this joint!

Lexus: What are you talking about, kid? We are NOT boyfriend and girlfriend.

Butters: … What? Lexus, what are you saying? Are you saying … you don't want to be together anymore?

Lexus: I'm sorry, sweetie.

Butters: So that's it? We're broken up now?

Lexus: I gotta get these curly fries to Table 12. [walks off]

Butters: Well go ahead and go. It's best we don't say anything more. There's nothing left to say. It's over. [walks off dejected] Our relationship is o-over.

What a painful scene to watch as Butters matures before our very eyes. His world is destroyed and he experiences loss like most have. You feel for Butters and see that the relationships we discussed earlier are in full display, *South Park* is there to say, in President Bill Clinton's terminology: "I feel your pain." That's what a lot of these episodes are about—understanding the suffering those in society are enduring, whether it be economic pain in "Margaritaville," political frustrations in "Douche & Turd," or religious hypocrisy in "Red Hot Catholic Love," and others. This is why the show has been so popular all these years—the vulgarities and the ability to shock their audience contribution—but if the show lacked all heart, like their amateurish competition *Family Guy*, *South Park* would just be amusing and nothing more. This element takes the emotions of the show to another level and this sequence is indicative of that.

Butters is now in Stan's shoes, heartbroken and completely spun off his axis. To mirror the two, Matt and Trey put Butters in the exact scene Stan was in while sitting on the curb in the rain. There's a different song, but the sentiment is the same.

[Run-down part of town, night. The conditions surrounding Stan's presence there a week ago are present again, and Butters sobs at the same spot Stan did, at the curb under a working street light. Some shadows move in on him and stop when they cover most of his head]

Goth Voice: Look at this. Another tortured soul. Another life of pain. [Butters looks up to see the Goths. Stan isn't shown yet.] Hey Raven, check it out. [Stan, now named Raven, enters the picture]

Stan: Butters?

Butters: Oh [sniffs, wipes away his tears] Uh hey, hey Stan.

Stan: What's the matter with you?

Butters: [sobbing] Well, mu mu mu girlfriend broke up with me.

Henrietta: Did she step on your heart with stiletto heels?

Butters: Yeah. [sniff] It sure does hurt.

Goth Kid 2: That's cool. I guess you can join up with us if you want.

Goth Kid 1: Yeah. We're gonna go to the graveyard and write poems about death and how pointless life is.

Butters: Uh, uhm no thanks. I- I love life.

Stan: Huh? But you just got dumped—

Butters: Wuh-ell yeah, and I'm sad, but at the same time I'm really happy that somethin' could make me feel that sad. It's like, ih ih, ih it makes me feel alive, you know? It makes me feel human. And the only way I could feel this sad now is if I felt somethin' really good before. So I have to take the bad with the good, so I guess what I'm feelin' is like a, beautiful sadness. I guess that sounds stupid …

Goth Kid 1: Yeah.

Stan: No. No, Butters, that doesn't sound stupid at all.

Butters: Well, thanks for offerin' to let me in your clique, guys, uh but, to be honest, I'd rather be a cryin' little pussy than a faggy Goth kid. Well see ya, Stan. [walks off]

Stan: He's right. I don't even know who I am anymore. I like liking life a whole lot more than hating it. Screw you guys, I'm goin' home. [walks off]

Goth Kid 2: Go ahead and go back to your sunshine fairytale!

Butters's realization is that he actually loves life despite the incredible pain he is enduring at the moment. He doesn't look at the break-up in a negative light because he decides to focus on the positive experience. The yin and the yang of life, if something can make you feel that good, there must be a possibility for the exact opposite feeling when it comes to an end. If we, as people, can accept that duality in love and other emotional experiences, we can learn to appreciate everything. The truth is, and it's no secret, that we're going to lose the people we love in life, as Irving Townsend said,

We who choose to surround ourselves with lives even more temporary than our own, live within a fragile circle, easily and often breached. Unable to accept its awful gaps, we still would live no other way. We cherish memory as the only certain immortality, never fully understanding the necessary plan.

Butters understands Townsend's plan and if we could value them and understand relationships' transient nature and look back on them in a positive way, we could evolve as a society. Maybe we could function properly when things go haywire and won't morph into a Goth kid writing bad poetry. Or be better quipped when our heart is stepped on with stiletto shoes as Goth girl Raven says. This is what *South Park* is all about. They are arming today's youth with the education we lacked while growing up. They say youth is wasted on the young but maybe *South Park* can put a stop to the cyclical nature of regret. *South Park* is all about heart and they evoke sympathy and empathy for their characters, who are made real. Matt and Trey put everything into these characters. This allows for connections and trust, even when they're grinding up parents and feeding them to their kids, which Cartman did in "Scott Tenorman Must Die." There's something more here that keeps the audience tuned in and keeps the show fresh after all these years.

5

In an episode from Season Fifteen entitled "You're Getting Old," the audience sees a new wrinkle in the *South Park* universe. Stan has a birthday and is a year older and this is a rarity because animated characters rarely age—Bart Simpson has been eight years old for over twenty years now. Bart does not age, Stan does not age, but in this episode Stan celebrates a birthday. There are birthday parties in the show, "Casa Bonita" for example, and grade progression from third to fourth, but the boys' age is constant. However, in this episode, Stan turns ten and things immediately begin to change for him. He becomes bitter and cynical towards everything he loved before, as everything has turned to literal shit to him. He goes to the movies with his friends, and all the previews look like shit to him. Afterwards, he eats ice cream but the dessert looks and tastes like shit. Even his friends morph into big, walking, talking pieces of shit. And as the episode continues, one cannot help but wonder what is going on in Trey Parker's head, as his *South Park* avatar is usually represented with Stan. Has everything turned to shit for Trey too?

One of the most interesting subplots in *South Park*'s history is contained within "You're Getting Old," the dissolution of Sharon and Randy's marriage.

Watching "You're Getting Old," one begins to sense this has nothing to do with Randy and Sharon but more about Matt and Trey. The two animators have been friends and creative partners for over twenty years, meeting first in college and now are in their forties. "You're Getting Old" is the final episode of the half season, and Matt and Trey have spent seven straight weeks together. Complicating the relationship between the two, right before this half-season, they finished, rehearsed, premiered, and did all the press for their mega-hit Broadway show, "Book of Mormon." From the dialogue between Randy and Sharon, it truly sounded like Matt and Trey were done with each other and hence, the show. And to add to the drama, their Comedy Central contract was ending, leaving the show's future in doubt.

[The Marsh house, night. Randy and Sharon can be seen arguing through the living room windows]

Randy: You don't get it, Sharon! You never have! And that's supposed to be my fault?!

Sharon: Yes, it IS your fault, Randy, because you're a child!

Randy: I'm sick of everything I do being so wrong, Sharon!

Sharon: … You're 42 years old, Randy!

Randy: I'm not dead yet Sharon, but you might be!

Sharon: Oh is that what you think?! That I'm dead?!

[A moment later]

Sharon: You do this all the time! First you're obsessed with baseball fights! Then you need to play Warcraft! Then you gotta be a celebrity chef! [the two men slide a side window up ever so quietly, go in, and sneak upstairs]

Randy: Why can't you ever just support me?!

Sharon: Support what?! Another stupid dream of yours?!

Randy: Face it Sharon, our son turned 10 and you feel old!

Sharon: WHAT does our son turning 10 have to do with YOU making the same mistakes again and again?!

Randy: Because I'm unhappy, okay?! I've been unhappy for a long time! [Sharon reflects on this for a moment and her voice goes soft]

Sharon: I'm unhappy too. We both are, obviously. How much longer can we keep doing this? It's like, the same shit just happens over and over and, then in a week it just all resets until … it happens again. Every week it's kind of the same story in a different way but it, it just keeps getting more and more ridiculous.

Randy: I don't know if I've changed or you have. I just feel like I might not have a whole lot of time left and, I want to enjoy it.

Sharon: I want to enjoy it too, but … I can't fake it anymore. You just seem kind of shitty to me.

Randy: You kind of seem shitty to me too.

Sharon: People get older, Randy. People grow apart.

These are powerful statements from both characters; they're not funny but they are tragic. The scene's location is important as well. Having the marriage end in the typical family living room, Matt and Trey transport us into the scene, as we are the kids spying on our own parents fighting to understand one another. When Randy and Sharon revealed their unhappiness in their marriage and life, it's a devastating moment but also typical American television. This is the beginning of the end and if the show has only seven episodes left, this is the beginning of the South Park boys moving away. Friendships, like the one the boys have end because parents divorcing and relocating occurs in every town. In television, characters reveal their unhappiness or are forced to switch jobs, ultimately leading to their exit from the show. Helplessly, we watch as Randy and Sharon separate, taking the children to a new place and selling their home. And in case you ever believed *South Park* was incapable of drama, here is your answer in a beautifully created montage to end the season.

[Stevie Nicks' "Landslide" begins to play over the entire montage. Stan is seen at Stark's Pond looking at it from a bench. Kyle walks up to Stan, but keeps some distance from him, then turns around and walks away. Stan looks at a flower … which has a huge turd growing from it. A bee lands on it. At the house, Shelley and Sharon pack away everything in the kitchen. Later, Randy explains things to Stan as Stan's dresser is being moved. Later, a realtor sets a "FOR SALE" sign in place—four bedrooms, two bathrooms, kitchen, back yard. She finishes and walks away. Randy is driving a U-Haul truck and watches the house fade in the distance through the driver's rear-view mirror. Sharon and her kids move into a new place. Sharon works on her room and gives Stan the box for his room. Stan later sits in a swing in the new yard. A small sandlot is nearby. Instead of a wooden fence, the new place has a wrought-iron fence. Stan looks up at the sun, which is a glowing massive turd. Stan is then seen at the cafeteria sitting at a table with a bunch of turds that are supposed to be his classmates. All the food looks like shit too. At night the police arrest the Britches Bandits, the two men who stole Randy's underwear, and take the underwear in for evidence. Cartman and Kyle play a game on Kyle's sofa. They look at each other and seem to reach a mutual understanding, since they smile at each other. Stan walks all alone in South Park and passes a duck in a tux. He stops and looks at the duck, who keeps walking. It looks at him and quacks out shit, which lands on him. The last scene is Stan lying in his new bed, in his new bedroom, looking up at the ceiling. The episode fades out and the credits roll in silence for the first few moments.]

The silent fade-out is brutal. The show had never done that before because usually, in television, an ending like this is reserved for a major character dying in an episode. The silence is used as a small gesture to eulogize the fallen character. Rest in peace, Edgar from *24*. Could this silence be the eulogizing of the show as Matt and Trey's contract was ending in seven short episodes? Reactions were swift and rumors circulated of the show's now seemingly eminent end. A few weeks later, Matt and Trey were on *The Daily Show with Jon Stewart* and Stewart's first question was: "Are you guys okay, is the show ending?" They responded by saying no the show is not ending, and they loved doing that episode. They were actually surprised by the response from the audience but everything was fine between the two longtime friends. Later, Comedy Central announced that Trey and Matt signed another mega contract running through what would be *South Park*'s twentieth season.

Emotion from a foul-mouthed cartoon is not expected by critics and dismissed by those who ignore cartoons. Throughout the years, the show has experienced heartache, divorce, aging, pain, loss, and confusion. These things aren't controversial—although most viewers expect controversy from the show—but its true worth lies in its heart. This is where *South Park* does its best work, even if it is not the most popular or discussed aspect. The show's creators are able to infuse real-world problems with family relationships, utilizing the entire episode to design their narrative.

In "Bloody Mary," Season Nine, episode fourteen, the show features several major themes of the show: family, familial relations, religion, religious dependency, the belief in miracles but also, this idea of giving oneself over to god. And this theme of the parents being the children and the children being the parents is constant throughout the show's run. In the episode, Randy gets arrested for drunk driving and utters the brilliant line, "what seems to be the officer, problem?" After the arrest, Randy is forcibly sent to Alcoholics Anonymous or (AA), where the people in charge tell him that he suffers from a disease and is powerless to cure himself unless he follows God. To those in AA, Randy doesn't drink too much; he made an error in judgment, and has a disease because alcohol is a chemical that people can become dependent on. Since alcoholism is a disease, they are absolved of any and all responsibility for their actions. *South Park* immediately dismisses that by spoofing Randy and all his subsequent actions. Randy runs home, shaves his head and puts himself in a wheelchair because he is suffering from a disease. Stan is fed up with his father's actions and marches down to the AA meeting and starts arguing with them. The AA members claim that they are afflicted with a disease, and Stan, acting as the parent responds, "No it's not, cancer is a disease. My dad just needs to drink less."

As this is happening, a subplot forms in the neighboring town of Bailey, Colorado, where a statue of the Virgin Mary is bleeding out its ass. And what ends up happening of course, in a typically religious country, people flock to the statue to behold the miracle. The media arrives and interviews worshippers asking them why they believe the Virgin Mary is bleeding out her ass. True to form, a baptism line forms with a priest putting the "Virgin Mary's divine ass-blood" on each person's forehead while saying, "Praise Christ." All the people are there to hopefully cure their deadly diseases, to heal their deformities, or abnormalities, or even stop their bodies from aging. Randy sees this on television, believing this is only hope for a cure—and once again, the common theme of religion taking the place of personal responsibility—he forces Stan to drive to him Bailey, Colorado. In a wheelchair, Randy starts at the back of the line and meets a man with brain cancer. Randy feels his pain and actually says, "I know, I have alcoholism." Impatient and still drinking, Randy is somehow able to finagle his way a little bit closer by cutting the line and waiting next to a girl with elephantitis and remarks with a straight face, "We are the same she and I." Finally, a security guard comes over because an argument erupts over Randy's obvious cutting of the baptism line.

Officer: What's goin' on here?

Man 9: This kid's cutting in line!

Randy: Please, officer, you have to understand. I need a miracle waaay more than these people. I'm an alcoholic, and I'm powerless over it.

Officer: … I understand. My, my brother's an alcoholic. Here, let me push you to the front of the line. [Stan looks on a bit stunned]

Randy: Oh bless you, sir! Bless you! [the line parts as the officer moves him] 'Scuse me, out of the way, alcoholic coming through! [the officer moves him into position. Randy wheels himself closer] She's … beautiful. [the statue squirts a long stream of blood on him and he rejoices in it] Aaaah. AAAAAaaaaah! [opens his eyes, and the statue quickly squirts him one more time. He then wheels himself into view and struggles to get up from the wheelchair. He still has a bottle with him] I'm … not … going … to drink this. I'm not going to drink this! [throws the bottle off somewhere] It's a miracle! I'm cured! [begins to dance away. Stan is embarrassed and stewing]

Yoohoohoo! Praise Jesus! Praise Mary the Blessed Virgin Mother! Thank you! Thank you God! [runs off]

Some time later in the episode, after Randy has transformed himself into a born-again believer, he is at an AA meeting, drinking lemonade and watching television. He's praising Christ and his disease- and alcohol-free self. However, while at the meeting, a news report breaks that gets Randy's full attention.

[News Report from St. Peter's Church in Bailey]

Field Reporter: An update from the bleeding Virgin Mary statue!

Randy: [turns around and reacts] Oh wait. Sh sh. Hold on a second, gang. [the group quiets down]

Field Reporter: Earlier today, the new pope, Pope Benedict the 16th himself, visited the statue here in Bailey to witness the miracle firsthand. [Footage of the pope walking through the crowd. People left and right kneel before him in reverence] It was an amazing sight to behold as Pope Benedict made his way through the throngs of people.

Cardinal Mallory: Right this way, Your Holiness.

Field Reporter: The pope then examined the statue closely. [the pope draws closer … closer … blinks, gets closer … looks at the camera and raises his eyebrows quickly twice, turns back and gets closer, gets a stream of blood on his face, about as much as Randy got] After witnessing the phenomenon firsthand, the pope then cleaned himself off and then declared that the bleeding Virgin Mary statue is not a miracle!

Randy: What?

Field Reporter: Having investigated closely, the pope determined that the blood was not coming from the Virgin Mary's ass, but rather, from her vagina. And the pope said quote, "A chick bleeding out her vagina is no miracle. Chicks bleed out their vaginas all the time." [a graphic with those words appears on screen, along with an image of the pope and his name, Pope Benedict XVI] Back to you, Tom.

Pope Benedict who had been pope less than six months, and has since retired, was a prime candidate for *South Park*'s scorn. But Randy is severely affected by this news as it dawns on him that he's not cured and still suffers from alcoholism. He immediately drops his lemonade and orders "three shots of McAllen, two small bottles of vodka, three bottles of beer, and some Jell-O shooters!" This influences all the other AA members to turn their back on Christ, religion, and God, succumbing to their "disease." Randy runs out of the restaurant and we get another lesson from *South Park* delivered by Stan fulfilling his role as parent throughout the episode and into the final scene.

Whistlin' Willy's, outside. Randy staggers out with his drinks]

Stan: Dad, Dad, Stop!

Randy: [turns around, dropping an empty bottle] I'm sorry, son! I'm off the wagon!

Stan: Dad, you don't have to do this! You have the power. You haven't drank since seeing the statue.

Randy: But the statue wasn't a miracle!

Stan: Yeah. The statue wasn't a miracle, Dad. So that means you did it. That means you didn't have a drink for five days all on your own.

Randy: You're right, Stan. If God didn't make me stop drinking then … I did. Maybe … Maybe I can force myself to never drink again. [throws off all his drinks, and they shatter on the pavement.]

Stan: No!

Randy: No??

Stan: Dad, you like to drink. So have a drink once in a while. Have two. If you devote your whole life to completely avoiding something you like, then that thing still controls your life and, 'n you've never learned any discipline at all.

Randy: But, maybe … I'm just the kind of person who needs to have it all or nothing.

Stan: Naw. All or nothing is easy. But learning to drink a little bit, responsibly, that's a discipline. Discipline … come from within. [Randy looks at Stan for a moment, then walks up to his side and kneels next to him.]

Randy: How did I manage to raise such a smart kid?

Stan: I've had a great teacher.

Randy: Thanks, son.

Stan: No not you, my karate teacher. He's really smart.

Randy: Oh. Well, tell you what: let's leave the car here, walk home, and watch the game. Like to have another beer or two.

Stan: All right!

Randy: [lifts up his son and places him on his shoulders] Come on! [they begin to walk] Or maybe I'll have three beers. [they walk off towards the sunset in the street. Their shadows are long on the pavement as the sun blazes on the horizon]

Stan: That's probably okay if you spread it out.

Randy: Well how about four?

Stan: I think you're pushing it.

Randy: How about twenty?

Stan: That's not discipline.

Randy: Right, right. Does vodka count?

Stan: Dad!!!

It's an incredibly touching father-son bonding moment but there is an important lesson, one of moderation and excess. *South Park*'s lesson is vices are expected and acceptable as long as there's a limit to them. It's obvious that Stan is more in tune with reality than Randy ever is. Moderation, decency, acts of kindness, and aging gracefully are not exclusive topics to every episode but certainly the most memorable. Of course, there are episodes where Randy does an admirable job as a parent, as in the Emmy award–winning "Make Love, Not Warcraft" episode. Randy, wanting to join the latest fad of online gaming to grow closer to his son, enters the online World of Warcraft world in order to save his avatar's son's life. Stan and his friends are fighting a "rogue" gamer who is destroying everyone's gaming experience but as good as they are, defeat is nearing. However, the creators of the game send Randy into the game to help in what appears to be a losing battle with the rogue gamer. Randy has been given access to "the sword of a thousand truths" and the weapon will tip the scales of the battle, enabling Stan and his friends to achieve an improbable victory. Randy rushes over to his son's fight, and Stan dismisses him but then realizes what Randy has. Randy hands his son the sword and immediately after the weapon is transferred, the Rogue gamer stabs Randy.

[The Rogue gamer (ganker) stabs Randy and Randy goes down, mortally wounded]

Randy: Augh!

Stan: Dad!

Randy: Stan ... [falls down face first]

Stan: Dad, no! [turns around to face the ganker] You killed my father. [walks up to the ganker and strikes him with one blow of the sword. The ganker's defenses start to crack.]

[Few moments later after the ganker has been defeated. Stan throws away the Sword of a Thousand Truths and rushes up to his father's dying character. He shakes the character around a bit]

Stan: Dad? Dad?

Randy: [answers] Staaan. [falters a bit, but Stan holds him up] I've never been able to say this before, but ... I love you, son.

Stan: I know you do, Dad.

Randy: [swats Stan's hand away] Augh! Aaaaaaaaaaaaaaaaaaaa. ...

[Randy continues the melodramatic act of dying at the demo desk in Best Buy.]

Randy was able to be the father he always wanted to be and had a heroic death while saving his son. Isn't that what every good father would want to be able to save their child in the most dramatic way? Here, Randy gets that satisfaction and moment even if it is only a video game. But the scene provides a genuine opportunity for Randy and Stan to share their true feelings and emotions. *South Park* has heart and establishes the importance of relationships. This enables them to explore the wedge issues that were discussed earlier as the things that divide us and pit Americans versus Americans. The perfect episode for this is one of their most talked about and relevant: "Best Friends

Forever" from Season Nine. This aired actually in 2005 during the height of the Terri Schiavo incident and for those who don't know or remember, Terri Schiavo was a woman who got into a horrible car accident and for seven years she was in a permanent vegetative state. She had no chance of recovery. Her parents and her husband wanted to keep her alive on respirators and eventually the husband after seven years decided it was time to move on and let Terri go. The parents didn't approve and fought Michael's decision. There were court injunctions allowing the plug to be pulled and Terri removed from life-support, and then another court disagreed and forced the doctors to reinstate the machine. Then the media grabs hold of the story and do what they do best and that is to make the story into the typical left versus right with no room for nuance or middle ground. The sides featured those who want to save Terri on one side, and those who want to let her die on the other. The Republicans and Democrats both get involved—hoping to cash in on the media's attention—spouting support for or against the husband, Terri's parents, and/or the court's decisions. In fact, George W. Bush left his vacation home in Texas to return to Washington to sign a bill written by the Republican Congress to force the courts to give Terri's rights back to her parents, so Terri's husband, Michael cannot take her off life support.

As this is going on, *South Park* has its show to do and with six days to air, the creative provocateurs decided it's their turn to weigh in on the controversy. What would their approach be? How would *South Park* endure a Terri Schiavo controversy that remains inside the *South Park* universe? The only way they can is by killing Kenny, but they're not killing Kenny just to kill Kenny this time. An ice cream truck kills Kenny and he ascends to Heaven because he is actually a grandmaster at the PlayStation portable game "Heaven versus Hell." While in Heaven, the Angel Peter explains what is happening and why Kenny is the universe's only hope.

Peter: There isn't much time, Kenny. You're dead, but, your death was no accident. Heaven needs you.

Kenny: (Me??)

Peter: Come! There is much to discuss. [they both enter and behold a gleaming city on a hill. Inside, the city has all the appearance of a super-basilica, built with gold and marble. Angels flit around doing stuff] Things are not good in Heaven, Kenny. Satan is planning a massive attack and he knows we are too few in number to stop him! God has changed the rules here. For ages, only Mormons were allowed into Heaven. [they pass the Mormons, who greet them] But knowing that Hell was becoming much larger, God decided to let more people cross over so that he could build an army as well, an army that YOU must command.

Kenny: (That I what??)

Peter: The Sony PSP was built by God, to determine who on Earth had the best skills to defeat the armies of Satan. You … are the best. YOU, are the only hope for the universe.

[In a great courtyard outside the super-basilica. An angel addresses the others]

Angel 3: Satan's army grows as we speak. The Dark Lord knows that our armies are few in number, and unorganized. So our only hope … is perfect strategy. [steps aside to show Kenny off]

Angel 4: A child? This is God's solution?

Peter: He beat Satan's army in over three thousand separate simulations.

Angel 4: Archangel Michael, what say you?

Michael: [looks out into space, then turns around] The child did something none of us could: Reach level sixty on the PSP. Now I don't know if that's luck or perseverance, but it's Goddamned impressive. All right, Kenny, let me show you what we're up against. [two other angels roll a whiteboard to him, and he begins drawing up strategies.] This is the Kingdom of Heaven. Satan's armies will attack the gate … here. They are … ten billion in number. Maybe more. [sniffs the fumes from the dry-erase pen] Our armies are here, here, and here. Just under … ten thousand strong. [sniffs again] We are outnumbered and in need of someone who can singlehandedly bring the whole Dark Empire down. Basically, Kenny, you … are Keanu Reeves. [Kenny just sits there.]

Kenny is about to start preparing for the fight and all of a sudden disappears from heaven, because the doctors were able to revive him down on earth after being legally dead for a day. However, the doctor says Kenny is more of a tomato than a real person because being dead so long, all his brain cells died—he has ended up exactly like Terri Schiavo. The details of his return don't concern Stan and Kyle who are elated their friend is still alive. In this episode, Kenny's parents, Stan, and Kyle will come to represent Terri's parents and the side of keeping Kenny/Terri alive on life support. Cartman on the other hand is angry not because he loves Kenny and does not want to see him suffer, but Kenny left Cartman his PSP in his last will and testament. This is similar to the "Cartoon Wars" episodes where Cartman was standing up for religious sensitivity but his real agenda was to get the juvenile *Family Guy* off the air. Cartman, Kenny, and the PSP trace back to the opening sequence when Kenny was able to purchase a PSP portable and Cartman wasn't. Obviously, Cartman wants Kenny to die so he can have Kenny's PSP but Kenny's parents have the right to determine Kenny's life. Undeterred, Cartman is determined to overturn the decision and takes his fight all the way to the Colorado Supreme Court.

[The Colorado Supreme Court, day.]

Cartman: You see, Your Honor, I was the only one that Kenny McCormick told his wishes to. And Kenny told me specifically that he would never want to be kept alive on a machine. What they're doing to him … is not right.

Chief Justice: Well I'm sorry, young man, but the parents want their child kept alive. I don't believe you have any legal authority here.

Cartman: I do have legal authority, Your Honor. You see, I was Kenny's … BFF.

Judge 2: Best friends forever?

Cartman: That's right. Kenny and I have been BFFs since first grade. Here, look. [brings forth a necklace with the left half of a BFF heart medallion] Kenny has the other half of this BFF necklace. I believe you all know what that means, and how serious this is.

[Hell's Pass hospital, Kenny's room. Kenny's parents keep vigil with Stan and Kyle.]

Mrs. McCormick: Look, Kenny, your friends are here to visit you again.

The Doctor: [entering with a policeman] But this just doesn't seem right.

Stuart: Wha, what's the matter, doctor?

The Doctor: I'm afraid I've been given a court order to remove Kenny's feeding tube.

Mrs. McCormick: What?

Cartman: [comes in with the Chief Justice] He's right in here.

Kyle: Cartman!

Chief Justice: Kenny's BFF says that Kenny didn't want to be kept alive artificially. The courts have determined we must obey his wish.

Kyle: Cartman is NOT Kenny's BFF!

Police Officer: Sir, take a look at this. [has Kenny's necklace in hand and points to the other half of the BFF medallion. The justice walks over the officer puts the two halves together]

Chief Justice: [steps back] That's all the verification we need. Pull the feeding tube, doctor.

Mrs. McCormick: No doctor! You can't!

The Doctor: I'm sorry. I have no choice. [pulls the tube and drops it on the floor]

Is this not Matt and Trey giving their opinions about marriage and the institution of marriage as nothing more than a Best Friends Forever or a BFF necklace? How can a system be set up where a spouse has rights over the parents, the people who created the person we're debating about? Cartman has his full rights over Kenny and pulls the plug, returning Kenny to Heaven. What happens next? The media latches onto the story, just like in the real world and a "right to die debate" begins. Should Cartman be allowed to pull the plug as court- and state-sanctioned BFF? Should we respect the authority of the BFF? At the same time, on the other side, we have those who want to save Kenny and keep him alive. Stan and Kyle start their counter protest chanting: "Don't kill Kenny, you bastards." During the protests an argument emerges from one of the characters repeating a common trope: "You bureaucrats are playing god by taking the feeding tube out." That was the argument from the "right" side, bureaucrats are playing god by taking the feeding tube out of Terri Schiavo and Kenny.

As the protest and debate is going on down on Earth, Kenny is supposed to be in Heaven leading the forces of Heaven against the much larger army of Hell. The archangel Gabriel devises a plan to send down two angels who must figure out how to remove the feeding tube and save the world. Down on Earth, they overhear that Cartman has already done the work for them; ah, the irony! Because Cartman successfully removes the feeding tube and allows Kenny to die, then Heaven will be saved. An angel affectionately calls Cartman "a blessed child" even though Cartman doesn't know what he's done but it's certainly one of the more amusing twists in the episode. But the Forces of Hell will not go down without a fight, as Satan watches the events unfold on television.

[Satan watches on his TV, which is much nicer than the one in his bedroom. The hooded figure stands nearby]

Satan: What mockery is this?!

Hooded Figure: My Lord …

Satan: The feeding tube has been pulled! If the child dies and his soul returns to heaven, God will have his Keanu Reeves!

Hooded Figure: Perhaps the child won't die in time.

Satan: Forget it! I'm calling the attack off!

Hooded Figure: No! Keep your army marching, my Lord. I will get that feeding tube put back in. [turns and walks off]

Satan: How?

Hooded Figure: I will do what we always do: Use the Republicans.

[The White House, a press conference on the lawn. People carry signs saying "Kenny Is Alive" "Murder Is Not A Choice" and "Don't Kill Kenny"]

George Bush: We Republicans are deeply saddened by the tragic events in Colorado. [the crowd cheers]

Hooded Figure: [appears and whispers into Bush's right ear] Removing the feeding tube is murder, hughughughughughugh …

George Bush: Removing the feeding tube is murder!

Hooded Figure: [whispers into Bush's left ear] Who are we to decide if Kenny should live or die?

George Bush: Who are we to decide if Kenny should live or die?

Hooded Figure: [whispers into Bush's right ear] It is God's will that he live!

George Bush: It is God's will that he LIVE! [the hooded figure hisses into Bush's left ear] Haaghaghaghaghaghagha …

Hooded Figure: No no, you don't say that part. [hisses into Bush's right ear]

George Bush: No no, you don't say that part, haghaghaghagha. [the crowd looks at him in stunned silence]

Whether Matt and Trey are saying Satan's right hand man is influencing George W. Bush and the religious right is up for your interpretation, but it really did feel as if they were being led to this for some bizarre reason. Considering Republicans want government out of any health care decision, yet here their hypocrisy on this issue apparently knows no limit. In the episode's most poignant scene, *South Park* contributes a new wrinkle in the Schiavo situation instead of merely satirizing it. While the angels are attempting to remove the feeding tube, they end up in the protest of the side that wants to keep Kenny alive. The protest line of "you bureaucrats are trying to play god by pulling the feeding tube out" is uttered by one of the protesters. The two angels try to plead with the protesters to understand it's more complicated than they think, and Matt and Trey answer that angle of the debate as one angel says:

Angel: No, no, see, they were playing God when they put the feeding tube IN!

The writers of *South Park* decided not to tackle whether or not a spouse/parent should have the right to remove a feeding tube but actually that modern medicine was already playing god by putting the feeding tube in. They're not talking about "should we or should we not take the feeding tube out," they're talking about the problems and issues related to contemporary medical advances. They are bringing forth the notion that sometimes people are chosen to die for whatever reason. In this case, Kenny was chosen to die to save Heaven from the forces of Hell. But humans don't get to see that because ironically, or on purpose, the angels are not heard by anyone on Earth, so this extremely valid and correct argument is ignored completely. What happens at the end of the episode is vintage Matt and Trey as the debate over whether Kenny should live or die ends up in Kenny's hospital room. The two sides are arguing because no one knows what Kenny's wish was in the event of him being in a vegetative state. Finally, Kenny's lawyer enters the hospital room because he found the missing page to Kenny's will. He reads it for everyone to hear and once again the audience receives the episode's lesson.

Lawyer: [clears his throat] If I should ever be in a vegetative state and kept alive on life support, please … [flips to the last page] for the love of God, don't ever show me in that condition on national television. [not a word is uttered for a few seconds]

Stan: Oooo.

Man: Oowhoops

Kyle: Oh geez. Maybe we let this thing get out of hand. This issue is so complicated, but … mmaybe we shhhould just let Kenny go in peace.

Stan: You mean, Cartman's side is right?

Kyle: Cartman's side is right, for the wrong reasons. But we're wrong, for the right reasons.

Both sides: Yeah.

Kyle: Come on, everybody. I think Kenny wants to be left alone. [everyone walks out.]

It's a beautiful sentiment with real heart and understanding of the situation. Kyle and Stan and Terri's parents just wanted to keep their friend and daughter alive because they love them so much. They do not want to lose them because they know once the machines are turned off, they will never see their friend and daughter again. The debate from this side is from a place of love. Cartman, and Terri's husband Michael, wanted to let Kenny die so they can move on with life, and of course get the PSP. This mentality was used during the "Raisins" episode and Butters's reaction to the end of his relationship. *South Park* wants us to value the good, value life, but know it's fleeting and appreciate it while you can because nothing lasts forever. They want us to make the best of the cards we are dealt, another theme throughout the series, which is featured in such episodes as "Death" and "Eek, A Penis!"

Kenny's feeding tube is removed and he is taken off life support. The media announces shortly after that Kenny has died and hopefully he's in a much better place. The episode cuts to Heaven being overrun by the army of Hell but Kenny arrives in the nick of time to save Heaven from the invading horde. One of the most incredible parts of the episode is that the audience never sees the battle, but instead the angel Gabriel only remarks how epic the battle is and how it's bigger than the final battle in *The Lord of the Rings* movie. This episode aired on Wednesday, as the show always does, and the next morning, Terri Schiavo passed away after being taken off life support. *South Park* was able to get in their philosophy just in time on what was a huge debate in America. This is what Matt and Trey try to do: they attempt to figure out what's going on with America and illustrate our shortcomings. The episode also carries another *South Park* trademark with religion and the idea of God's will and those who are chosen to die. And how do they do all these things? With the show's innate ability to capture the American experience, they are able to accomplish their goals. Through having their characters encounter the same dilemmas that we Americans are going through except with a bit more humor and a necessary amount of nuance, *South Park* adds to the debate.

Though now not as relevant, one of the most important wedge issues was over a decade ago as America debated whether or not to preemptively invade Iraq and alter our foreign policy for years to come. *South Park*'s "I'm a Little Bit Country" from Season Seven aired at the height of the highly volatile debate. There was the pro-war side, and those engaging in global anti-war protests. The American debate got extremely heated and the boys, as per usual, end up getting thrown smack-dab in the middle of it.

Anti-War Protesters: No war! No war! [a sea of them mill around on South Park Avenue waving various signs around] No war! No war! [One man wields an American flag. He lowers it while another reaches for a lighter and sets the flag aflame.] No war! No war! [three men break into Tele's through its large window and steal various TVs] No war! No war! No war!

Mr. Mackey: [walks up to the boys with several signs in his hands] No war, m'kay?! No war, m'kay?! Oh uh, here you go, boys. [hands each of them a sign] These will help you protest. It's good to see that you care about peace, boys, m'kay? No war, m'kay?!

A voice: Excuse me, boys. [the boys look and the adult is shown] Tom Stansel, HBC News. Can you kids tell me why you marched out of school today? [behind him is the cameraman and an assistant, and behind her, the news van]

Stan: [pause] Uh … war?

Tom: Right. What about the war?

Kyle: [pause] Ih ih ih-t's g-gay?

Tom: Uh huh, and what aspect of it do you think is most gay?

Kyle: [looks at his sign] Uuuh, n-no blood for oil.

Stan: Yeah. [the mic moves back to him as he looks at his sign] War is not my voice.

Cartman: [reading Kenny's sign] Bush is a Naizi.

Even though Cartman has dressed up as Hitler before, he can't even pronounce Nazi correctly. Once again, *South Park* proves the point that the media has failed, as they are always looking for the easy story and in this instance interviewing children. As if fourth-graders would know whether to go to war or not is a sound foreign policy! But to counter the anti-war protesters, Matt and Trey have the pro-war side join the fray with their standard and clichéd argument.

Skeeter: [arrives with a crowd] Hey all you un-American bastards! If you don't like America, why don't you git out?! [moves his right thumb in front of his shoulder and to his right. With him are Jimbo, Ned, Stuart, and Craig's father Tom]

Mr. Mackey: Don't you call us un-American! This country was founded on the right to protest! M'kay?

Protesters: Yeah! Right!

Stuart: If the Founding Fathers saw you burning your flag an' callin' the president a Nazi, they'd roll over in their grave!

Supporters: Yeah! Right!

Randy: The Founding Fathers would agree with our right to protest!

Skeeter: Foundin' Fathers would kick all your asses!

Tom: Boys, what do you think the Founding Fathers would say?

Cartman: … Eh the … Founding who?

This "what would the founding fathers do?" would be a common utterance in America during this time. What would George Washington, Thomas Jefferson, Ben Franklin say about this impending war? Would they go to war or choose diplomacy? The constant refrain of "The Founding fathers would do this!" is the easiest thing to say and the hardest to refute because they are not alive today. We also get another common trope: "If you don't like America, then you can get out." The argument being the second you criticize America you should leave. That's what some people say and the clichéd line is used all the time! What does one have to do with the other? Why is criticism considered unpatriotic? Why should a disagreement about the merits of war lead to self-imposed exile for those who prefer peace? So, what do the pro-war and anti-war sides do next after brawling with one another: they split the town down the middle. One side of the town is the pro-war side, and the other is the anti-war side, but problems begin to erupt as they realize splitting a town or a city or a country for that matter in two isn't as straightforward as it sounds.

South Park Avenue. The opposing groups face each other in front of the tallest building in town. Skeeter paints a line across the span of the street and looks up]

Skeeter: There! All finished. From now on, this is the pro-war side of town, and that's the unpatriotic side. [the war supporters begin to clamor]

Randy: How about we call this the rational side of town, and that the redneck side?!

Protesters: Hahahaha, yeah.

Jimbo: You just keep all your flag burnin' and your hippie-rock protest songs on YOUR side o' the town!

Protester: Hey wait a minute, your side of town has the post office.

Stuart: Well your side has the grocery store.

Jimbo: Well you can come to our side of town to use the post office and we can go to your side to use the grocery store.

Gerald: Aaah, can we cross the line to take our kids to school?

Jimbo: W-hell, naturally you could cross the line for that. Just like ... we could cross the line for hardware, supplies, gas, and pharmaceutical needs.

Townsfolk: Yup, yes sir, yeah, right, uh huh.

Skeeter: Hey everybody, this is never going to work. Don't you see? All this dividin' up the town, it's just ridiculous. What we really should be doing, is just beatin' the hell out of each other like we were.

Randy: He's right. [looks at Sheila] Boy, do I feel like a fool. [moments later, both sides attack each other again. Among the skirmishes: Kenny's mom attacks Gerald, Sheila attacks Ned]

As the South Park citizens war with one another, the boys have an assignment to figure out where the founding fathers would stand with regards to the war. But Cartman is Cartman and as expected, he doesn't want to do the project. To get out of any real research, Cartman devises one of the most ingenious plans ever: He fills up his TiVo with fifty hours of the History Channel's *American Revolution* specials and at the moment the TiVo reaches its memory capacity, Cartman will be dropped into a bath of water along with the TiVo and be magically transported, hopefully back to 1776. Does it work? Somewhat. Cartman ends up in a coma, but while in the coma he flashes back to 1776. During these sequences, Cartman and the audience receive the answer to what the Founding Fathers would say and what preemptive war means for American foreign policy.

[Cartman enters Independence Hall, awed by the people he sees around him, and approaches the main desk. He hands the document to the man waiting there] I am John Hancock, President of the Congress.

Cartman: Wow.

Hancock: Mr. John Adams?

Adams: Aye. [rises and approaches the table]

Hancock: Will you do the honors of reading the document to Congress, please? [Cartman takes an empty chair nearby]

Adams: [reading from the Declaration] WHEN in the Course of human Events, it becomes necessary for one Person to rise up—[cut to the end of the Declaration]—we mutually pledge to each other our Lives, our Fortunes, and our sacred Honor. P.S. Every Thursday should be Free Ice Cream Day. [rolls up the Declaration. Cartman looks around]

A Congressman: Excuse me, but does this Declaration actually suggest that we should go to go war with England?

Adams: We have no choice, Mr. Dickinson. [chatter erupts in the same manner it did in South Park earlier in the episode]

[Later in the episode, as South Park is holding a shared pro-war, anti-war rally with rock 'n' roll serving as the anti-war music of choice and country music as the pro-war preference]

[Philadelphia, day, Independence Hall. There's plenty of argument going on]

Adams: We must go to war!

Dickinson: But what about the violence?! The lives lost?! If we found a country, it should be founded on peace and diplomacy.

Congressman 1: England will only understand one thing: Force.

Congressman 2: [rises] I must state again for the record that South Carolina, North Carolina, Pennsylvania, Maryland, and Georgia are against war! [pounds the table with his fist]

Congressman 3 (with Southern Redneck accent): Yeah, because you don't care about the fate of the Colonies like we do! You're all unpatriotic! And if you don't like the Colonies, then you can git out!

Dickinson: Don't you call us unpatriotic! We're protesting this war because we care so deeply for the fate of our Colonies! You are all unpatriotic for leading the Colonies into a war that half of them don't want! [the various Congressmen begin squabbling with each other]

Cartman: [observing] Whoa, how very very relevant.

[Later still with the rally is still going on and Cartman still in 1776]

[Philadelphia, day, Independence Hall. There's plenty of argument still going on]

Congressmen: Rabble Rabble Rabble Rabble Rabble Rabble Rabble Rabble Rabble Rabble Rabble Rabble!

Dickinson: We cannot found a country based on war!

Adams: We cannot found a country that is afraid to fight!

Congressman: Rabble!

Congressmen: Rabble Rabble Rabble Rabble Rabble Rabble Rabble! [the doors open and in walks an august figure. The boisterous voices become hushed] Oh my, it's Benjamin Franklin. It's Benjamin Franklin. It's Benjamin Franklin. [they keep murmuring this as Franklin walks towards the main desk]

Cartman: Oh, it's Benjamin Franklin. It's Benjamin Franklin. It's Benjamin Franklin.

Hancock: Mr. Franklin, where do you stand on the war issue?

Franklin (voiced by TV legend Norman Lear): I believe that if we are to form a new country, we cannot be a country that appears war-hungry and violent to the rest of the world. However, we also cannot be a country that appears weak and unwilling to fight to the rest of the world. So, what if we form a country that appears to want both?

Jefferson: Yes. Yes of course. We go to war, and protest going to war at the same time.

Dickinson: Right. If the people of our new country are allowed to do whatever they wish, then some will support the war and some will protest it.

Franklin: And that means that as a nation, we could go to war with whomever we wished, but at the same time, act like we didn't want to. If we allow the people to protest what the government does, then the country will be forever blameless.

Adams: [holding a slice of chocolate cake] It's like having your cake, and eating it, too.

Congressman 2: Think of it: an entire nation founded on saying one thing and doing another.

Hancock: And we will call that country the United States of America.

Scholars have dedicated their lives to understanding and explaining American Foreign Policy, and those living abroad attempt to grasp America's seemingly contradictory stand on a bevy of international issues. Yet here is America's foreign policy summed up by *South Park*'s creators in one line: Having your cake and eating it too. While simplistic, it does seem as if the US does do that—as they've helped Libya during their revolution yet haven't assisted Syrian rebels or been able to stop the massacre. Or how the US occasionally allows certain countries to skirt international law, while invading or bombing others that have violated the same regulations. But from an optics standpoint, the US does seem to always act in its best interest—then again, doesn't everyone? Cartman's flashback ends and he immediately wakes up. He runs to the center of the town to stop the town from tearing itself apart and its citizens from slaughtering and massacring each other. Cartman, just like "Best Friends Forever" saves the day as he goes on stage getting everyone's attention because he "would like to do his report now."

Cartman: I learned somethin' today. This country was founded by some of the smartest thinkers the world has ever seen. And they knew one thing: that a truly great country can go to war, and at the same time, act like it doesn't want to. [a shot of the crowd] You people who are for the war, you need the protesters. Because they make the country look like it's made of sane, caring individuals. And you people who are anti-war, you need these flag-wavers, because, if our whole country was made up of nothing but soft pussy protesters, we'd get taken down in a second. That's why the founding fathers decided we should have both. It's called "having your cake and eating it too."

Randy: He's right. The strength of this country is the ability to do one thing and say another.

Skeeter: Yeah, but ... if it weren't for all you guys protesting, why, everyone around the world would hate the American people instead of just the president.

Gerald: And if it weren't for you people flexing your arms, America could easily get taken over by terrorists or … or China.

Mr. Mackey: I guess we … owe you an apology.

Stuart: Eh-ah, I guess we owe you one.

And like that, everything is fine, as the entire town understands what protests and debates are really about. The survivors then gather on stage to finish singing, "I'm a little bit country, I'm a little bit rock and roll" with some important lyrics: "Let the flag of hypocrisy fly high from every pole!"

6

Edward R. Murrow said, "To be persuasive we must be believable. To be believable we must be credible. To be credible we must be truthful." *South Park* is all of these things. They are credible. They are believable. They are truthful. And what have they given us? What gifts have they given us? They've given us life lessons of guidance, opinions, dissent, war, peace, rebellion, and conformity. But Matt and Trey have bestowed upon us reality; granted it's a different reality than we're used to, but it's reality. *South Park* has a reality where we actually have community and people know each other. There's a reality where children rarely age and stay young forever. A reality where characters die and come back the next week, where their town and sometimes other towns can be destroyed and fixed the very next week with no issue or consequences. The creators have provided us with a world where friendship reigns supreme and where happiness and pain are real for everyone. But at its core is the story of these four boys, these four friends. This is what it is all about: friendship. And it's the four boys who act as the adults and the adults act as the children educating us along the way. These four boys, they're what the show truly comes down to. Cartman, Stan, Kyle, and Kenny and everyone else in this show are more accurate than anyone who's representing Fox News or CNN or MSNBC. Mainly because they are real, yes, these characters are real. They're real because Matt and Trey put every ounce of themselves into these characters. It's who we are and for that much, they deserve our trust.

As humans we are flawed, passionate, confused, humane, unreasonable, frustrated, charitable, egotistical, sympathetic, and apathetic, and *South Park* represents the best and worst of our nature. Every split, every connection, every agreement, and every disagreement *South Park* has in some shape or form weighed in on. If viewed through the proper prism, Matt and Trey have catalogued the American experience as they've emerged as the voice in the middle of a nation divided. They are the return to reason in a country that has lost its rationality and continues to spiral seemingly out of control. They are the animated face of the minority in a nation ruled by majority. The show is the fifth estate in response to the damaged fourth estate. And all they're trying to do is hope that we understand America and the American experience a little more. They want us to trust, to connect, to grow, to evolve, and to attain knowledge to be better in every facet of our lives. And of course, the audience is there with them anxiously looking forward to seeing what's going to happen next in that tiny little mountain town known as South Park.

LAST FIKA

"Fika?!" I yell with an unstrained happiness that only twenty straight hours of sun, three hours of sleep, and what is seemingly endless cups of coffee can provide. Each time I call out the word, the Swedes in earshot cheer me on, obliging me my exuberance. Cecilia laughs while shaking her head—she's too amused to be completely embarrassed, and too entertained to stop me. I was wrong: her laugh is absolutely infectious, one that makes you wish you were a comedian so you can hear it constantly. There's no cackle to it that disturbs everyone around us, but instead her laugh draws people closer. They want to be part of whatever fun she is engaged in. She knows it's a good one too, which is probably why she doesn't give it up to just anyone and why it took so long for me to break.

She finally stops laughing, "Today is midsummer. It's an all-day Fika, if you want. Will that satisfy you?" What a direct question to ask, but that's Cecilia: direct. Over the past few days we both promised that there would be no reservations, no filter. She loved that idea, I gather because she would have been that way anyway, and now she has complete freedom from any repercussions.

We're seated outside the bar Boule & Bersa on the banks of a channel from the eastern sea that divides Stockholm, drinking and basking in the sun's glory. I never made it north to see twenty-four hours of sunlight: that will have to wait for the next trip. All definitive plans changed after The Pelikan and the second night's lecture. The benches, the sand, and the river make Boule & Bersa an ideal backdrop. The sun is strong. Cecilia chose the place because her good friends are the owners. I thought this would get us free drinks for the rest of the day (especially considering how expensive liquor is here), but it's against the law to give drinks on the house. I'm not sure if she's just messing with me or the owners are not as friendly as she believed.

"Yes, an all-day Fika will satisfy," I say, teasing her usage of the word. Her guard, which was sky-high three days ago, is almost nonexistent now. My thoughts take me to Wirstroms Pub, where after the second successful lecture, all the organizers left and the two of us stayed out all night. We won each other over there. While the restaurant was the beginning, our conversations didn't start until that second night. I noticed her in the back of the second lecture as she made faces at me, trying to distract me and make me laugh. It worked several times as I lost concentration, but fortunately not many noticed. Throughout the night she would challenge me, but I would give it right back to her. I'd never tell her but she's smarter than I am in every way. Good thing is, she knows it but doesn't flaunt it. Wirstroms was definitely a highlight, and we descended into its ancient tombs where there were old couches pushed up against white stone walls. Each nook and cranny had its own personality and plenty of privacy, yet everyone is in full view. It's a contradiction but an accurate one. We moved from niche to niche, pretending that every new couch was a new date or another time seeing one another. By my count we had seven. I didn't want to leave without the promise of spending more time with her. Once I made the declaration, she followed suit by emailing work to let them know she was sick, and that was that.

We walked around Old Town, struggling on the cobblestones, past the shops, bars, and life. All we did was talk. We ran the gamut of politics to philosophy to sports and yet we both knew there were more sights to explore. Similar to the cab driver who drove me to the first lecture, Cecilia is seduced by Stockholm. The way she speaks about it, even when she complains about the winter, makes you fall for the place even further than I already had. Hard to not want to move here but those winters are probably worse than they say. Right now, day three, we are outside, as time is ticking away. Cecilia takes a sip of her coffee, and then a sip of beer.

"But yes, to answer your question, the lectures were as good for me as they were for those in the audience. Even if you were in the back making faces and doing whatever that was—

"It was a dance," she remarks with confidence in her ballroom skills.

"So you keep telling me. But I think it's the ideal time to retire *South Park*," as I finish replying to her earlier query.

"You're getting old," she says, referencing the *South Park* episode I discussed in the lecture. "Best to retire on top." She's so sharp. Am I as blinded by her as Butters was by Lexus? Does it really matter?

"I don't know about that, but if I'm not mistaken, you're eight days older than me plus one year," I counter as the verbal jousting continues.

Her nerves have dissipated, no more jitters. It could be the constant flow of coffee. I've never had THIS many cups in this short amount of time. Hope this doesn't become a pattern. The longest we've gone is three hours without a cup. Cecilia is looking around the bar, smiling at her country-men, then points to the American flag near the bar to the left of us.

"Imperialist," she says, getting me back for the "satisfy" comment from before.

"Socialist," I respond in kind. Neither of us committed to the stereotype or insult but the banter seems to be working just fine. Ah, that mellifluous laugh of hers. A work of art, an exquisite cup of coffee not made from elephant dung but from the most expensive beans in the world.

"Americans throw that word around quite a bit. Orwell said the most misunderstood word was 'fascism' but I think if he were alive today, he may designate America for over-using and improperly using the word 'socialism.'"

"It is a very dirty word."

We sit staring at one another, and it feels as if people are watching us, yet we're too distracted to care. Though the place is jammed and every seat is taken, we're alone, this is our place and no amount of sun or noise can change that. It's the way I've felt since the restaurant. I'm careful not to ask if she feels that, too. So much for no filter. She glances at her watch and yawns. An embarrassed smile crosses her lips. She takes another sip of coffee.

"This is it, you know," Cecilia declares with equal parts regret, hope, sadness, and realism reserved for people who can no longer fantasize on where their lives will end up. A statement like that reflects on where your lives truly are.

Everything stops. Her words reverberate through me. Whether Cecilia knew it or not she had just had summed up my life and my existence in a way no one else had. Those words are the end of one life I've been leading and the beginnings of another, and we don't even have the wolf at the door to make us aware of the occurrence. It just happens, there's no signal, no warning, it just happens. One part begins, another part ends, and we're given zero indication. "This is it" reminded me of the day my childhood ceased and adulthood commenced, all without notification. This is it; a day I replaced someone who had just left a section of life with someone older. The ebb and flow as we're replaced to keep humanity moving forward are in these details. Had she known those words conferred finality to so much, she may not have said them. But knowing her, she probably would have just because she could to remind me that fantasy is left for the dreamers and for the less-than-ambitious. There's a tragedy that we can't have years back, or in this case, hours. Everything we had done led us to the realization that we cannot stop momentum, even if we don't have any. Observing Cecilia, there's so much to say, so much more to do and even more to explore. We both said yes to everything, foregoing sleep to delay the inevitable. I sat mindlessly stirring my coffee, reflecting on all that had ended and started—not a life less ordinary but life less spectacular—but if honest wishful thinking peeked through my soul, maybe this was the end of ordinary and the spectacular was just beginning. No way Cecilia could have imagined those words, while true, had more effect on me than the moment we first spoke had had. I suppose as parts of us die, we reflect on the experiences we never will have again. Like a piercing ring in our ear as that sound will never be heard again, as our ear cells die, we pray for it to end, but forget that's the last time we will ever hear that frequency. Fortunately, there's recognition here from both parties involved—I touch her hand, she squeezes tight; maybe the harder she squeezes, the more it says. The grip reveals enough: "This is it, you know," but she should have said: "Why didn't we meet when all this was possible? When we were young enough to make fantasy a reality, even for a little while?" From simply walking around to stopping at coffee shops and her regaling me with her knowledge of what seemed to be every subject possible. Nothing mattered, I just wanted more from her. Even as I thought it,

I knew there was only a small amount of time, yet she finally acknowledged it. I never would have. She's better than me.

"I know," I finally say, realizing this isn't going to end well. She gives one last squeeze and takes her hand away. Her disappointment reveals all—she feels the same, thinks the same, and feels a lustful connection unlike any we could have imagined. Logic is out the window here; all education of mistakes of the past does not matter. We need another drink. I smile at her. Is there a way to skirt the issue, delay the obvious, or if I'm really lucky, the clock will stop moving, if only for a minute. I knew what time it was before she checked her watch. Though the sun is shining like it's four in the afternoon, it's actually seven AM. We've been out all night going from place to place with the hope the longer we stayed awake, the slower time would go. But she didn't have to confirm the time. Even if my senses are off from the lack of sleep, I still knew our time was setting even if the sun wasn't.

Her shirt is this seductive red satin—whether or not she knows it, it will be burned into my brain forever—that flows with the wind. It's as if the blouse was made specifically for her and for me to remember her by. She leans in. The red contrasting with her skin and green eyes brings my thoughts to Christmas and how incredible it was when I was a child. She makes me feel like a kid again. Excited for life and anxious for it to hurry up and get going. Cici is desperate to ask a question but stops herself. I egg her on.

"You know, Cici, I always found you can learn more about people by the questions they ask than the answers they give." My coffee is cold. Need a refill. While it is summer, it's still morning and a slight chill is in the air. No one, myself included, seems to mind in any way. After today, the days will slowly get darker and colder, leading to winter solstice. The all-night partying is motivated by that very fact.

"Ah, so by that rationale you know who I am because I'm interested in what you're thinking or what you enjoyed most about your time here."

We both like the challenge. A gust of wind moves her hair over her eyes, she places it back, but more wind comes. She puts her hair up in a bun. She seduces me with every movement, every quirk, every mannerism, whether awkward or graceful. If only I knew I was having the same effect on her.

"I could say that from your questions, you are concerned about my happiness and want to be sure you were able to fulfill it," I tell her. She looks at me, and all I can think of is the ticking clock. My silence and sudden frown is unmistakable: time continues. "Do you think you're going to remember this in the same way as I will?"

"If I didn't, I wouldn't know it. I can only hope."

"If we both told our story to the same person ten years from now, I wonder what you would focus on."

The proposition is fascinating. Will I have mythologized her or will I portray her accurately? Will she do the same? Will we write about the identical moments or experiences? Selective retention, remembering the same event differently, is never more apparent than right here.

She traces her finger on my hand through the grooves of my knuckles then whacks me on the hand. "Answer me."

"I would talk about you warmly and accurately without any flaws."

"You'll write it like you did everything perfectly and I was helpless against you," she says, putting on an innocent voice to play up the charm. "You Americans are so full of shit." She doesn't play innocent for very long.

"That we are." There's a pause between us, a silence where each moment says something, yet we're left to our own devices to interpret them. "I can't believe you took me to that bar with the ping-pong circle game."

She laughs that laugh—I may never get sick of hearing it. "Ugglan on Narkesgatan." She says the name as if I would know how to give directions to a tourist and recognize the name.

"That street was like The Village in New York. Restaurants, bars, cafés. Everything looks great but instead you lead me into this bar and down into the basement. And all I'm thinking is 'why are we inside when the sun is out so late?' And there it was—a ping-pong table and thirty people surrounding the people who were hitting the ball. Not well I might add—"

"There's a method to losing that game."

"And apparently, you've perfected it, considering you were the first eliminated every time." Another laugh. I wish I had better material. "I just had to sit back and watch as these drunken Swedish people attempted to hit a ping-pong ball to each other as they circled the table. I think the longest go-round was seven hits. Eight at most."

"I was long gone by then." She smiles, almost proud of her ping-pong inadequacies.

"I was surprised that someone was willing to show how poor a ping-pong player they were and unashamed to flaunt it in front of all those people."

Another laugh as we raise our glasses to each other. The sun continues to ascend in the sky as the time to leave creeps closer and closer. Even if it has been three days, there's been something to our time together that is not unexplainable but tricky to fully explain. The words can do it justice, but not much more than that. The setting certainly helps, the whirlwind tour, the weather, everything makes this that much more heightened. Like finding a new coffee blend with just the right additive and flow. Everything is intense, with every bit of fantasy and no reality. Two people alike, yet worlds apart, engaged in a discourse and playfulness that while seemingly trite and clichéd is nothing of the sort. For having known each other only three days, it's incredible how much we understand each other. The ticking clock sheds most of the inhibitions—all relationships should start knowing the end is near. I would have been that much more successful had I dealt with them as if I was searching for someone to share the end of the world with. It'll stop all the games and allow each of us to open up sooner.

"Tell me your favorite part of the last three days," I say to her as if the statement is more a question that is easy to answer. It's a set-up, she knows it, and I can't wait to see how she handles it. With time winding down, sometimes it's the most basic question that makes the most sense.

Cecilia nods her head going through all the things we've done over the past few days. She doesn't say a word but observes the setting, then tilts her head to the sun, absorbing the warmth and comfort of the morning.

"I'm weighing all the options," she says to me.

"You know what I've noticed." A moment of clarity comes over me.

"Yeah, what's that?" she responds, squinting just a little when the sun hits her eyes.

"I've had way too much coffee and may never sleep again. But it's what I said before, you can't lie with a question. Asking a question reveals what you're thinking, it reveals who you are and what direction your mind wanders towards. You cannot hide who you are when you ask a question or as much as you would want to."

"But you can with an answer. So, in essence, I could be fabricating all of this." She's toying with me just like that first night. This is who she is, and it's a huge element of her personality. She continues to probe, to test, to push. "But I won't. Not today," Cecilia says, as she takes a sip and stares right into me. "I'd say, right now as clichéd as it sounds." Her guard is almost completely obliterated, mine following close behind.

"Yes clichéd and an easy answer. I'm less than impressed."

"Sometimes the easiest answers are the truest and most clichéd. And sometimes, impressing someone isn't needed anymore. Witty banter be damned. But as easy as you think that answer is, it isn't. It's right now."

"I wasn't fishing."

"I was," she says with that mischievous smile that is her calling card. It's a smile that says she knows who she is, she knows what she is, and where her strengths and weaknesses are. Her confidence makes me confident. It's a smile I've studied for seventy-plus hours.

"I did notice the fishing pole and tackle box you've been carrying around since we left your place yesterday." She leans over and picks up her bag.

"You mean this? Hard to get a fishing rod in there but actually, it's a present for you, and no, not salmon, so don't even ask."

We share a quick laugh and the waitress exchanges our old drinks for new ones. She reaches into her bag, taking out six small plastic bags all with coffee beans in them. She hands each of them to me.

"Couldn't let you leave without imprinting myself on you."

"Too late" pops into my head and she knows it: there's that confidence again. Each plastic bag has enough for about two cups of coffee, maybe three, depending on the strength. They're marked with the coffee's name, location, elevation of origin, and a brief description. I study each one intently as Cecilia watches me. I can't imagine any of these is anything less than stellar.

"I assume you have a favorite," I say as I investigate the bags a little further.

"If I were to pick a favorite and tell you, I'd influence you and we can't have that," she says, once again playing with me. Her coyness is anything but irritating—it's maximizing her affect and effect on her surroundings. I bet it's a trick she learned when she was very young and it's only evolved since then. It works on me as it's worked on everyone before me.

"Fine. Select one for me for the first cup when I arrive home."

"Ah ha! Now that's a worthy challenge!" She's excited as she takes the bags back, studying each one, contemplating her decision. At the same time, remembering the physical toll of flying across the Atlantic, checking in two to three hours before take-off, the meals, the flight itself, the average coffee that we're told not to drink in a vain attempt to overcome jet lag, yet the flight attendants still serve through the trip. The restless last forty-five minutes and the realization that there's much more traveling to do after the plane lands. She makes her selection and hands a bag to me but immediately grabs it back from me. "No, I don't want you to doubt my selection. Put it away, separate from the others, and when you get home, then you'll see my choice."

"Ah, the confidence breaks, you think I'll doubt your choice."

"Or maybe you'll reveal yourself to have no sense of what is good coffee and ruin any good will I had towards you. So, for your own image and the American image, just promise you won't."

I promise her that I'll do just that and she checks her watch again. Time refuses to stop, no matter how much we pretend otherwise. I notice her phone is face down and she glanced at it only once since we've been sitting here and that was for the taxi update. Has to be a good sign. We sit in silence, and the people around us are enjoying the midsummer celebration. There's so much more to discuss, to say, to test, but right now, all that matters are those few more minutes before the car arrives.

"I could just miss the flight and deal with the penalties and fees later on. But what's one more day?" I say with all the honesty and vulnerability I have inside me.

"Or one more hour," she says, with the understanding of the situation equaling my sentiment.

It's time to go. Yet one last thing has yet to be decided: will we see each other again? The ticking clock elevates my courage but before I'm able to speak, Cecilia looks at me with those glittering eyes I've stared into for three days straight. The beauty mark on her cheek close to her ear highlights the right side of her porcelain face. It was a detail I didn't notice the first night, but fell for the second night.

"Just say it," she reassures me. The probing is over, the exams are finished, and she has laid her cards out there for me to call or fold. But she still did it in her way. Encouraging me that it'll be all right mixed with the confidence she has to make a declarative statement. I couldn't have answered any other way.

I see in the distance the taxi pull up like a grim reaper waiting to escort me to the other side, and Cici's phone starts vibrating with an incoming call from the driver.

These are the shadows of forthcoming events that Beckett warned me about while we were sitting on the bridge in Amsterdam a decade ago. He was referring to his decisions, fatal and otherwise; I'm now thinking about my own. He spoke of the shadows of forthcoming events as a harbinger to all that follows. It's the point where clarity reigns. Where you can see everything laid out for you piece by piece. All the issues that will follow, all the falls that will break you, and all your options will suddenly become limited. This "event" between Cecilia and me will continue for a few weeks, a few months, and then determinations will have to be made.

"But what if we had just this?" she says, breaking the moment. It was an honest question, or was it a statement? Either way, it was mixed with logic and survival, foregoing any chance of disappointment. "Maybe this was exactly what we're supposed to have. These three days." I can tell it's not a cover: it's two people looking into the future and the adult selves will have to win out, the adult self always wins out. We'll never be on the same page more than we are right now. I wish I was twenty-three years old again but I'm not.

"And anything more may ruin it. Or it may lose its luster," I chime in, starting to understand she may be right, "this is it, you know," still rattling around my brain. "We could just live our lives on this and wonder what should or could have been, but ultimately realize this is all it was supposed to be."

We gaze into each other's eyes, and I wish I could say something worthy of the moment, something that we both will never forget.

"Onsra," I say, as I put my head down almost as if I'm ashamed that's the best I could do. She picks my head up to kisses my forehead and temple.

"Onsra." She kisses me one more time and glances at the phone. She motions to the driver. He waves back in understanding. She stares at me, soaking in the moment, and says, "We're being very mature about this. I don't like it."

"More than you know, Cecilia. The younger me would buy a return ticket to Stockholm right now, or convince you to come with me. But I'm not that person anymore."

"Nor am I. Too many things have changed."

"We're adults."

I stand up. It's time to go. We walk slowly towards the taxi. I hold her hand probably for the last time.

"I'm glad Jonas arranged for the taxi to pick up my stuff," I tell her, deflecting from the death march we're currently engaged in. The driver sits in the car and allows us our goodbyes. Neither of us is prepared for this moment, no one ever really is. Two people who make their living on preparing, and we're not doing good jobs of thinking on our feet. My thoughts go to Beckett and all he taught me. Even four years after his death in Iraq, I'm still in awe of how influential he was. Beckett had his moment with a beautiful journalist and I now have mine with Cecilia as our last silence together etches itself onto everything inside me.

"I could stay," I tell her, hoping the illogical becomes logical, knowing that a student always rebels against the teacher no matter how influential. "But—"

"Eventually, you'd have to leave and we'd have to do this again."

"And I'd say the same thing and you'd say the same thing."

She smiles. "By then I'd want you to leave." We both give a small nervous laugh. She's perfect. This is how I'd prefer to remember her—plus the red satin shirt. You can live a lifetime on three days. "This is where you say something meaningful."

"I already did say, 'onsra.'"

"Yeah, I know. But this is where you say something meaningful. Right now."

The pressure. The push.

"And if you say 'something meaningful' I'm going to slap you." She consistently manages to take me further than I planned to go. Was I going to say it? Probably.

"Apparently, the proper Swedish massage was from a Dutch guy named Johan Georg Mezger," I say with a childish, sheepish, yet confident grin. "But some Internet websites say it was created by Peter Henry Ling, a Swede. So my reality is still alive and well."

"You shouldn't believe everything you read on the Internet."

"So, I should avoid the 'Swedish Girls Are Easy dot com' website?" I say with a huge smile indicating it's all a joke.

Her facial expression is priceless—nice one. She pinches my arm and scrunches her face. I'm going to miss her. The clock on the driver's dashboard alerts us to the end. We both know and finally concede: this is it.

She squeezes my hand. "Send me your next lecture whenever it comes out." She keeps the connection but just barely. It's a safe one because this could be the last one.

"Deal, only if you send me some more coffee samples."

"Using me for my coffee access," she says with that snark I'm going to wish for tomorrow morning.

"That's what this has been all about."

"As if I didn't know what you were about—why do you think I told Jonas I wanted to go to dinner?"

Her secret is out. She planned this from the beginning. She supplied the coffee to her brother, and she asked to join us for dinner. Her devilish nod confirms as much. It was the lecture that surprised her and kept her off balance. She wanted to discuss coffee but the lecture veered her off course, directing us to where we are now. I couldn't be happier with this beautiful sadness that Butters from *South Park* spoke about.

"Any man who requests a coffee in that manner, and with such details—"

"Should be mocked—"

"Or congratulated for making a truly creative and delicious cup. I had to try it out myself."

The puzzle I didn't know I was putting together begins to take shape. "You made me the cup." She smiles at me, confirming my guess. We give each other one more last kiss, no goodbye, just go. I step into the car. We smile at one another as the car slowly pulls away.

I put the window down and look out to her, one last time: "Hey Cici, FIKA!!!"

"It's not Fika!!" she responds with a smile as the driver speeds up, leaving her to fade in the increasing distance.

We should not have been adults about this, we should have forgotten where we were in life, there's always time to correct that mistake. I look on the seat next to me and there is a package of peanut M&Ms from Jonas and Co. with a note attached:

> Thank you for the lectures and we look forward to working with you again in the near future.
> Hopefully, these will suffice—the corner store was out of blue pretzel M&Ms.

The shadows of forthcoming events. Onsra. Stockholm. Midsummer. Cici.

This is going to be the worst flight, but at least I have her coffee when I return home. I wonder which one she picked. I have fifteen hours to guess.

LECTURE FOUR: COMEDY OF OUTRAGE

The Satirical Representation of the American Presidency

I can see nothing, no shadows, no events, nothing. My mind and body crave the coffee already—those caffeinated thoughts woke before I did. The darkness encompassing my European hotel room is like a black hole. I scan the room for any sign of life. Where's the alarm clock and where's my phone? These simple questions go unanswered but a small bit of sun creeps through the blackout blinds, alerting me that morning has painfully arrived. I can tell the room faces east and behind the curtain is undoubtedly a gorgeous European view. They're all gorgeous views in Europe. A late hotel arrival and check-in due to an impressive thunderstorm that shook the countryside, causing massive delays to rail, air, and road travel. Though that last coffee was quite good, I do remember that.

Last night. Passengers were making videos of the lightning show and complaining yet again about the train system, but not about the weather. One that they can "control" while the other they're seemingly powerless against, yet they're pretty powerless against both—wait, what time is it? I inspect the room for the alarm clock and my phone but both are still doing an excellent job hiding. My body calls for the coffee. Get it now. But first the geography needs to be determined: What city am I in? Last night I was in … where was I last night? That's the worst—though I could only imagine not knowing what country you're in would be even worse. I know I'm in The Netherlands—that much is certain. It has finally stopped raining. There's been four days straight of downpours but it seems as if the countrywide cloud cover has dissipated. Maybe a day of sunshine will hit the country soon? The Dutch have been waiting months, if not years, for the sun.

I have to be up and dressed to do the hour prep before the lecture, though this early, a lightning jolt would be most welcomed. The morning coffee's enjoyment is an absolute must but things have changed. As these trips have proven, sacrifices have been frighteningly necessary and absolutes have been shattered bitterly. A promise was made and subsequently broken about doing these cross-Atlantic lectures anymore and certainly not after midsummer in Sweden. To be so close to Cecilia and knowing we're unable to meet was not easy to handle. The proximity reminds me how right we were. Our three days will have to last a lifetime. No time for sentimental thoughts. She's not here and I have a job to do—coffee. We drank coffee all day for three days and now I need it constantly. Even a scant four months ago, before my time with Cecilia, I drank coffee, but now I *need* to drink coffee. Use any analogy you want, but this is beyond acceptable.

Maybe it's the coffee that gets all of us going. Maybe this is why New Yorkers are so hyper? It doesn't help that Manhattan has a coffee shop on almost every corner. I think the caffeine keeps us from falling down or dropping dead—I'm starting to understand what withdrawal feels like. The caffeine keeps us going, but I wonder at what cost. New York City has evolved to suit our coffee addiction, opening a shop on what seems to be every block. But I'm not in New York. I'm in The Netherlands … I think. No, I am. How can I forget that storm while boarding the train leaving Eindhoven? However, the city I'm in right now, I'm not so sure about. Finally, I'm starting to stir and making my way. Where is that alarm clock? I set it last night for seven AM for an ungodly nine AM lecture. Didn't set the iPhone because the battery was dead, I need an upgrade. I started charging it but I just couldn't wait. I needed sleep.

Nine AM? Who scheduled the talk at this time? Jonas would never do that. I don't function well in the mornings. Eleven, if I'm lucky. Regardless, time to roll out, can't stall any longer, but my vision is still impaired. The struggle from the bed to the small light is way more taxing than it should be. Fortunately, the light guides me and it's as if the sun was eavesdropping on my sleep, hoping to influence last night's dreams. Try as I might, there were no dreams on the meaning of life or anything vaguely resembling that discussion. So much has changed. There are no more dreams like that. They've stopped and I haven't been able to re-create that dream since I returned home, and the Cecilia dreams sporadically rise up from my subconscious when I'm at my most powerless. But the coffee cravings have only grown. Before we left she said she wanted to leave an imprint on me. I thought she meant on my mind and soul, not a full-body craving for coffee. But she did that, too.

One deep breath and I open the blinds. Just pull it off like a band-aid, as my mother used to say: "Just do it quickly and it won't hurt."

The blinds slide across with that sound of a day commencing, and contrary to what my mother said, the band-aid rip really hurt. Blinds that are opening have a distinctive sound versus blinds that are closing—wait. In the distance, there's a clock tower with a red face and gold hands. I can't read the year but I can read the time clearly—8:40 … what the …

Someone at the door knocks, at first gently. Confusion overwhelms, yet the story seems to be taking shape. Another knock, then another, and another, each one more aggressive than the last. I'm rummaging through the half-opened suitcase, and there's another knock at the door. "ONE SECOND!" I yell out.

T-shirt? T-shirt? No. No. Where, oh, where are the coffee beans in my suitcase? Right! Cecilia sent them to my hotel the first night, apologizing for being in Kenya and not being able to meet. She's a peach, and a plum, and a pearl. The beans are crushed too! One of my better packing jobs this was not. I'm sure those will be good but not now … t-shirt? T-shirt! I throw it on and answer the door.

Waiting in the hallway is the classic Dutch woman. She's tall, slender, blonde, with long hair, and I mean really long. She has that determined Dutch face and her outfit screams rebellion, yet also whispers of dressing incompetence. A Dutch balance for sure with her hair a bit wet from the rain she had to bike through. Even though from the looks of it, there was only a passing shower.

"Sorry to disturb you, I'm Kirsten from the Center. We were wondering if all was OK? You missed breakfast. We tried your phone and the hotel room but no answer."

"Is it really 8:40?" My mind can't get a grasp on things. Wait—I slept through the ringing of a landline? Please let it be that a previous guest turned off the ringer. Too many wheels turning as Kirsten looks at her watch, and immediately we both understand what is happening.

"You have to hurry. We have only a few minutes," she tells me.

This is precisely what I did not want to do! OK. Focus. Coffee. No time. I have to get dressed—and fast. But I need to be more than presentable because I remembered that after the lecture there are some media interviews.

Kirsten stares as I give her the motion to come in. "Are you OK?" she cautiously inquires wondering about the answer.

Without answering, I take my clothes into the bathroom and shut the door behind me. I splash some water on my face to wake up. The mouthwash first, so I can get dressed and then brush. Nice bathroom at this hotel, shower, no tub, with marble countertops. And it's real, not some marble imitation. They did a really good job putting it in here too, no uneven corners or the "good enough" philosophy my father used to rail against. What's the name of this hotel? I always believed the nicer the hotel I'm put in, the more the organizer is a fan of my work and the opposite being true, too. UGH! FOCUS!!

Spit. Shirt goes on. Brush teeth. I feel like I'm going through withdrawal already. It's too early to meet people and play the role. Especially without coffee! I've been up for not even five minutes and all I am thinking about is one cup. Just one.

Ready to go. Kirsten waits patiently as the bathroom door swings open. She's looking at the coffee beans.

"You carry coffee beans with you?"

"Yeah," I say, as if that is the most natural thing in the world. Wonder what she would say if she saw how the French press was packed. But no coffee today. This is a travesty. Thanks for the reminder, Kirsten. God, her hair is long and extraordinary. She must go through a bottle of hair conditioner a week.

I grab my bag, but can't find anything else. The bag is empty.

"Do you see my computer? My notes?"

Kirsten turns around searching, but is just as lost as I am. Where is my iPhone for the remote presentation? Where is everything? At least I know what country I'm in. Kirsten must be observing me as some stereotypical American, something along the lines of being scatterbrained and unorganized. Though at the moment, she'd be right. I'm dropping everything; nothing is going right, and I know why—coffee, or the lack of coffee coursing through me. I'm stuck in the wrong gear and this is not going to work. My hands are actually shaking.

"Can you heat that water? I can down a cup right now." Desperate times call for desperate measures. How bad can it be to down a cup once in a while?

"Sorry, but there's no power in the hotel from the storm last night," she says apologetically. My world begins to crumble as the mystery reveals itself bit by bit. The lightning storm last night knocked out power, hence the train delay from Eindhoven. The alarm was set last night, but I got in too late, forgetting to request a wake-up call. Power knocked out in the hotel, knocking out the alarm clock, and the battery charger for the phone. I should be a detective.

Focus. Stop thinking about last night and this morning. Where are my notes?

This isn't working. This is a nightmare—it's why early lectures are the worst! But hey, the money was good, fuels the Galapagos coffee I found for $25 per pound, better than $500 a pound elephant dung–fermented coffee. I didn't want to like that Galapagos coffee or the Black Ivory for that matter, but I knew I would on both counts. Setting myself up for failure.

Kirsten steps closer and I'm not shocked how tall she is. A majority of the Dutch are and proud of it. They're the tallest people in the world and they flaunt it at every opportunity, but then apologize profusely for flaunting said height.

"What can I do?" Kirsten asks, trying to help as best she can.

"I need a solid cup of coffee."

"Solid?" Her confused look says enough.

"Not shit. Not disgusting. Not German or from cat piss. It's why I have these—"

"I can get you one after the talk, the coffee here is certainly not … solid." Emphasizing the word "solid" like a small child who just learned a word that impressed the family.

"No, I need it now. I need to get my mind in order, it's my ritual—never mind."

Notes. Notes. Notes. The floor isn't giving any hint to where these notes are. The wallpaper with its bizarre flower, windmill, and anvil patterns with a pink background suddenly distracts me. Who has wallpaper anymore? Why did I work on this lecture last night? Should have never changed it but after the other night … . I should have known better, even though the changes are needed and made the piece that much better, I won't be comfortable with the language or timing. The absence of coffee is making me regret life choices right now. I'm jittery, just like Cecilia at The Pelikan. She did this to me! Yes, I'll blame her for this.

"I just need coffee." I reaffirm my desperation to the gods of coffee.

"There's a solid, not-shitty place about ten minutes from here—but it's in the opposite direction," she says, now using my vernacular to no doubt mock me. I bet Jonas would have had a cup waiting for me, easing my pain of a nine AM start.

"Of course it is. Everything in The Netherlands is ten minutes away. Can we delay the start?"

"Sadly, no. It's being streamed and starting on time is essential for hits, plus the interviews after. It's a tight schedule, and then your train departs. It's why the lecture is so early."

"I can't concentrate. I need coffee."

Kirsten bends down and picks up the coffee beans Cecilia sent to me, a small smirk crosses her face, and says, "Will these do?" She tosses the bag; my stab at it is pathetic, at best, as it hits the wall and falls to the floor.

"Yeah, I'm pathetic enough to grind them up and snort them." Warranted sarcasm that's dipped within a living nightmare. If James heard that, a large bet would be made immediately. I thought surviving power outages in New York was it for me, but here, my vow is going to be broken, and I'm not going to get my coffee. That would have been acceptable for sure before Cecilia—but not now, now it's a necessity! The clear plastic bag lies on the floor, and the beans have been crushed from the travel. Probably from being in the top of the suitcase and not being packed properly. A lapse in judgment there; I should have packed them more securely. But I have time to live with that mistake just not now. I am in a dark place right now.

Cecilia's crushed beans distract me, as they look like they've been ground up to what seems to be a fine grain. Talk about a metaphor. Where has this suitcase been?! There's been too much traveling, too many trains in a short amount of time, but no complaints. Back to the search for my notes and worst of all, I keep dropping things and making mistakes. If this is what coffee does to me, or even scarier what no coffee does to me, I'm in deep trouble. I just need it right now for these three hours. Just the feeling.

I stare at the crushed beans and turn to Kirsten. The realization crosses my face that this is really about to happen. As if the shadows of forthcoming events were any clearer, the sun just went behind a huge cloud, darkening the room. I clear the table as fast as I can without regard for anything that was in the way. I grab my wallet from the floor. The American Express would do in the "normal" situation, but it's too flimsy here and lacks the thickness required. A room key is usually a harder plastic. It should do, but no way am I finding it now and have no time to waste.

"Are you ... " Kirsten's facial expression says it all. My lack of reaction gives her all she needs to know: yes this is really happening. Everything that Beckett taught me is ignored in every which way—to prophetically see the future, a ticking clock will obscure even the clearest vision. And the clock is ticking. No time to think about the after-effects, there is only time only to act. Maybe that's the flaw of man, a ticking clock. Mistakes are made in such haste and so are the greatest decisions known to man.

I'm skimming through my wallet as the sun catches a card ever so perfectly: The Chase Sapphire Preferred card is illuminated like it's been sent from heaven. It's double the heft of the other cards and is blue with gold letters. There's hardly a logo on the front compared to the others, but the thickness is incredibly appealing. The Chase Sapphire card is a conversation starter when cashiers, waiters, or basically anyone sees it. They have to ask about the design (I think it's aluminum) and the benefits and advantages are explained. I should get paid for this type of promotion but basically its prime use is right here, right now as the hard plastic goes over the bean almost begging to be crushed. I wonder if the card was designed for just this purpose. And I'm sure Chase will be thrilled. Furiously, tapping the card over the grinds, I remember that "efficiency is job one, people." I'm way too good at this, as it takes less than twenty seconds.

Kirsten observes with equal weights of horror and astonishment. "Are you really going to do what I think you are doing?"

"You can watch or you can stay. Either way, this is happening." And they say the Dutch are adept at utilizing their surroundings! The beans are crushed and pretty fine, too. I have to admit the travel did a bunch of the work and damage as the grinds are quickly separated into three even lines about three inches long.

I take a twenty-euro bill off the floor, rolling it tightly with surprising efficiency. A sigh of "don't try this at home, kids" fills the room and I take another deep breath. Here we go without a second's regret or disgust. How did I go from having coffee on a bridge to drinking elephant-dung coffee, buying another pound of it three days later because we drank it all, to snorting three lines because it seems like the only logical thing to do at the moment? There's no way this is healthy and no way this is NOT going to hurt later. After eating the elephant beans with Declan and James last year, I thought I'd hit a bizarre rock bottom that night. Today, I found there are still more depths to explore. This day will definitely not be a highlight of these trips. Chewing didn't do the job last time I was here; however, that was before my brainwaves were altered—maybe this is exactly the remedy I need. You'd think I would have learned something but when it comes to this type of dedication, there are no lessons, no morals, just actions, and stupid actions. James and Declan are going to be quite displeased knowing they missed this one. And for some reason, I'm quite comfortable with that and this.

Here we … OH GOD THAT FEELS GOOD AND AWFUL. The second line disappears with a long sniff, and the third goes down, way way too well, but I'm already feeling sick—this was a big mistake, what is going on here? Why would a grown-ass man go to such lengths—OH, the notes! There they are! Right under the suitcase and clothes! The computer is in the gift bag I received from the organizers last night and the phone is charging by the bed. It all starts to come together. The tunnel contracts and everything becomes clear. I grab all the necessary materials, throw them into the bag, and turn to Kirsten, "Let's go."

"Yeah …" Kirsten's lack of motion verbalizes it all.

2

I have the jitters like never before as the coffee grinds through my body … what's next, mainlining? No way … I don't like needles—said the desperate man who just snorted three lines of crushed coffee beans. Did you know there are people who get coffee enemas? Lines have been drawn and some will not cross—add me to that list. Honesty time. Either way, I affirm to all of you, I am officially an addict.

The realization seems more like a foregone conclusion than some epiphany, especially after the last few months. I think today was the slap in the face but that was necessary even if the act reeks of overindulgence. I chug some water while walking into the lecture hall. I wonder what's to happen next as I make my way on this caffeinated downward spiral?

Walking behind Kirsten I'm trying to keep pace; her long legs give her an advantage as we go through a lobby area into the main hall of the building. The room is remarkable with stadium seating and a nice raised stage with a wood podium. Kirsten turns to face me, "We just had this renovated. You're the first person to use it. All new equipment."

"I like the podium. The balance of modern technology but an old-time lectern. Exactly what I would have purchased, it's a classy choice." Just like my classy move in the hotel room.

"That was the precise reason for this purchase. My colleague indicated that a podium matters. It gives the speaker confidence in the oddest way. And the room. We had several prominent speakers give us suggestions to make the room as inviting as possible," she tells me as she turns to walk down the aisle closer to the stage.

She's one hundred percent correct, the room gives confidence or takes it away. Too small and not filled, there's a deflated feeling that no one wants to sit through the work. If it is too big and not filled enough, the same feeling consumes and penetrates the thoughts. Picking a venue is key here and this will do. A cursory glance and there are about three hundred to four hundred seats.

"It's really a nice space. I like the colors in the room, too, like a purple or something." I don't think Kirsten heard me because the lights and sound are being tested. On then off, dim, dimmer, and dimmest, then the lights go back on with the music fading in and out. Walking onto the stage, I see that the table holds several options for today's production. There's a very stylish silver wireless microphone, next to that is a wireless head microphone, and a basic black handheld. The tech guy, who has to be the shortest Dutch guy I have ever seen, presents the options to me as if he's presenting one of his daughters for marriage.

"I prefer the wireless microphone whose receiver we can attach to your suit jacket. Free of motion, minimal feedback," he proclaims with a deep confident voice.

"I hope I don't disappoint you, but besides needing my hands to be free, I like the wireless head mic." He's not disappointed. He's crushed. He puts the wireless head mic on as pleasantries are exchanged with the organizers, crew, and some faculty. This caffeine coursing through my veins is actually not bad. The back of my throat has a hint of mild citrus and the acidity is definitely on the low ends. Cici does know her coffee. There's some caramel and maybe a hint of cocoa, as well; obviously a nice blend. Wonder how it would taste if I drank it? As if there is any doubt Cecilia would send me anything less than top-notch. I make it back to Europe and she's away on business in Africa. The shadows didn't lie.

The tech guy finishes the set-up, stuffing the battery pack into my jacket pocket like a jaded lover putting clothes in a bag to leave for the night after an argument. I walk around the stage and in the back of the room. I notice Kirsten, as she is overly animated, speaking to a short Dutch woman. She's gesturing with her hands as the other woman takes notes—a journalist perhaps? No doubt I'll have to answer for the hotel-room scene but hey, it's a good story.

"Check one two three," I say into the mic. All seems good, as I continue walking around the stage making sure the crew doesn't think stationary is an option. "Check. Check. Hello."

Perfect.

"How close to the crowd can the mic get picked up?" I ask anyone in earshot.

Another tech guys yells, "Keep going until we don't get a signal or some feedback."

Walking midway through the seats, I'm still able to get a signal. Then about three-fourths of the way up, the mic cuts out on me. "So, about here."

"The other mic would go further," the microphone guy says loud enough for me to hear. The rest of the crew ignores the barb; he's been spurned before and the crew knows not to engage in his bitterness by now. So, I ignore him as well, and walk back onto the stage. At least there'll be interaction and I can walk freely.

Kirsten is still gesturing in the back of the lecture hall, and is quite demonstrative for a Dutch girl, which I've observed is usually not their forte. Matter of fact, she had a wedding ring on, maybe she's not Dutch after all or just that different from all the rest? The Dutch are "determined yet reserved," that's the way to classify them with as much stereotyping as possible. The saying, "Doe maar normaal dan doe je al gek genoeg" or in English, "Just act normal, that's crazy enough" is a common here and the Dutch really do abide by that. How can I possibly achieve normalcy when I just snorted those lines of an African blend with a surprisingly high elevation? The drip in the back of my throat sparks an inner debate on whether or not the coffee is fair trade and organic. I'll venture to guess it's both fair trade and organic. Cici didn't seem like the exploitative type.

The crowd begins to file in, apparently a full house, but who knows? As if it matters. This place, unlike the hotel, was spared from the power outrage even if it is in the same building. Hopefully, there will be a balance within the audience to add to the flavor. I think I'm grinding my teeth right now. Does anyone notice? Water and some more water. I gesture to a member of the crew for another bottle as I make my way to the front row while the seats fill. Ignore this terrible feeling as the noise gets louder, or is it the beans altering my perception? If this story gets out I wonder what will happen. Oh, Raoul. Desperation makes an interesting bedfellow to logic. I should really get new idols.

"Looks like it worked, no?" Kirsten says as she investigates me with her eyes, trying to catch any glimpse of a side effect from the little show I just put on in the hotel.

"Seems as such," I respond with confidence that is lacking in common sense but steeped in bullshit. Elephant shit is better, but try convincing any of the ninety-nine percenters of that.

"You've done that before, no?" She smiles at me.

"Would you believe me if I said there's a first time for everything and hopefully this will be the last?" Before she has a chance to answer, the lights dim, followed by a small round of applause as the organizer, Martina comes on stage. I check my watch, I made it before nine AM but now the real question—will I make it through this lecture before descending into a coffee abyss?

"Thank you for coming to this morning's lecture. We're quite pleased to bring you a lecture on the Presidents of the United States and Comedy in America. I want to say to our lecturer today, welcome back to The Netherlands, it's been a whirlwind tour or so I'm hearing."

She knows. Kirsten told her, she had to. My teeth are chattering. Does anyone hear it?

"He survived the storm and the train delays from last night's weather. He's now an official Dutchman after that experience. So, please welcome—"

Here it comes, the pronunciation and she nailed it like a gymnast off the high beam. And she did so without the slightest hint of her northern Dutch accent. The crowd breaks into a polite applause but they should be applauding her. I walk on stage and all I'm thinking about is: I should have crushed up more beans.

The lights go dark and the keynote goes up. The grinds make their way through.

"Good morning … alles goed? Everyone good?" I avoid saying "hi" to the city, just to be safe, because what if I'm wrong? The audience does not notice but I do—the coffee inside me is making me perspire and my mouth is dry. I take a big gulp of water. Showtime.

3

Today we're going to discuss the satirical representation of the American presidency by investigating the media and parallel realities. For the sake of this lecture, parallel realities will be defined as "an exploration of alter egos and impersonations, and how they present an alternate reality to the audience." In comedy and other forms of entertainment, a persona is devised as a way to comprehend the people, and to understand the other side of the public. To put oneself in another's shoes allows for a new appreciation of the plights and successes of others and in turn, a greater appreciation for everyone. Hopefully, our inherent apathy is replaced with more human emotions such as empathy and sympathy towards the current human condition. And in this, a new reality is created where the audience receives a version of the truth that normally would not have been received. While attempting to grasp the notion of parallel realities, as was defined just before, I thought of William Shakespeare's *Henry V*.

In the pivotal Act IV, scene I, Henry, the highly recognizable and popular monarch, dons a hood and travels around incognito to talk to the troops about the upcoming battle they seem certain to lose. First, the king meets Pistol, who calls him a bawcock or a fine fellow with a heart of gold. Pistol remarks that Henry had good parents—so much so that he would be willing to kiss the king's dirty shoe. Pistol has real affection for the king, and not in some abstract medieval way, because he has a real and personal connection with Henry's family. However, Pistol also calls him a "lovely bully," a fascinating insult that precedes the verbal fireworks of Henry's next encounter with John Bates, Alexander Court, and Michael Williams in the camp. Could these three have the most un-unique names Shakespeare ever created? Yet, there was a method here, Shakespeare was creating "an everyman" with no royalty name or otherwise to speak of, but simply men in the king's army who would reflect the soldiers' and subjects' feelings. Once again, like Pistol, the soldiers do not know this is King Henry. Instead, the men believe Henry is just another soldier in the army and with that level of safety and freedom in mind, Bates remarks that the king "may show what outward courage he will, but I believe, as cold a night as 'tis, he could wish himself in Thames up to the neck" (IV, I, 110–112). The king, still keeping his identity a secret, feels the need to calmly respond by saying: "I think he would not wish himself anywhere but where he is." The men continue challenging the king, still ignorant to his true identity, about royal leadership and questioning how Henry would react if he were captured. The men come to the conclusion that the king would allow himself to be ransomed to save his own life. Of course, the king disagrees, promising "he would not be ransomed," yet the soldiers keep attacking Henry's dignity, complacent in the fact that this stranger is just another soldier. The thought of royal slander never enters their minds.

The soldiers discuss the notion of royal infallibility and accountability because Henry is the one making the decisions. Henry is the one who has to live with the consequences, as Williams comments: "But if the cause be not good, the king himself hath a heavy reckoning to make, when all those legs, and arms, and heads, chopped off in a battle." The men continue questioning the king and the conversation becomes more and more heated until Henry and Williams challenge each other to fight, throwing down their gloves—their gauntlets—ready to kill one another. The scene's poignancy is captured perfectly by Kenneth Branagh, in his 1988 film interpretation of Henry. This essential confrontation contributed to Henry's evolution as not only a king but also a man who understands the sacrifices soldiers make for the crown and England. The king's maturity began in *Henry IV*, Part I, as Henry grew from the wild child known as Prince Hal, roaming the countryside partying with his good friend Falstaff, to a man ready for his epic battle with Prince Hotspur in Act V, scene iv of the play. In another vital scene regarding Henry's development, he understands nobility for the first time, praising the mortally wounded Hotspur for his courage. Hotspur is what Prince Hal will strive to be and ultimately become—reminiscent of Hamlet's view of Fortinbras's army in *Hamlet*, though Henry had more success and less tragedy. In this scene, the dying Hotspur is bequeathed a classic Shakespearean death, prophesying the carnage to come with Henry's ascension to the crown, but in a twist, stops, saying: "O, I could prophesy, but that the earthy and cold hand of death lies on my tongue. No, Percy, thou art dust, and food for—" (Henry IV, Act V, sc. iv, 181–84). But before he can finish, Hotspur dies and Henry, as if understanding the true meaning of being a prince, finishes Hotspur's words and realizes what honor and royalty truly mean.

> Henry: "For worms, brave Percy. Fare thee well, great heart … adieu, and take thy praise with
> thee to heaven!" (L85–99)

Henry realizes he has to grow up, as everyone does, and officially retire the boy he currently is. Only then will Henry be capable to receive ownership of his title of prince and then king seriously. Henry does this by ending his friendship with his childhood friend Falstaff in *Henry IV*, Part II. This split with his wild companion was foreshadowed in Part I, Act II, scene, iv, when Falstaff asks Prince Hal if, when he becomes king, he would ever hang a thief or banish him. Hal responds, saying he would, and this actually happens when Hal ascends to the throne in *Henry V*. All of these scenes, from Falstaff's eventual exile to the French insults at court to the incognito trip around the camp, lead King Henry to deliver his famous St. Crispin's Day speech. This epic speech rallied the English troops to achieve an improbable victory over the French on October 25th. Henry stands in front of his men with a bombastic voice and inspires the troops to fight alongside him:

> King: If we are mark'd to die, we are enow
> To do our country loss; and if to live,
> The fewer men, the greater share of honour.
> God's will! I pray thee, wish not one man more … .

And later in the speech, the king addresses those who wish to flee the battle because victory seems improbable and to those who stay that immortality and legend awaits them:

> King: That he which hath no stomach to this fight,
> Let him depart; his passport shall be made,
> And crowns for convoy put into his purse;
> We would not die in that man's company
> That fears his fellowship to die with us.
>
> This day is call'd the feast of Crispian.
> He that outlives this day, and comes safe home,
> Will stand a tip-toe when this day is nam'd,

And rouse him at the name of Crispian.
He that shall live this day, and see old age,
Will yearly on the vigil feast his neighbours,
And say "To-morrow is Saint Crispian."
Then will he strip his sleeve and show his scars,
And say "These wounds I had on Crispian's day."

By being a man of the people at his young age and walking among his men the night before, Henry was able to deliver the monologue. The king experienced a parallel reality that enabled him to find the words for inspiration. Henry was not the king of privilege but instead, a soldier fighting in the muck with the rest of the men. This is where those in power are educated by the powerless and hopefully they learn from these experiences and WE, the audience, learn more about those who wear the crown. Similar to a jester's approach, but this is a more direct and personal education as opposed to the jester's roasting at court. Taking on a persona and creating a parallel reality, no matter how briefly, as Henry did, allow for a new and unseen truth to be revealed about the world to the king. By removing the name and creating something else, the person, in this case the king, is able to explore more about humanity. Later on in *Henry V*, Act IV, sc viii, the king has a scene with Williams to retrieve the glove Henry gave to him when they challenged each other to a fight. Williams begs forgiveness while Henry toys with him his wilder days as a trickster are still inside him and instead of punishing him, the king rewards Williams for his honesty. King Henry understood that without Williams's honesty, he would have never connected to the people on a deeper level than ruler–subject that most kings have had. His time with Williams was invaluable to his victory and reign in England. By disguising the king as a commoner, Shakespeare finished the transformation of boy to king he began two plays earlier. Henry matured to become the king he was destined to be, conquering not only France in the later scenes, "once more unto the breach" dear Englishman, but also winning the hearts and minds of his people, an absolute necessity to be among the most beloved and immortal kings.

The coffee's intensity, or the coffee grinds' intensity, I should say, is still doing the job, except the thirst is overwhelming. Two bottles of water are finished in only a few minutes as I motion for another one. More importantly, the crowd seems to connect to the Shakespeare part. They have to be wondering what this has to do with presidential satire. I pause to reassess the lecture, but the additions seem to be working. I peruse the notes, moving the lecture forward.

The foundation is laid and now there has to be a connection to contemporary history times using the parallel reality. When we discuss famous American personalities, Samuel Clemens has to come to mind. Clemens would free himself from who he was; he unshackled himself from his namesake and adopted the Mark Twain persona. The name Mark Twain derived from a nautical term that measured the depth of a river. Clemens embraced the term, humanizing it, enabling his writing to measure the depth, stage, and condition of America. Mark Twain, not Samuel Clemens, assisted his readers to navigate the American experience in the nineteenth century, ranging from literary smackdowns in the hilarious "Fenimore Cooper's Literary Offenses" to the abomination that was slavery in the incredible epic novel, *The Adventures of Huckleberry Finn*.

Adopting a pseudonym frees the author from the constraints of a family name, hesitation towards a subject or fear of retribution to name a few—like a superhero wearing a mask who knows he can do more with an alter ego than he can as just a person. Bruce Wayne could accomplish only so much but his alter ego Batman knows no limits. Eric Arthur Blair was born with an English imperialistic name steeped in tragedy and torture and changed his name to George Orwell. This freed Blair to become a citizen of the world, a literary and political rebel who was able to make commentary on the state of the lower classes, political philosophies, and the dystopian future that lay ahead. Others have done the same though for a myriad of reasons—Hunter S. Thompson had Raoul Duke and Dr. Gonzo, and more recently Salman Rushdie adopted the moniker Joseph Anton for his own protection from Islamic radicals during "The Satanic Verses" crisis, and later wrote a memoir using that name in the title. The name change allowed for Mr. Rushdie's perspective on the horrors he and his family endured for two decades without the burden of his true last name. A pseudonym, an alter ego, a parallel reality; these are all done to allow for commentary for an unspoken truth to be revealed, for the satire to do its work, and for power to have yet another nemesis. By examining the idea of alternate personae, and moving that towards those who do impressions of real people, a new part of the person they're impersonating where the media, parallel realities, and satire mix is revealed to everyone. Gilbert Highet said, "satire is a blade with not one but two sharp edges and those who engage in the acrobatics of satire have to describe, decry, and denounce the here and now." Satirical work has to be topical and the most topical subject in today's media world is the head of state. The tone towards the leader is usually not serious but the intent is and the work is sarcastic, ironic, shocking, and inappropriate to the subject. Powerful satire reveals humanity and alters our perceptions of what we once believed. Effective satire holds up the mirror to society and makes us laugh at what we are as a culture and society. Other words that have been used to describe satire are parody, spoof, invective, lampoon, and caricature. While all of these serve their purpose, political satire will be our main focus.

Utilizing all these elements is *Saturday Night Live*, one of the longest-running American shows in TV history. Premiering in 1975, the show immediately began satirizing the presidency, politicians, and American culture week in and week out. From their weekend update skits to their powerful impressions, *SNL* exaggerated known characteristics of the commander in chief; however, they also created an alternate version of the president as *SNL* mocked the office, in an attempt to circumvent the immense power it had accumulated under the treacherous leadership of President Nixon. With *SNL*'s debut just one year after the Nixon resignation, satirizing the president became a necessity. Sometimes satirizing the president was child's play, as Gerald Ford, who actually fell down a flight of stairs, can attest. The lampooning begins with Chevy Chase not even bothering to look or sound like President Ford but to make Ford a clumsy, incompetent bozo, who was not only incapable of being president, but also according to *SNL*, really wasn't. It was successful satire because it established what *SNL* would do to presidents and others in the political world. Chase would have his "Ford" answer a glass of water, thinking it was the phone, or falling down constantly as Chase was quoted saying: "He had never been elected to higher office … so I never felt that he deserved to be there to begin with." Vice President Ford became president under the 25th Amendment after Nixon's previous vice president resigned in 1973 and Nixon resigned in 1974, becoming the first man to become president without being elected by the Electoral College. Chase's sentiments towards the man are understandable, considering the turmoil the country was engulfed in. The tracing of presidential satire is explored further in *Satire TV: Politics & Comedy in the Post-Network Era* in the chapter by Jeffrey P. Jones titled: "With All Due Respect: Satirizing Presidents from *Saturday Night Live* to *Lil' Bush*."

In 1976, Democratic challenger Jimmy Carter defeats "incumbent" Gerald Ford, and ascends to the presidency. *SNL*'s Dan Aykroyd ventures in the opposite direction from Chase, taking his impersonation seriously by putting on a wig and adopting Carter's southern drawl. The most vital aspect was Aykroyd taking on Carter's personality as a know-it-all micromanager trying to solve every problem that comes his way. To illustrate this, Carter attempts to reach the people with a call-in chat show, in a *SNL* segment called "Ask President Carter …" with Bill Murray as the iconic Walter Cronkite hosting.

Walter Cronkite: Mrs. Horbath, do you have a question for the president?

Mrs. Edward Horbath (on phone): Yes, sir. I'm an employee of the U.S. Postal Service in Kansas. Last year they installed an automated letter-sorting system called the Marvex-3000, here in our branch …

President Jimmy Carter: Yes.

Mrs. Edward Horbath (on phone): … but the system doesn't work too good. Letters keep getting clogged in the first-level sorting grid. Is there anything that can be done about this?

President Jimmy Carter: Well, Mrs. Horbath, Vice President Mondale and I were just talking about the Morvex-3000 this morning … uh … I do have a suggestion—you know the caliber poised on the first grid sliding armiture?

Mrs. Edward Horbath (on phone): Yes.

President Jimmy Carter: Okay, there's a three-digit setting there, where the post and the armiture meet. Now, when the system was installed, the angle of cross-slide was put at a maximum setting of 1. If you reset it at the three-mark like it says in the assembly instructions, I think it will solve any clogging problems in the machine.

Mrs. Edward Horbath (on phone): Oh, thanks, Mr. President! Oh, by the way, I think you're doing a great job!

Later on in the skit, Carter is faced with a troubled youth named Peter, who is in the midst of negative reaction to drugs.

Walter Cronkite: Thank you, Mr. President, ha ha! Our next caller is Peter Elkin of Westbrook, Oregon, whom I am told is 17 years of age.

Peter (on phone): Hello? Hello?

President Jimmy Carter: Yes. Hello, Peter?

Peter (on phone): Is this the president?

President Jimmy Carter: Yes, it is.

Walter Cronkite: Do you have a question for the president?

Peter (on phone): Uh … I, uh … I took some acid … I'm afraid to leave my apartment, and I can't wear any clothes … and the ceiling is dripping, and uh … I, uh …

Walter Cronkite: Well, thank you very much for calling, sir.

President Jimmy Carter: Just a minute, Walter, this guy's in trouble. I think I better try to talk him down. Peter?

Peter (on phone): Yeah..?

President Jimmy Carter: Peter, what did the acid look like?

Peter (on phone): They were these little orange pills.

President Jimmy Carter: Were they barrel shaped?

Peter (on phone): Uh … yes.

President Jimmy Carter: Okay, right, you did some orange sunshine, Peter.

Walter Cronkite: Very good of you to know that, sir.

President Jimmy Carter: How long ago did you take it, Peter?

Peter (on phone): Uh … I don't know. I can't read my watch.

President Jimmy Carter: All right, Peter, just listen. Everything is going to be fine. You're very high right now. You will probably be that way for about five more hours. Try taking some vitamin B complex, vitamin C complex … if you have a beer, go ahead and drink it.

Peter (on phone): Okay.

President Jimmy Carter: Just remember you're a living organism on this planet, and you're very safe. You've just taken a heavy drug. Relax, stay inside and listen to some music, Okay? Do you have any Allman Brothers?

Peter (on phone): Yes, I do, sir. Everything is okay, huh, Jimmy?

President Jimmy Carter: It sure is, Peter. You know, I'm against drug use myself, but I'm not going to lay that on you right now. Just mellow out the best you can, okay?

Peter (on phone): Okay … !

The basic questions that should be asked are: How does Carter know the answer to everything? How does he know basic mechanical operations of a sorter and how to talk a kid down off a bad acid trip? How would Carter know to change a setting for a more efficient machine or to listen to the Allman Brothers to mellow out? The know-it-all is on full display in the skit. The parody satirizing Carter's attitude of believing only he knew what was best would cost him the 1980 election, as public approval of his job performance was one of the lowest in modern history. The confidence shown by Aykroyd's Carter would not translate, as the real President Carter was powerless to stop the oil, economic, and Iranian hostage crises; the know-it-all didn't seem to know what to do at all and was a one-term president because of it.

In the 1980s, one of the most versatile cast members, Phil Hartman, created a version of Ronald Reagan that was hapless in one moment, and a plotter the next. Hartman plays the senile old man for the people and the press but once alone, Reagan morphs into someone we've never seen before. He becomes a mad mathematical genius, a real-world Wizard of Oz working behind the (iron) curtain, gathering knowledge of intimate information happening around the globe. Reagan's assistants can't keep up with all the information, and one interrupts him saying he doesn't understand, to which Reagan responds: "I'm the president, only I need to understand." What this satirical skit does is allow the audience to question who and what President Reagan really is. Considering Reagan was the first Hollywood actor to become president, the question is begging to be asked: is Reagan as the kindly great communicator his true persona or was this one big act to fool the American people? By Hartman's creating an egomaniacal tyrant, it gives the audience a new version of President Reagan and allows for a parallel reality to be entered, where it's not "morning in Reagan's America," as the Reagan political slogan goes, but instead we should be *mourning* because Hartman's Reagan is running America. Sadly, Hartman's take on Reagan never really penetrated the zeitgeist, as President Reagan was and still is revered decades after he left political life.

In 1988, vice president and eventual 41st president George H.W. Bush had to endure Dana Carvey's caricaturing of his mannerisms and intelligence (or lack thereof) at a near-pitch-perfect clip. The impression was so incredibly accurate that Mr. Carvey received an invitation to the White House by Bush 41 himself. But even before that happened, *SNL* and Carvey took the American people and the vice president to task as the skit highlights Bush's incoherence in his debates with Massachusetts governor and Democratic presidential candidate Michael Dukakis, and Bush's inability to form sentences without carefully crafted sound bites to help him along. The entire skit is satire at its best as Bush fumbles through each question and Dukakis answers with sound, albeit frustrated logic, but in the end has only one statement to make.

Sam Donaldson: Vice President Bush, there are millions of homeless in this country—children who go hungry and are lacking in other basic necessities. How would the Bush Administration achieve your stated goal of making this a kinder, gentler nation?

George Bush: Well, that is a big problem, Sam, and unfortunately the format of these debates makes it hard to give you a complete answer. If I had more time, I could spell out the program in greater detail, but I'm afraid, in a short answer like this, all I can say is we're on track—we can do more—but we're getting the job done, so let's stay the course, a thousand points of light. Well, unfortunately, I guess my time is up.

Diane Sawyer: Mr. Vice President, you still have a minute-twenty.

George Bush: What? That can't be right. I must have spoken for at *least* two minutes.

Diane Sawyer: No, just forty seconds, Mr. Vice President.

George Bush: Really? Well, if I didn't use the time then, I must have just used the time now, talking about it.

Diane Sawyer: No, no, Mr. Vice President, it's not being counted against you.

George Bush: Well, I just don't want it to count against Governor Dukakis's time.

Diane Sawyer: It won't. It will come out of the post-debate commentary.

George Bush: Do you think that's a good idea?

Diane Sawyer: You still have a minute-twenty, Mr. Vice President.

George Bush: Well, more has to be done, sure. But the programs we have in place are doing the job, so let's keep on track and stay the course.

Diane Sawyer: You have fifty seconds left, Mr. Vice President.

George Bush: Let me sum up. On track, stay the course. Thousand points of light.

Diane Sawyer: Governor Dukakis. Rebuttal?

Michael Dukakis: I can't believe I'm losing to this guy!

The vice president is at a complete loss for words and has nothing to say or add to this policy, or any for that matter. Instead of revealing new ideas, Bush simply regurgitates all the famous catch-phrases that made him the Republican candidate for president. In the end, where Jon Lovitz as the Democratic challenger Michael Dukakis says, "I can't believe I'm losing to this guy," is where *SNL* used satire's mirror and held it up to the people and Dukakis is that mirror. The writers and those on the show were generally confused about how the American public could possibly vote for Bush and not see Dukakis's value. How could the citizens be fooled by Bush and not impressed by Dukakis? It's not that Dukakis can't believe he's losing to this guy, this is *SNL* saying: "*we* can't believe Bush is going to become the president and all of you are letting it happen." It's a rare moment for *SNL* to be THAT obvious in their preference for a candidate, but if you watched the actual debates, you could understand why. Carvey would have four years of mocking President Bush but while Jeffrey Jones says Carvey's impression "lacked any real politics," looking back Carvey presented Bush as a gentle man-child amazed at the position he held because he'd wanted it for so many years, yet he was completely overwhelmed by twentieth-century technology. Carvey's Bush 41 was a relic of a bygone Cold War era and not equipped to handle the world today, like an 88-year-old using an iPad for the first time. In Bush, the comedian found a perfect vessel to illuminate that Bush 41 is not the right man to lead America into the twenty-first century. While it is certainly not as overtly political as other *SNL* impressions, by creating such an accurate impersonation coupled with the continued onslaught of the "absent-minded president," the label stuck. I'd love to say that more people remember Bush 41 for what Carvey made fun of than what Bush 41 accomplished or failed to accomplish. The memorable "not gunna do it" and the "Bush laugh" he usurped them from the president have become Carvey's signatures—Carvey's impression is iconic. In another sketch, Carvey, by mocking the president's facial and hand gestures, announces Bush 41's plan to attack Saddam Hussein, starting the 1991 Gulf War, or Desert Storm. Then like a child with a new toy, Bush puts on the new infrared night-vision goggles as he warns the image might be too frightening for children. The lights are turned off and only Carvey's night-vision red Cujo-like eyes are illuminated and "it's scary, it's very scary!" He begins to taunt Hussein in an immature way but Carvey's Bush then gets scared as a second pair of "eyes" comes into the Oval Office. However, it's his vice president Dan Quayle but instead of an adult, Quayle is a 12-year-old boy. This Bush version actually stuck and continues to be THE impression of Bush 41 with the public, contrary to Hartman's Reagan. Interestingly enough, the real President Bush embraced the mockery and appeared on *SNL* several times attempting to connect to the younger audiences. While Bush 41 saw a brief rise in popularity during the Gulf War, he ultimately lost his 1992 reelection bid to Arkansas governor Bill Clinton.

Candidate and President Clinton was a comedic dream for *SNL*. From his love of fast food to his southern accent to his numerous trysts with several women, there was plenty to satirize. Once again, Phil Hartman tackles the role as a president and *SNL* makes an incredibly accurate commentary on the president and his many strengths and flaws. Known for his appetite in more ways than one, Clinton, wearing an Arkansas Razorbacks sweatshirt and a Georgetown hat, visits a McDonald's fast food joint after jogging for a mere three blocks with his Secret Service agents. Hartman, like Aykroyd before him, adopts the Clinton hometown drawl but also the charm and Southern goodness, as the president's secret service agents question why they're at a McDonald's—again. All President Clinton craves is "to mingle with the American people, meet some real folks, and maybe get a Diet Coke or something." This line typifies everything that Clinton is about and this *SNL* "cold open skit" lays out what type of man Clinton is and what kind of president Clinton will be. The agents, only following orders from their boss, say, "Fine, but please don't tell Mrs. Clinton."

Clinton responds in an absolutely perfect way, reminding the agent who he really is:

Clinton: Jim, let me tell you something, there's going to be a whole bunch of things we're not going to tell Mrs. Clinton. Fast food is the least of our worries ok, buddy?

The crowd cheers knowing what kind of president we have—one who connects to the people and is a big-time philanderer. The Clinton line also nods to the sexual exploits of the newly elected president and more importantly, foretelling the X-rated scandals to come in his second term and the unwarranted impeachment. But what the satire presents to the audience is a parodied version of the president while at the same gets to the core of his appeal, his brand, and what made him then and makes him still a beloved man and president. Hartman's Clinton works the room exactly like Bill would, by reaching out to the people, but at the same time, taking their food as he wins the crowd over. First, he meets a black woman with a baby whose name is Shakira. Clinton, well versed in African American culture, immediately knows the name means "African Princess"; the mother is stunned and impressed, and Clinton continues to charm her while eating her french fries. Clinton tells Shakira, the baby, "to take care of your mom for me," getting a nervous giggle from the mother as Clinton moves on to the next table of patrons.

Clinton sits down next to Les Holmgren, a hardware store owner played by Chris Farley who tells the president: "We voted for you, sir." Hartman's Clinton turns up the charm and explains his policies for small business owners, a direct repudiation of Bush 41's inability to explain even the minutest details.

Bill Clinton: Thank you, Les. So you own your own hardware store?

Les Holmgren: Yes indeed, sir. Since 1972.

Bill Clinton: Well, good for you. You know, we want to create a network of community development banks that lend to small businesses like yourself. I see your boy doesn't like pickles.

Les Holmgren: Nah, he hates them!

Bill Clinton: You mind? [grabs the pickles] Attaboy! So, good luck to you. I'm gonna wake up every day thinking about you. Oops! Missed one. [grabs remaining pickle]

The skit is played for laughs but that's satire and there is satire's double-edged sword. While working within the Clinton reality of an over-sexed glutton, he truly is a real man of the people with a tremendous ability to seduce everyone he comes in contact with. Everyone knows Clinton is not going to "wake up every morning" thinking about Les Holmgren, but it doesn't matter to Holmgren: the bond is made for life. Everyone knows Holmgren is being lied to but Holmgren accepts the lie because he likes Clinton. Consequently, this scene makes us look at ourselves and how we are in awe of Clinton: The patrons are fawning over the president even though he's eating all their food, but no one seems to mind. Clinton's ability to remain the everyman even when he became president was the key to his success. Seeing this skit alone explains why he left office at an approval rating of over 60%, still one of the highest in modern history. This skit truly encompasses who Clinton is: in 2012, President Obama remarked after Clinton's Democratic National Convention speech that Clinton should be the "Secretary of Explaining Stuff"; Clinton manages through all the distractions food, in this skit; sex, drugs, and women in others to still be coherent in explaining his plan for the country and the issues at home and abroad. It's a perfect skit meshing everything there is about the Clinton mystique into one hilarious scene.

If Hartman's President Reagan was a cold calculating genius and Carvey's President Bush was a man-child enamored with power and overwhelmed with his new toys, then Clinton was and still is the common man we wanted to be president. Clinton was the popular guy in high school, yet he wasn't the bully; instead he was the one who got everyone together to party. Though a Southern president like Carter, Clinton may have known it all but he did not overwhelm people with it—instead, he brought them up to his level as he was simultaneously dropping below—way below—theirs. Clinton was more "us" than any other president with "real" problems and "real issues." This could be the reason that he is still an influential figure a decade-plus after he left office. Though I have to admit, his wife Hillary had a lot to do with his rehabilitation and re-emergence.

I should have done another one in the hotel room. Four would be the magic number. Wonder if anyone would notice if I knelt down and just did it right here behind the podium? It would suit the next bit of the lecture.

As the Clinton years came to an end in 2000, the American electorate experienced the polarizing Bush vs. Gore election. The political unrest, instability, scandals, and the numerous events that followed opened a golden opportunity for satirists and surrealists. If Clinton opened a comic goldmine, then satirists struck oil with George W. Bush! What made George W. Bush fascinating and doomed him from the start was that he was a punch line BEFORE becoming president. While satirists will always mock those seeking power and influence, there was something different about the W satire. Was it his speech? Mannerisms? His child-like wonder at things? Was it his perceived but unfounded lack of intelligence? Or was it his unique ability to not be presidential while seeking the presidency? He was "the man you wanted to have a beer with"; contrast that with Al Gore's lack of personality, and you can begin to understand Bush's successful run. On an additional note: The Florida voting purge investigated extensively by Greg Palast and Ralph Nader's entry notwithstanding, if Al Gore had won his own home state of Tennessee, he would have been president. Let's all admit, right here and right now, Gore was a poor candidate who did not even manage come across as a passionate environmentalist in his award-winning film *An Inconvenient Truth*. If he had been that candidate, our country would have possibly gone in a different direction.

Regardless, once President Bush took office he was continuously seen as a buffoon or simpleton. *W: The First Hundred Days, a White House Journal*, brilliantly conceived and written by DB Gilles and Sheldon Woodbury, was just one of the satires on Bush's apparent lack of intelligence. The "journal" was written in Bush's own handwriting with secret doodles and several blank pages "revealing his thoughts." Several other books such as *George W. Bushisms: The Slate Book of Accidental*

Wit and Wisdom of Our 43rd President continued to mock the president, but even serious ones like *Bush's Brain* continued with the "Bush is stupid" theme and motif.

As mentioned before, a lot of the television history is covered in *Satire TV: Politics & Comedy in the Post-Network Era* in the chapter by Jeffrey P. Jones titled: "With All Due Respect: Satirizing Presidents from *Saturday Night Live* to *Lil' Bush*" as he discusses the fall of 2000, *South Park* creators Matt Stone and Trey Parker produced a TV show about the Bush presidency called: "That's My Bush!" starring a Bush lookalike portrayed as a moron who means well but has no business being anywhere near the White House. The spoof was more a sitcom spoof than presidential satire, as Matt Stone and Trey Parker had "Everybody Loves Al" ready to go into production had Gore been victorious. Jones also discusses the mood in America as Bush's second term ended, when an animated TV show called *Lil' Bush* premiered. The show had Bush and his cronies—Cheney, Rumsfeld, Rice—as angry and destructive children who are completely oblivious to any consequences their actions may have. The show's obvious hatred towards Bush and his administration mirrored the negative public opinion in 2007 and 2008. But it was *SNL* and Will Ferrell who created the most iconic version of the 43rd president: a somewhat lovable yet completely inept college frat boy who influenced the nighttime comedy landscape in a way no other *SNL* player had been able to.

Variety magazine wrote that Ferrell made no apologies for Bush, yet reveled in Bush's blissful ineptitude and irresponsibility. Ferrell's Bush is somehow endearing, as the comedian refused to demonize the president or portray him as being so awful that he's worse than an actual human. This delicate balance is essential in satire or the comedy of outrage, as satiric scholar Gilbert Highet called it. But if satire is filled only with hatred or amusement, then it's not satire and will have no lasting legacy. Ferrell portrayed W on *SNL* full time for only the first two years of the Bush Administration, but returned frequently to reprise the role, as no other *SNL* player was able to capture the Ferrell/Bush magic. There were several memorable skits over the two full seasons and remaining eight years, but one of the more controversial skits was aired during a special "Thursday Night Weekend Update" on October 23, 2008 just before the presidential election.

In the "cold open" skit, Ferrell begins discussing the coming election between "the hot lady" and "the Tiger Woods guy." He's completely ignorant to the economic disaster that had recently befallen the country, declaring that the oval office is "a bummer-free zone" and he doesn't care because he's out of office in a few weeks. Bush then reveals why he's speaking on national television at this time—he wants to help Sarah Palin and John McCain "by giving them what every candidate wants most: a prime-time heavily publicized network endorsement from George W. Bush." The crowd laughs, as they understand the way Ferrell portrays Bush as the good-hearted simpleton who has no clue how things really are or the image he projects. No way would McCain want a prime-time endorsement, but W brings out Sarah Palin, played brilliantly by Tina Fey, instead of John McCain because as Palin tells the president, "upon hearing you wanted to give him a super public endorsement, he cannot be found. He was last seen travelin' on foot through the Adirondacks." Speaking of Palin and Tina Fey's role in bringing down the former VP candidate by Fey's simply reading

Palin's exact words: Palin never held national office or served a full term as Alaska's governor. For the consistency of this lecture and time, the discussion will only be about viable politicians and their satirical doppelgangers. Also, maybe if we don't speak about her, she'll go away.

Back to the skit, Bush confidently declares they'll find McCain and "we'll smoke him out because George Bush always finds his man save for one huge exception." Another loud cheer erupts from the crowd as Ferrell and the *SNL* writing staff remind everyone that Bush never kept his promise of finding Public Enemy Number One, Osama bin Laden. After a bit of small talk, W endorses Sarah Palin:

> W: The office of vice president is the most important office in the land. The vice president decides when we go to war, how we tax the citizens, and how we interpret the Constitution. The president can do nothing without checking with the vice president.

Once again, the crowd enjoys the joke and image of the all-powerful Dick Cheney schooling and manipulating the lesser-minded Bush for the past eight years, convincing him to cede power. Americans who have a negative opinion of the Bush Administration believed this was the case, and to hear Ferrell say it, it hits the mark perfectly. As a matter of fact, there are several books dedicated to this subject of a Cheney presidency, *Vice: Dick Cheney and the Hijacking of the American Presidency* and *The Co-Presidency of Bush and Cheney* to name a few. In the skit, Palin corrects W not trying to go all "Katie Couric on ya,"—a reference to Palin's disastrous interview with Katie Couric on *60 Minutes*, where Palin was incapable of naming one newspaper she read or having a grasp of any policies national, foreign or otherwise—saying the vice president is supposed answer to the president. Then Todd Palin, Sarah's husband, brings in John McCain played by Darrell Hammond. However, a fascinating development occurred during the research, because none of the online videos continued past this point in the skit. In fact, most, if not all, videos were scrubbed out completely, removed with a content advisory or ended before McCain walked in the door and started speaking. Why? Why would the skit end here? The removal could be because of the scathing commentary delivered by Ferrell a few moments later as W takes McCain's hand, looks into the camera, affirming his unflinching support. Fortunately, the text was available in full:

> W: I, George W. Bush, endorse John McCain and Sarah Palin with all my heart. John was there for me ninety percent of the time over the last eight years. When you think of John McCain, think of me, George W. Bush. Think of this face. When you're in the voting booth, before you vote—picture this face right here. A vote for John McCain is a vote for George W. Bush. You're welcome. So, I want to be there for you, John for the next eight years.

The words do not in any way do the satire justice! From Hammond's McCain's facial expressions to Ferrell's pauses to let the words sink into the public's mind—it was satire at its sharpest and a proud moment for *SNL*, which was in the midst of a ratings boom during the election season. Ferrell takes the facts about McCain's record and reminds the voters what McCain really stands for and what type of president he would be. Ferrell points at his own face while saying: "Think of this face. When you're in the voting booth …" it's powerful because the political slant is so obvious. The audience knows where *SNL* stands, and it harkens back to Jon Lovitz as Michael Dukakis stated in exasperated disbelief: "I can't believe I'm losing to this guy."

So where is the clip? What happened to it? Considering almost every *SNL* clip is on Hulu.com or some other website, for some reason this skit is edited before this sequence plays out. The only way to access the skit was to buy the entire episode off iTunes. There is little doubt ONE person can scroll through whatever website they illegally download and find the clip, but that is beside the point. The regular Internet user who does not know enhanced search techniques, or want to pay for it, will not be able to see this clip in its entirety. The only full free clip was on an obscure website, Hark.com, but that was only an audio. While listening you can get a sense of what Ferrell does in the skit, but it's difficult to appreciate the moment without the visual. The questions have to be asked: Did Ferrell veer off script and improvise where he no longer was W but instead revealed his own personal political preference towards Barack Obama or more against McCain, Bush, and Palin? Did NBC-Universal warn Ferrell NOT to be so overt with the final part and Ferrell did anyway? Why would this clip be removed otherwise? If it is because the endorsement is too politically motivated or scathing, then what's the point in having presidential satire or free speech? Yet through all of this, Ferrell created a W who has outlasted the president in some ways, but was this appearance the final straw? Ferrell would come back throughout the years reprising his role, but this is the only appearance that is missing from the Internet.

There are several other iconic moments of Will Ferrell as George W. Bush, but this 2008 appearance on *SNL* was also during rehearsals for the comedian's one-man show on Broadway, "You're Welcome America: A Final Night with George W. Bush." The show premiered on Broadway in 2009 as Ferrell continues to lose himself in being the frat-boy-turned-president. The advantage is Ferrell that has more than a simple 5- to 8-minute skit to explore the man and the myth. On stage, Ferrell immerses himself in W in a show that is balanced between facts, half-truths, exaggerations, and some moments of satiric genius. To open the show, Ferrell's George W. Bush arrives in the theater via helicopter and welcomes everyone to the "gay theater district." But there is something different about Bush: he is extremely relaxed but instead of worrying about the office of the president, all Ferrell's Bush has to do is worry about being funny and entertaining the crowd. W then says the election is over, and with the new president in, he is now "Former President Bush." This is received with a raucous cheer from the crowd, which surprises Bush as he holds his heart saying: "thank you, that's unexpected, and very sweet of you." Continuing from his 2008 appearance of being oblivious to everything, Bush never realizes that the crowd is cheering that he's gone and now a seemingly competent and educated man is in the White House. His arrogance and ignorance about the American majority is summed up flawlessly in the statement.

W admits once again that he's a fan of "the Tiger Woods guy" and is so relieved to be out of office, because he can now do whatever he wants as an ordinary citizen. And what does an ordinary citizen do? For Bush it's drink a beer or smoke a joint "or spleef, as they say in the hip-hop community," but because he's "such a wildcard right now," he might even show a picture of his penis for everyone to see. True to satirical form, on the screen behind Bush is a picture of a man's penis and Bush walks around the stage astonished by his own exceptional manhood. This is the Bush that we know! Running around, full of ego, and wants zero responsibilities but at the same time is very impressed with everything that is George W. Bush. Ferrell's Bush is willing to expose his penis for everyone to see—similar to how the real man seemingly walked and talked—as if everything that was done during his presidency was about the size of his penis. The crowd is still in shock by the gratuitous display and then W tells the crowd it wasn't a mirage and they weren't imagining seeing his penis, so for good measure, he threatens to show it again—"I'll show it again! Do it again!" W shows his penis once again on the big screen remarking, "That's what you call shock and awe, right there. That's my stimulus package," as he gloats to the crowd.

As the show progresses, Ferrell explores Bush's rise from his early years to college frat boy and the secret Skull & Bones club he joined, or as W called it: "Skull and Boners." And then in 2000 W wins the White House as Ferrell re-enters the stage "shaking hands" with imaginary people and making chitchat. But he also can't resist being the joker as he pulls his hand away from a "person" and says, "too slow!" Or W sees someone in the crowd and asks if they lost weight—because "you need to." He sits at the president's desk in the Oval Office and says, "Shit, I actually have to do this now." W then tells how it was on his first day as a cacophony of voices overwhelms and fills the theater. Bush gets more and more frightened and uncomfortable because certain names like Bob Galligan of Halliburton and Ken Lay of Enron are louder than others—letting the audience know who is in charge—and a deep voice letting W know that "Freddy Kruger is a fictional character and poses no threat," which W gives a thumbs-up to. Finally, the voices get to be too much for Bush and he screams as loud as he can. His screaming stops and he comments: "You see how annoying that can be, especially when you have no idea of what you're doing?" The crowd cheers again because maybe this was what was going on in Bush's head on that first day. Maybe this is who Bush is—a man in too deep, who has all the responsibility he never seemed to want or was prepared for. What Ferrell does is manage to give the American public the Bush we wished he would admit to being—a man who owned up to his lack of skills and intelligence, but also kept the all-important "Bush swagger." W questions the crowd:

W: But who in their right mind would know what the job of the president entails? Would you? (Points to an audience member.) Would you? (Points to another.)

Man in Crowd: I would.

W: You're full of shit.

A preplanned stage fight breaks out as "Jerry the secret service officer" on duty removes the man from the theater. The man curses at Bush and shouts: "I want my 401k back!" to which Bush responds: "I want *my* 401k back—I lost like a thousand bucks!" While the line gets a good laugh, it does cut right to Bush's core—a rich man who has no concept of the middle or lower class plight, especially after the economic catastrophe at the end of his presidency. Unlike Hartman's Clinton, who told Les Holmgren that he's going to go wake up every morning thinking about him, or later in the skit telling the student that he's going to create a national service that allows every student to attend college, Ferrell's Bush has no idea of everyday American problems and what the loss of a thousand dollars reflects. Several other sequences within the performance expose that sentiment as well, but then Ferrell does the most important thing: he attempts to transform our impression of George W. Bush. In the show's most surprising section, the audience is given a moment to pause, allowing us to contemplate the disastrous Iraq War and all the harm it has caused for the world. During this moment, the audience gets yet another look into the Bush persona and Bush legacy as the man grapples with the fact that he is and always will be considered "a wartime president." During this crucial scene, Ferrell is dressed in the infamous fighter pilot jumpsuit, the same one Bush wore when he declared "Mission Accomplished" on an aircraft carrier. But Ferrell's Bush remains steadfast in his decision to invade Iraq, but what makes this dramatic monologue so vital and incredible is that Ferrell gives the real President Bush the one thing W seemed to be missing after 9/11 and the Iraq invasion: a soul that feels pain, has humility, and understands loss on a real level.

> W: But in the choice between freedom and tyranny, we must always choose freedom. (Pause.) Has the war weighed heavily on me? (Pause.) Sure, it has … I think about it every day. (Another pause.) Do I cry about it? Yeah, without a doubt, I cry a lot. I feel for the families who have lost loved ones (holding back the tears) and I cry for the parents who have lost a son or daughter. (Another pause.) I cry for the kids who will never get to know their mom or dad. I also feel for the hundreds and thousands of Iraqi civilians who've lost their lives. A lot of this crying is done alone because I'm the one who made the call and I … I must live with that. (Another pause.) So at this moment and time, I'd like to honor all those who died as a result of this war with a moment of silence.

The moment of silence lasts for about 20 seconds and eventually a phone rings, breaking away from the emotional scene and back into comedy, but in this brief two minutes of stage time, Ferrell gave the people everything they've wanted from the president. This Bush version is the compassionate conservative he ran as in 2000 and the one who seemingly disappeared once he became president and then became a "wartime" president after 9/11. While watching Ferrell on stage, the audience is stunned into silence though an occasional laugh breaks through, expressing some form of catharsis towards the situation or quite possibly having a new appreciation or emotion towards

George W. Bush. People, like myself, went to the show to laugh and mock W with Ferrell leading the way, but this sequence changed everything, if only for a fleeting moment. And this is the best kind of art where the artist takes the audience on a journey to reveal the best truth into someone's soul and makes us reflect on ourselves. This is satire holding up the mirror to once again have the people look into it to see who we are and what we think of the man, rightfully earned or not. This wonderful and tragic moment makes Will Ferrell's George W. Bush a better W than the real W—a man who understands pain and suffering, and a person who actually feels more than he allows the people to see. But someone who as president, while seemingly absent-minded, is also a very lonely person and Ferrell finds that in his searching of the Bush psyche. In fact, if THIS Bush were the real Bush, would the world would be more accepting of the things he did? It always seemed that it was Bush's presentation more than his ideas that alienated people. This holds to the satire definition—Ferrell seems to believe our hatred is somewhat misguided towards the man but rightfully so towards the man in the office. And this is not a tremendous leap, especially when you look at the work done by presidents while in office and then when they are out of the office. Former President Carter won the Nobel Peace Prize and Bill Clinton has launched a global initiative covering all sorts of world and environmental issues, to name just two.

If anything, this is a new parallel reality that has been created because it is such a detailed impression: if W could have watched Will Ferrell, maybe he would have been able to connect more with the American people. Thinking back to Henry V visiting his troops, which helped him become a better king, maybe Bush could have been a better leader had he carefully weighed his many impersonators and critics. The similarities between the two certainly do not end there. Shakespeare's Henry V and the real George W. Bush have other connections—both come from powerful families where the father was the leader and then the son took over. Both men had wilder days, getting into trouble, and eventually reformed themselves to take over their country. Lastly, both men invaded another country, though their reasoning was quite different. In truth, Ferrell managed to bring a sense of tragedy and sadness to Bush that no other satirist had done before or has since.

To remove any doubt or to create more, since leaving office, former President Bush has become quite an avid painter. The irony is, according to many critics, he's actually quite skilled. Marc Tracy wrote in *The New Republic* that, "Bush's paintings show a withdrawing side that is paralleled by his lack of substantial post-presidential public activity; they revel in clean, nice things like bathing and animals; they cast the president in an unequivocally sympathetic role (particularly since he is not trying to cash in, wealth- or fame-wise, and is in fact the victim of a hacker.) However, in his piece, Tracy attempts to simplify the idea by quoting others who critiqued Bush's paintings, but then realizes something greater than that:

> The paintings are proof that Bush is an artist—that he invests his energies and imagination
> in creating works that are meant to be aesthetically pleasing and serve no utilitarian purpose.
> And being an artist is proof that Bush is an honest-to-God person, not the nightmarish,

vague presence we all remember. It's not even that Bush has a soul, just as it's not even that the paintings are all that good. (And, I mean, are they, really?) It's that he is of the same species as we are. He possesses an inner life—the very thing whose apparent absence seemed to connect all of his worst outer traits, from his intellectual incuriousness to his bullying nature (the nicknames!) to his economic cruelty to his foreign militarism. The paintings are a reminder that—as Philip Roth wrote of the White House during the Clinton years—a human being lived there. Someone who provided unprecedented funding for combating AIDS in Africa and evinced tolerance at a personal level. A son, a husband, a father.

4

However, not ALL George W Bush impressions, or critiques, created an endearing, reflective, or Shakespearean tragedy. Some satirists and comedians used the parallel reality to discuss the inherent injustices of the Bush Administration and the world at large. In Season Two, episode thirteen of the extremely popular sketch comedy show *Chappelle's Show*, Dave Chappelle conjures a world where President Bush was not the Texas cowboy but instead a black gangbanger from the inner city. Chappelle introduces "President Black Bush" by saying, "if our president were black, we would not be at war right now … because America wouldn't let a black person do something like that, without asking them a million questions." To prove his controversial point Chappelle envisions President Black Bush making the case for the Iraq invasion during the first scene entitled: "The Lead-Up to War." Throughout the sketch Chappelle uses President Bush's words, replacing the Texas twang with the inner-city slang. He tells the press not only is the "area right for regime change" but if he could be "real" with everyone:

> President Black Bush: He tried to kill my father, man. I don't play that shit.

> Black Vice President: Say the word he tried to kill your father, son.

> President Black Bush: (grabbing the boom mic above his head): THAT N***A TRIED TO KILL MY FATHA!

What makes this so shocking is that Black Bush is calm in the beginning but then Chappelle uses a similar President Bush sound bite from September 2002 when he said: "After all, this is the guy who tried to kill my dad." This will be the skit's theme throughout the piece: Use George W.

Bush's words and translate them to the hip-hop/gangster vernacular. This will allow Chappelle to explore not only race relations (a favorite topic for him) and the language of war, but also the presentation of language from white to black.

This continues in the next sequence titled, "British Intelligence"; a news report brings the audience up to speed on the relationship between Bush, British Prime Minister Tony Blair, and their intelligence about Saddam Hussein's weapons of mass destruction. Chappelle, who has created this alternate reality with Black Bush, has to continue abiding by the rules of this universe by portraying PM Blair in a similar vein. Actor Jaime Foxx, adopting a British accent, becomes Black Tony Blair, using comparable "Black Bush language" to back up the president because as Blair says: "We don't know what he has." As Bush and Blair are seated next to each other, Bush passionately defends the invasion because Saddam may have weapons of mass destruction and he can't let that go, not "on my watch!" he says. To Bush this is serious, but if you don't believe him, he has Black Tony Blair supporting him with "a whole new set of intelligence":

> Black Tony Blair: We don't know much about these things but we can't trust "random n***as" with things like that as George so eloquently put it. I'm with him 100% of the way; we don't know what he has.

When Black Tony Blair says this, Chappelle's mocking the entire country who accepted the WMD narrative because Blair added "rhetorical nuance and diplomatic finesse" to the president's blunt decrees. Chappelle is not only questioning the war's rationale but also America's liberals who seem to like Blair because he has a regal British accent. Blair became "Bush's ambassador to America" not because he was right but because his oratory skills far exceed the president's, as Andrew Sullivan wrote in October, 2002:

> For Bush in turn, Blair is a very useful—perhaps even indispensable—domestic tool. Without Blair, it would be far easier for the Democrats to portray the president as a reckless provoca-teur in world affairs. But where Blair really comes in handy is persuading wobbly American elites—especially liberal ones—that the case for war is not necessarily a conservative one. Blair reminds American liberals of their own principles. When he describes the way Saddam has gassed his own citizens, invaded his neighbors, fomented terrorism around the globe, and now aims to develop potent chemical, biological, and nuclear arms, American liberals get to hear a strong voice speaking their own language in the pursuit of security. This matters.

After Black Tony Blair, Chappelle continues with his alternate reality by having his cabinet members assist him in making the case for war. Here during the "Proof" sequence, Black Bush once again uses the real words/arguments from the president's 2003 State of the Union address when he used scare tactics of foreign-sounding pastries to help his cause for the war. Black Bush is begrudgingly answering the media's questions, this time during a White House briefing, as he stands behind a podium with the presidential seal on it and American flags on each side of him. Animated as per usual, Black Bush explains that the United Nations doesn't have all the facts and that:

> President Black Bush: The n***a bought aluminum tubes! Do I need to tell you what the fuck you can do with aluminum tube? Aluminum! That don't scare you? Fine! I didn't want to say this but … (scary music) The motherfucker bought some yellow cake, ok, in Africa. He went to Africa and bought some yellow cake.

The press questions this damning piece of evidence and Bush confidently brings out his CIA chief to help convince the reporters in the room that he is telling the truth. Of course, this is Chappelle's reality and the CIA chief is played by rapper/actor Mos Def wearing oversized sunglasses, a do-rag, gold chains, and several rings, and carrying a bottle of hard liquor. The Black CIA chief walks on stage annoyed that he has to answer questions saying, "it's ridiculous." He reveals he just came back from Africa, along with "some Black Dude" who adds that Africa is "the cradle of fuckin' civilization" and that Saddam Hussein is out there buying yellow cake. The press is skeptical and the Black head of the CIA takes out a real piece of yellow cake—which looks just like an Entenmann's pound cake—wrapped up in a "special CIA napkin" so unless he "drops that shit," everyone is safe. But everyone better pray he doesn't. Chappelle is satirizing the term "yellow cake" and the situation to magnify the weak and absurd case the Bush Administration was making to launch a pre-emptive war with Iraq. Chappelle used Bush's infamous "16 words" from the president's 2003 State of the Union where he said: "The British government has learned that Saddam Hussein recently sought significant quantities of uranium from Africa" to create this outrageous scene. Later that year, Bush's statement was proven completely false by former ambassador Joseph Wilson, in his opinion piece in *The New York Times* titled: "What I Didn't Find in Africa." But it is Chappelle who is penetrating deep here and doing his best satirical work, and even though there are funnier Chappelle skits, this happens to be a rare political and topical one. Chappelle, following Highet's lead, decries the here and now and uses satire's double-edged sword to illustrate his points. The skit remains contemporary with Chappelle exploring America's racial issues, as there is a definite double standard given to the white/black dynamic—but also acceptable language and how a politician presents their ideas plays a role. Chappelle not only satirizes the notion of "yellow cake" but also the concept that the Bush Administration was exaggerating the supposed imminent Iraqi threat during the lead-up to war. Bush's cabinet members were actually irritated because they had to provide evidence against Saddam Hussein. This annoyance and irritation at having to answer to the press is perfectly captured by Mos Def's facial expressions as he played "The Black head of the CIA" And was also indicative of the Bush Administration's contempt for transparency as well as for the press.

The skit continues as Bush tries to persuade the American public that this is NOT about controlling Iraq's oil supply. This charge was and still is a common theory about the US invasion of Iraq. In a conference room, the media accuses Black Bush of wanting control of Iraq's oil and he reacts first by acting shocked, "Who said something about oil, bitch, you cookin'?" After that outburst Black Bush knocks over a pitcher of water and runs out of the room. Obviously, the real President Bush acted in such a way, but deflecting or flat out refusing to answer questions and walking out of an interview can certainly be classified under the "knock and run" approach. Another question was whether or not the US would seek permission from the UN to go into Iraq and disarm Saddam. Black Bush answers that as well, standing behind a podium in the White House Rose Garden with five microphones, he tells the UN what he thinks should happen.

> Black Bush: You know what you (the UN) should do—you should sanction me, sanction me with your army. OH! Wait a minute, you don't have an army—I guess that means you need to shut the fuck up! That's what I think about it, about no army. I would shut the fuck up! (Chappelle leans into each microphone.) Shut-The-Fuck-Up! That's right, Kofi Annan! Think I'm going to take orders from an African?

Even though the real President Bush would NEVER say these exact words, didn't W act the same way by completely disregarding the UN? Wasn't Bush essentially saying the same thing to the UN by invading Iraq even though the UN was skeptical and said not to? Regardless of the United Nation's flaws or strengths, this was an unprecedented maneuver by a US president. What Chappelle is doing here is holding that mirror up to the people as only satire can do: Did President Bush get away with disrespecting the UN in this manner because he was white and presented his rationale a bit more eloquently than Black Bush did? Weren't Black Bush's arguments exactly the same as George W. Bush's arguments? But the only difference was Black Bush is using a more aggressive vocabulary. Does the *way* something is said make it more acceptable than *what* is being said? To relate to a real world, would the world have been more accepting of the Iraq War had President Clinton pitched the invasion in the Slick Willie voice and charm? In the skit, Black Bush finishes dressing down the UN leader Kofi Annan, and gloats that he has a "Coalition of the Willing" prepared to join in with the Iraq invasion. He's asked by an off-camera journalist to list countries within the coalition. At first, Bush is shocked someone can question him but he recovers to start the list of the coalition.

> Black Bush: ENGLAND! Japan's sending Playstations … Stankonia said they are willing to drop bombs over Baghdad … Rickety Raw is coming … Afrika Bambaataa and the Zulu Nation … but I am not doing this by myself! And I am not disrespecting the UN even though they got no army.

The sheer ridiculousness of Black Bush's coalition emphasizes the simple fact that the US really did seem to be alone in their intent to invade Iraq. Chappelle ridicules this flawlessly, telling the UN "to go sell some medicine, bitches" and that he's "not going to take orders from an African." What makes these lines so fascinating is that Chappelle may be attempting to channel the real Bush's thoughts on the black community, considering how the events in New Orleans and Hurricane Katrina would unfold several years later. To say that the relationship between Bush and the African American community is strained is putting it mildly. Ferrell's Bush during his Broadway Show explored this as well when he reacted to Kanye West's comments that Bush hates black people, to which he responded: "I don't hate black people, I don't even think about them … No, not in my day to day." Was Chappelle already predicting what would happen when Bush had to react to a crisis in the African American community or was he simply reacting to Kofi Annan's African heritage?

The next title card in the skit is "Invasion," where news reports give the audience the grounding of the events in the war and then the next card: "Victory" comes on the screen. The new reports show a fighter jet landing on an aircraft carrier and cuts to a gloating Black Bush dressed in the fighter pilot jumpsuit. He's joined on stage with a friend adorned with the infamous "Mission Accomplished" banner and several navy personnel behind him. Black Bush shows off to his friend, asking him if he saw him land the fighter jet on the aircraft carrier. Chappelle is reinterpreting the actual things George W. Bush did and illuminating the audience with the truth behind his words. As the war goes south, the media begins to ask more grueling questions and all Black Bush wants to do is change the conversation to more important issues. The war isn't important because "gay people are getting married, folks." Chappelle is reacting to Bush's endorsement of constitutional amendment restricting marriage to two people of the opposite sex, a controversial social issue in 2003, 2004, and today. By the end of the sketch, Black Bush is back in the White House briefing room, but this time he has an imposing bodyguard and another friend, who's eating out of a basket, standing on stage for support. The bodyguard stares at the press corps, hoping to scare the public with his physical presence, while Bush totally dismisses Iraq because has a new plan for America's future:

> Black Bush: I'm focusing on other things, namely the Moon. Yes, I said it: The Moon. Can't be distracted what's going on with the war or what's going on with the economy … . STOP WORRYING about that! I got that shit under control. Let's focus on space, n****s, the United States of Space. 'Cos I ain't stopping at the moon. Write this down … M-A-R-S, Mars bitches. That's where we are going! MARS! RED ROCKS!! YAY! YAY!

What makes this ending and everything else so incredibly funny is that it ACTUALLY happened! Unlike Will Ferrell giving America an imaginary heartfelt apology from President Bush for the pain his actions have caused, Chappelle simply uses what Bush said and did to show the president's ineptitude. The plan to go to the Moon and to Mars was during the 2004 state of the union address when the real President Bush presented the plan in a transparent and futile attempt to try to distract the country from the Iraq disaster. Chappelle presents the president as the angry black man, but instead of a parody of action, Black Bush is doing what the real president had previously done, just with a remix of language and attitude. Chappelle's understanding of Bush's lack of nuance is key here and it allows for a new reality and certainly a worthy addition to the Bush satirical library.

If we were to be honest, a black president in the early 2000s seemed more Hollywood fiction—just like a Hollywood-actor-cum-US-president had—but all that changed when Barack Obama became president in 2008. How would the satirical media world handle the first half-white and half-black president? Obama has always been considered cool, calm, and collected, no matter the situation. Some media critics say it's a weakness, others say it's his strength. But his lack of anger or outward emotion has been the crux of the satire towards him. Obama, usually on an even keel with his emotions, is the exact opposite of George W. Bush's cowboy persona—a man who refuses to let his emotions get the best of him. If Bush was an over-reactor-in-chief, Obama is the under-reactor-in-chief and the satire responds accordingly. Even when engulfed in scandal or negative information comes to light, Obama seemingly remains under control.

Saturday Night Live has struggled with Obama since his meteoric rise from unknown community organizer to US senator to candidate for president. Fred Armisen would attempt to mimic Obama's cadence, but unlike the previous presidential satires, this lacked any real edge. The show would mock Obama's calm and whimsical orations but nothing compared to the work Tina Fey was doing with Sarah Palin, destroying her credibility by just showing up and speaking Palin's own words. The closest the show came was Obama morphing into the Incredible Hulk played by Dwayne "The Rock" Johnson, but there was nothing substantive or penetrable there. His chief of staff Rahm Emanuel played by Andy Samberg just wants Obama to get angry and he morphs into The Rock Obama, who "finally gets angry" and starts throwing senators out the window. The show has been unable to cut to the core of Obama like Hartman did with Clinton or Aykroyd did with Jimmy Carter, where they affectively satirized who he was as a man and president. Though *SNL* will keep trying, as Jay Pharoah has assumed the role over the past few years.

It was Comedy Central's new sketch comedy show *Key & Peele* that was able to get the Obama satire right. The two comedians Jordan Peele and Keegan-Michael Key were the perfect avatars for the Obama satire because both men, like Obama, come from an interracial families and this connection gives the two men an advantage with dealing with Obama's duality and the comedians have to deal with this duality as well. The two performers approached the "Obama anger" a bit differently, while seemingly taking their cues from Chappelle's Black Bush, Key and Peele give the audience a flesh-and-blood personification of Obama played by Peele and Obama's repressed rage named Luther, Obama's Anger Translator performed by Key. There have been numerous incarnations of this skit, usually reflecting on news that occurred within the previous week or two. But the one that accurately sums up all that Obama has endured was the premiere sketch as Obama introduces the

American people to Luther. First, the camera focuses in on Peele as Obama, almost a dead ringer for the commander in chief, where he explains himself and his lack of anger.

> Obama: Before I begin, I just want to say that I know a lot of people out there think that I don't get angry. That's just not true, I get angry a lot. It's just the way I express passion is different from most. So just there's no more confusion, I've hired Luther here to be my anger translator.

Luther will articulate ALL the things Obama and his supporters, and ironically his detractors, think he wants to verbalize but know he cannot because he is the president. But Luther also represents what some people want from Obama, either in support of his decision-making or in hopes of his making a fatal mistake in revealing his true nature: the angry black man. But the real Barack Obama simply does not express himself in this way, no matter how much people want him to. Instead, the audience is treated to a parallel reality revealing how President Obama's Freudian id, aka Luther, might be operating as the two react to the various issues confronting his administration from the Middle East dictators to the Tea Party to the birth certificate scandal:

> Obama (cool as can be): To the governments of Iran and North Korea, we once again urge you to discontinue your uranium enrichment program.

> Luther (stepping forward aggressively): Mahmood, Kim Jong, I think I done both told y'all, eighty-six your shit, bitches, or I'm gonna come over there and do it for y'all! PLEASE TEST ME! And see what happens.

Luther steps back behind Obama and Obama calmly continues his speech about those who oppose Obama's policies:

> Obama: I hear your voices and am aware of your concerns … That goes for everybody, including members of the tea party.

> Luther (jumping up and down, running off camera): Oh, don't even get me started on these motherfuckers right here!

> Obama (remaining stoic): I can assure you we will be looking for new compromises with the GOP in the months ahead.

> Luther (running from one side of the frame to the other): And you know these motherfuckers are going to say no before I even suggest some shit!

Obama then lists his accomplishments in his classic monotone voice with the classic speech pattern, with Luther enunciating each one for maximum value and impact.

Obama: And my intentions as your president are coming from the right place.

Luther (gesturing, walking front and center): They're coming from Hawaii, which is where I'm from! Which is in the United States of America, y'all! OK?! This is ridiculous, I have a birth certificate!! (Jumping up and down.) I have a birth certificate!! I have a HOT DIGGITY DOGGITY MAMA SAY MAMA SAY COO SA BIRTH CERTIFICATE, ya dumb-ass crackers!!

Obama tells Luther to "rope it in" as the dumb-ass cracker line may have gone too far for the president's tastes. Luther berates himself by pointing his finger at his face telling himself to "dial it back, Luther, damn!" A lot of things are going on within the skit but the skit's genius is that it's not only satirizing Obama, but it's also going after the American people. This is how the citizens have handled the first half-black, half-white man occupying the office, expecting calmness and anger all in the same sentence. There is a large portion, namely Republicans, who believe Luther is the real Obama and they're waiting for him to expose himself to the world. Those who support Obama wish Obama would become Luther every so often to shoot down his critics and be more aggressive in touting his incredible accomplishments. It's a delicate balance as Luther's language like Chappelle's Black Bush is anything but presidential, but it does get to the heart of the satire and our acceptance of Obama. Obama is NOT Luther and the only moment we've witnessed Obama's "anger" was on April 17, 2013 after gun control failed to pass in the US Senate. Obama called out the National Rifle Association saying they "willfully lied" and repeated the word several times. He also said "too many senators failed" and "this was a pretty shameful day for Washington." Never once did we see Luther emerge from behind Obama in the Rose Garden ripping the rose buds from their stems, yelling and screaming at Congress and the press because there is no Luther inside Obama. Luther and all the Obama satire seem to be satirizing is the public's reaction to Obama's calm demeanor and his refusal to be the reactor-in-chief. Obama is not Bush in that sense, even if some would prefer that he become a president for only the people who voted for him and not a president of the United States. All of these impressions and interpretations are after an understanding of how the office and the man work—how Obama and the others before him managed to survive the minefield of the most arduous occupation in the world.

Key & Peele revisit Obama and Luther as often as possible, reacting to Mitt Romney's 47% comments, the debates during the 2012 election, and when Obama defeated Mitt Romney to win a second term. During this skit, Obama once again calm as can be, is about to thank those who voted for him, when Luther jumps in front of the camera, attempting to catch a football, yelling: "We won!" as he does a touchdown dance to celebrate the victory. Luther thanks "black people for making it to two elections in a row" while Obama thanks everyone who voted for him. One is all-inclusive; the other is all about pointing out the exclusivity between people, namely those who vote for and against him. Luther lets all the white people who voted for Obama know that they are now all honorary black people and he continues to celebrate. By the end of the sketch, Obama has joined Luther in a celebration: MC Hammer's "U Can't Touch This" dance and finally loosens up. The two comedians' hope is now that Obama has won reelection, his stoic nature will subside and he will display more passion and fire. As an amusing side note, President Obama was so impressed with Key and Peele's work that he invited the two men to the White House, similar to George H.W. Bush meeting *Saturday Night Live*'s Dana Carvey two decades earlier.

But all of these realities are fleeting, even if Key and Peele revisit Obama on a weekly basis. They are but a few minutes in a sketch, or maybe an evening on Broadway, because for as well as Will Ferrell impersonated George W. Bush, he still had other characters such as Ron Burgundy from "Anchorman" and Frank the Tank from "Old School" that made him famous. His Bush impression was not his only reality. Chappelle played Black Bush only once, as he created new versions of Rick James, Prince, and others. The *SNL* players had other characters, skits, and impersonations, as do the comedic duo Key and Peele. And even though they are in occasional realities, satirizing the presidency is effective in exposing new perspectives of existing realties and personas. At satire's core, coupled with these fabricated realities, are these men and women speaking truth to power. The reality we live in, the majority of us do not feel powerful and we feel left behind. Unless we're a part of a very elite club, we are limited in our scope of influence. When Henry V disguised himself and went among his men, opening himself up for criticism, the soldiers happily obliged. It was because of this that the king was able to deliver his speech on St. Crispin's Day.

The *SNL* presidential impersonations brought the politicians out of their bubble and into the fray with the common folk. But their scorn was not limited to presidents, as Sarah Palin and John McCain can attest. Will Ferrell's endearing George W. Bush allowed for catharsis but also questioned whether we should want revenge against the man or maybe realize he just wasn't talented enough to be president during times of crisis. Chappelle asked no such questions or allowed for such thoughts with Black Bush. There was nothing endearing about that reality; it was all about stopping the current farce being perpetuated. In the end, satire and parallel realities turn out to be about power, as things usually do. All the work investigated is about power: taking authority from those who have it, taking dominance from those who abused it or used their power improperly. Hopefully, the satire returns a small bit of power to the people, even for an ephemeral moment. Satire dulls the blade that's carving through those less fortunate and these satirists are excellent swordsmen. If we were to be honest, not one of these realities on its own changes an individual or a system, but working their satirical magic together over time alters and adjusts the reality.

In March 2010, the popular website "Funny or Die" organized a presidential reunion in the hopes of pushing President Obama to create "The Consumer Financial Protection Agency." All the remaining *Saturday Night Live* cast members reunite to convince Obama played by Fred Armisen and the American people about this important piece of government oversight and regulation. In the skit, Obama goes to bed, with former *SNL* player Maya Rudolph as Michelle Obama next to him, and has a dream where all the former presidents return to discuss the Consumer Financial Protection Agency's importance. Will Ferrell returns as W, Dana Carvey as Bush 41, Dan Aykroyd is back as Jimmy Carter, and Chevy Chase reprises the role of Gerald Ford. However, due to the untimely death years earlier of Phil Hartmann, Darrell Hammond, who had played the role for years, continues as Bill Clinton. Lastly, the comedic icon Jim Carrey steps in as ghost of President Ronald Reagan. After all the presidents return to their home, their personalities immediately come out, Ferrell's Bush pretends he's "the ghost of Dick Cheney" and remembered the code to get into the bedroom: "The security code is still 1-2-3-4 as it was when I was president, only it took me five times to remember it." At the same time, Clinton looks at Michelle making sexual advances towards her with cigar in hand, sitting on the bed but he also says all the former presidents are there to give Obama advice. Obama reminds the two ex-presidents that they were the reason we're in this financial crisis and then George H.W. Bush comes in and chides both men, saying they should have raised taxes.

W: Yeah, then I would have had one term.

Bush Sr.: Yeah, that second term of yours was a real victory lapper. Wasn't it Dubbers?

Carvey's Bush turns to "Borat," meaning Barack, and tells him he has to listen to the ex-presidents, and without the Consumer Financial Protection Agency, there will be more financial crises in the future. Bush 41 tells "Babar" that he has to look at the approval ratings and do what's right instead of what's popular. On cue, Jimmy Carter walks in saying he knows what it's like to do what's unpopular and immediately begins fixing something on the wall in the bedroom.

W: Oh great, well if it isn't Mr. Let's Get the Party Started. What do you say we open up a bag of malaise potato chips?

All the presidents laugh as each identity is perfectly sketched out and W jokes and gives Carter a Bushian nickname. Carter stops his handiwork and tells Obama that he has to establish the agency to protect the American people from the banks and credit card companies. Then Ronald Reagan shows up as a spirit to help Obama or as he calls him: "Mr. Reach-across-the-aisle to grow a pair" to get the agency set up, but of course tells a story about how he was able to get things done as president. After that, Chase's Gerald Ford comes in and immediately falls over the couch, bringing back the old joke while saying: "Live from New York, It's Saturday Night!" Bush 41 reminds him that this is "Funny or Die" and not *SNL*. The ex-presidents push Obama to create the agency and Obama responds:

> Obama: What you're saying is, I should clean up this mess you all created, take on the banks and all their trillions of dollars? How is this helpful?

> Reagan: It's a bitch. But as George Washington once said to John Adams: "Tag, you're it!"

Reagan runs out of the room as the other ex-presidents laugh as Obama gets back in bed. Each president then gives him one last piece of advice, or in Clinton's case, asks to be the ambassador to Cancun. Then Obama wakes up and realizes what he has to do: Create the agency for the good of the American people. The skit ends with its director Ron Howard asking people to call their senators to convince them to support the agency in Congress. While the satire isn't that memorable, the scene is, as is the message: President Obama has a real chance to change the direction of the country because the previous ones made terrible mistakes and things have to be corrected. Eventually, the power pendulum will have to swing back the other way and rational heads will prevail, but even when it does, satire needs to be there. All of these men involved are rooting for Obama to succeed but will go after him if they think he's not strong enough, hence the references to "growing a pair" by Reagan. Being a satirist and commenting on the power structure is a unique club that certainly welcomes all applicants, and as long as there are perceived flaws in government and media, satire becomes necessary. If the system were flawless then satire would be unnecessary, but that will never happen and it's safe to say that satire is not going anywhere anytime soon. The system has never been and will never be flawless as those throughout history work in concert with each other, as the presidential reunion illustrates. These comedians are banded together through the generations spanning over four decades as their work continues to inspire the people to be better, and to remind "the king" there are those watching him. It's a brave call to action by these comedians we return to Henry V's famous speech that inspired his troops to fight the French all those years ago. With these satirical impersonators coming together, they are hoping to make a difference in the world as they take the fight to the powerful. They do so knowing they're severely outnumbered, out-gunned, out-funded, and facing an uphill battle. But with their cause just, and their satirical blades sharpened, they join each other side by side, ready for combat with Henry's immortal words echoing in their minds that, "from this day to the ending of the world, but we in it … shall be remembered … we few, we happy few, we band of brothers."

5

I say "thank you" with the "Funny or Die" image of all the presidents remaining on the screen. Hopefully, it has the impact I'm looking to achieve, and the crowd applauds. I never hear the applause, or at least this time, I definitely do not. Either the coffee has worn off after the Q&A, or the shock to my system has. Sadly, there is no time for a question-and-answer period. Kirsten walks on stage and shakes my hand.

"Congratulations. You made it through."

I smile at her and nod, "I did. Just barely."

"I have to say, the lecture was very lucid."

"Lucid" is one of my favorite words in the English language, but to describe my lecture as lucid? Does she have any idea what is going on inside my body and brain at this moment? Lucid. Could have been worse. She could have said "caffeinated." I'm putting away my materials and giggling to myself over the number of bottles of water I drank throughout the lecture. The count is at nine.

A fascinating-looking woman dressed in a perfectly tailored power suit walks onto the stage. She moves towards me, "Sorry to bother you. My name is Daniella Renee Halsen—" Her accent puts me at a loss, is it English? Swedish? American? Seems like a mix of the three.

Looking at her, I instantly think one thing: she looks like a grown-up Disney princess character and I bet she looked exactly the same when she was a kid. Her incredibly curly hair is full of personality with different colors of red and brown and she has these big bright brown eyes making her age impossible to figure out but the suit she is wearing says, "successful, and in my twenties but with an education far exceeding that."

"A Swedish last name in the Netherlands but I hear some American influence in there," I say with a smile. I'm finished packing my things. Kirsten is trying to run interference in case I am not in the mood to continue chatting with Daniella. The irony of watching Kirsten act like a bouncer, after my hotel fireworks, makes this a story worth sharing with James and Declan. One can only assume they will be jealous.

"Yes, this is true. I wanted to know if you had time to chat for a few minutes," Daniella says as she steps forward and stands next to Kirsten.

Kirsten interjects before I have a chance to respond, "You have a few minutes before the interview. Just remember you have your train soon. I'll make sure to get you that solid cup of coffee." The cavalry will be here soon! I can hear the trumpets already. Or is that a death march?

"I will. Thank you."

Kirsten steps off the stage as Daniella and I follow behind her.

"That's a spectacularly posh British accent with a hint of living in the states." I'm totally guessing but she doesn't need to know that.

"Yes, on both counts. Father was born in America, and I lived there from middle school to college. Brilliant observation skills."

We walk outside the lecture room and Kirsten heads towards a journalist who's carrying a tripod. Behind her is the cameraman with his equipment. They motion to me, indicating they will be setting up in the room across the hall. I nod and return to Daniella.

"Have you been to Paris, recently?" Daniella asks.

"Not for a long time."

"I know you were in Sweden earlier this year."

"Yes, during midsummer."

"I'm sure you loved the experience of twenty-four-hour sunlight."

"It's certainly an experience." I pause and think about those three days with Cecilia and how logical we were. How silly it would sound to recap it for someone. I've already shared enough with friends and family all who said, "Go after her." That won't be happening. Ultimately, we'd have to choose each other's fate, either my fate or hers. The odds are not in our favor. Instead, we immortalized our time and when we discuss it years from now, we'll smile with only a grain of regret.

"Yeah, I did. But now I'm drinking way too much coffee." My mouth suddenly turns dry as a few last bits of coffee grinds make it down my throat and through my body. The stragglers kill me and turn my stomach.

"That's typical over there. I do enjoy Fika."

I can't help but smile. "I'm a huge fan. So, um—" I search for her name.

"Daniella."

"Yes, sorry, Daniella. What can I do for you?"

"Brilliant, well, the reason I am here is that we would love for you to come to speak at our organization and create a new lecture in Paris. Anything American will do."

"Of course!"

"My father used to lecture and he's constantly remarked how he was always thinking of his next lecture even during ones he was performing. I'm sure you do as well."

The newest idea for a lecture has been forming in my head for some time. The thought came to me during my flight over the Atlantic, sitting in first class. Without hesitation, I say, "I'd love to discuss Netflix and their show, *House of Cards*. Been thinking about that one for a while." My stomach is turning against me. The shock of what I did earlier coupled with the lack of a proper cup of coffee. Is this my life now? Did those three days really change my brainwaves to make me a full-blown addict? You know the answer; this was discovered in the hotel room. I need to stop or start fighting it now. Today. Today is the first day of the rest of my life. I will start anew.

I neglected to notice right away, but Daniella's face immediately lit up as if that was exactly what she was hoping I would say. "That would be really wonderful. I loved the series. We can talk about everything, price, dates, et cetera. Would you want to meet over a cup of coffee and a sandwich before you head home next week?"

My head is spinning as Kirsten comes into my view. She's behind Daniella, holding up a large coffee cup to show me she found a solid cup. The spinning stops but revulsion courses through my body. No more coffee. Not one bean. Not a grind. No French press, please. No milk and no sugar. There's only one thing to do and only one thing to say: "Absolutely, but I have a better idea, how about we discuss things over carrot cake and a nice non-caffeinated cup of hot chocolate?"

BIBLIOGRAPHY, REFERENCES & INFLUENCES

1. "'The Colbert Report' as part of 'The Fifth Estate'." *No Fact Zone: News Site for Fans of Stephen Colbert.* N.p., 14 Aprl 2008. Web. <http://www.nofactzone.net/2008/04/14/the-colbert-report-as-part-of-the-fifth-estate/>.

2. "Presidents Reunite." *Saturday Night Live.* Funny or Die: 02 Mar 2010. Web. <http://www.funnyordie.com/videos/f5a57185bd/funny-or-die-s-presidential-reunion>.

3. 2001: A Space Odyssey. Dir. Stanley Kubrick. Pref. Keir Dullea, Gary Lockwood, William Sylvester. MGM, 1968. Film.

4. Ackerman, Kenneth D., *Boss Tweed: The Rise and Fall of the Corrupt Pol Who Conceived the Soul of Modern New York.* New York: Carroll & Graf Publishers, 2005. Print.

5. Adler, John. *Doomed by Cartoon: How Cartoonist Thomas Nast and The New-York Times Brought down Boss Tweed and His Ring of Thieves.* New York: Morgan James Publishing, 2008. Print.

6. *Aladdin.* Dir. Ron Clements, John Musker. Pref. Scott Weinger, Robin Williams, Linda Larkin. Walt Disney Pictures, 1992. Film.

7. *All in the Family: Season Two.* Writ. Norman Lear. Sony Pictures, 2009. DVD.

8. Altman, Robert, dir. Writ. Gary Trudeau, and Perf. Michael Murphy. *Tanner on Tanner.* Sundance Channel : SUND, New York, 2004-present. Television.

9. *Anchorman: The Legend of Ron Burgundy.* Dir. Adam McKay. Pref. Will Ferrell, Christina Applegate, Steve Carell. DreamWorks, 2004. Film.

10. Anderson, Brian C., *South Park Conservatives: The Revolt against Liberal Media Bias.* Maryland: Regnery Publishing, 2005. Print.

11. Arp, Robert. *South Park and Philosophy: You Know, I Learned Something Today.* Massachusetts: Blackwell Publishing, 2007. Print.

12. Bakalar, Nicholas. *American Satire: An Anthology of Writings from Colonial Times to the Present.* New York: Penguin Group, 1997. Print.

13. Bakhtin, Mikhail. *Rabelais and His World.* Trans. Helene Iswolsky. Indiana: Indiana University Press, 1984. Print.

14. Barbera, Joseph, prod. *The New Tom & Jerry Show*. 1977-1979. Television.

15. Baym, Geoffrey. *From Cronkite to Colbert: The Evolution of Broadcast News*. New York: Paradigm Publishers/ Oxford University Press, 2009. Print.

16. Beecher Stowe, Harriet. *Uncle Tom's Cabin*. New York: Dover Thrift, 2005. Print.

17. Bennett, W. Lance. *News: The Politics of Illusion*. 8th ed. New York: Pearson/Longman, 2009. Print.

18. Bigelow Paine, Albert. *Thomas Nast: His Period and His Pictures*. New York: The Macmillan Company, 1904. Print.

19. Bourdieu, Pierre. *On Television*. Trans. Priscilla Parkhurst Ferguson. New York: The New Press, 1998. Print.

20. Bramble, J.C., *Persius and the Programmatic Satire: A Study in Form and Imagery*. New York: Cambridge University Press, 1974. Print.

21. Chappelle, Dave, writ. "Black Bush." *Chappelle's Show*. Comedy Central: 14 Apl 2004. Television. <http://www.comedycentral.com/video-clips/jmcxny/chappelle-s-show-black-bush>.

22. Chung, Peter, writ. *Æon Flux*. MTV: 1991-present. Television.

23. Conard, Mark T., and Irwin, William and Skoble, Aeon J., *The Simpsons and Philosophy: The D'oh! of Homer*. Illinois: Open Court Publishing Company, 2001. Print.

24. Davies, Andrew, writ. *House of Cards*. Dir. James Foley, and Kevin Spacey. Netflix, 2013. Web.

25. de Cervantes Saavedra, Miguel. *Don Quixote*. Trans. Rutherford, John. New York: Penguin Classics, 2003. Print.

26. *Der Fuehrer's Face*. Dir. Jack Kinney. Pref. Clarence Nash. Walt Disney Productions, 1942. Animation.

27. Doherty, Thomas. *Cold War, Cool Medium: Television, McCarthyism, and American Culture*. New York: Columbia University Press, 2003. Print.

28. Dyer, Gary. *British Satire and the Politics of Style, 1789-1832*. New York: Cambridge University Press, 1997. Print.

29. Fager, Jess, prod. *60 Minutes*. CBS: WCBS, New York, 1968-present. Television.

30. Ferguson, Kirby. "Embrace the Remix." TEDTalks, Aug 2011. Web.

31. *Finding Nemo*. Dir. Andrew Stanton, Lee Unkrich. Pref. Albert Brooks, Ellen DeGeneres, Alexander Gould. Walt Disney Pictures and Pixar Animation Studios, 2003. Film.

32. Franklin, Benjamin. "Rules by which a Great Empire may be reduced to a Small One." *Pennsylvania Gazette*15 12 1773, n. pag. Web. <http://nationalhumanitiescenter.org/pds/makingrev/crisis/text9/franklingreatempire.pdf>.

33. Frost, David, perf. Dir. Ned Sherrin. *This Was the Week That Was*. BBC: 1962-1963. Television.

34. *Gangs of New York*. Dir. Martin Scorsese. Pref. Leonardo DiCaprio, Cameron Diaz, Daniel Day-Lewis. Miramax Films, Initial Entertainment Group, 2002. Film.

35. Gilles, D.B., and Woodbury, Sheldon. *W: The First 100 Days: A White House Journal*. Missouri: Andrews McMeel Publishing, 2001. Print.

36. *Good Night and Good Luck*. Dir. George Clooney. Pref. David Strathairn, Patricia Clarkson, George Clooney, Jeff Daniels, Robert Downey Jr., Frank Langella. Warner Bros, 2006. DVD.

37. Gray, Jonathan and Jeffrey P. Jones and Ethan Thompson. *Satire TV: Politics and Comedy in Post-Network Era*. New York: New York University Press, 2009. Print.

38. Greenberg, Robert A., *Gulliver's Travels: Jonathan Swift*. 2nd ed. New York: W.W. Norton & Company, Inc., 1970. Print.

39. Griffin, Dustin. *Satire: A Critical Reintroduction*. Kentucky: The University Press of Kentucky, 1994. Print.

40. Groening, Matt, writ. *The Simpsons*. FOX: 1989-present. Television.

41. Halloran Deans, Fiona. *Thomas Nast: The Father of Modern Political Cartoons*. North Carolina: The University of North Carolina Press, 2012. Print.

42. Hanley, Richard. *South Park and Philosophy: Bigger, Longer, and More Penetrating*. Illinois: Carus Publishing Company, 2007. Print.

43. Hartman, Phil, perf. "Ron Reagan (Season 12, Ep 6)." *Saturday Night Live*. NBC: 06 Dec 1986. Television.

44. Hartman, Phil, pref. "President Bill Clinton At McDonald's (Season 18, Ep 8)." *Saturday Night Live*. NBC: 05 Dec 1992. Television.

45. Highet, Gilbert. *The Anatomy of Satire*. New Jersey: Princeton University Press, 1962. Print.

46. Jackson, Shirely. *The Lottery*. New York: Perfection Learning, 1990. Print.

47. Jenkins, Henry and Thorburn, David. *Democracy and New Media*. Cambridge, MA: MIT Press, 2004. Print.

48. Jones, Jeffrey P., *Entertaining Politics: Satire Television and Political Engagement*. 2nd ed. Maryland: Rowman & Littlefield Publishers, Inc., 2010. Print.

49. Jonhson-Woods, Toni. *Blame Canada: South Park and Contemporary Culture*. New York: The Continuum International Publishing Group, 2007. Print.

50. Judge, Mike, writ. "Nose Bleed." *Beavis and Butt-Head*. MTV: 21 Feb 1997. Television.

51. Judge, Mike, writ. *Beavis and Butt-Head*. MTV: 1993-present. Television.

52. Keane, John. *The Media and Democracy*. Cambridge: The Polity Press, 1991. Print.

53. Keller, Morton. The Art and Politics of Thomas Nast. New York: Oxford University Press, 1968. Print.

54. Kenny, Charles. "There Will Not Be Blood." *Foreign Policy*. 06 Feb 2012: n. page. Web.

55. Kerouac, Jack. *On The Road*. New York: Penguin Group, 1976. Print.

56. Key, Keegan-Michael, writ. "Obama's Anger Translator- Meet Luther." Writ. Jordan Peel. *Key & Peele*. Comedy Central: New York, 12 Jan 2011. Radio. <http://www.comedycentral.com/video-collections/mguivw/key-and-peele-key---peele--obama-loses-his-s--t/0py5fm>.

57. Key, Keegan-Michael, writ. "Obama's Anger Translator- The 47%." Writ. Jordan Peele. *Key & Peele*. Comedy Central: New York, 19 Sept 2012. Television. <http://www.comedycentral.com/video-clips/a15q18/key-and-peele-obama-s-anger-translator---the-47->.

58. Klein, Naomi. *The Shock Doctrine: The Rise of Disaster Capitalism*. New York: Picador, 2007. Print.

59. Knight, Charles A., *The Literature of Satire*. New York: Cambridge University Press, 2004. Print.

60. Krecher, Stephen E., *Revel with a Cause: Liberal Satire in Postwar America*. Chicago: The University of Chicago Press, 2006. Print.

61. Kricfalusi, John, writ. *The Ren & Stimpy Show*. Nickelodeon: 1991-1996. Television.

62. *Lil' Bush: Season One: The Invasion Begins*. Writ. Donick Cary. Viacom and Comedy Central, 2008. DVD.

63. *Lil' Bush: Season Two: Staying the Courses*. Writ. Donick Cary. Viacom and Comedy Central, 2008. DVD.

64. *Lost in La Mancha*. Dir. Keith Fulton and Louis Pepe. Pref. Terry Gilliam, Johnny Depp, Jeff Bridges. Quixote Films, 2002. Film.

65. Lovitz, Jon, perf. "Bush-Dukakis Debate (Season 14, Ep 1)." Perf. Dana Carvey. *Saturday Night Live*. NBC: 08 Oct 1988. Television.

66. *M*A*S*H*. Dir. Robert Altman. Pref. Donald Sutherland, Elliott Gould, Tom Skerritt. Aspen Production, 1970. Film.

67. Maddow, Rachel, perf. "Jon Stewart Interview ." *The Rachel Maddow Show*. MSNBC: New York, 12 Nov 2012. Television. <http://www.motherjones.com/mojo/2010/11/jon-stewart-vs-rachel-maddow-uncut-interview>.

68. Maddow, Rachel. *Drift: The Unmooring of American Military Power*. New York: Crown Publishers, 2012. Print.

69. Maher, Bill, writ. *Real Time with Bill Maher*. HBO: WCBS, Los Angeles , 2003-present. Television.

70. Maher, Bill. writ. *Politically Incorrect with Bill Maher*. Comedy Central and ABC: Los Angeles , 1993-2002. Television.

71. *Make 'Em Laugh: The Funny Business of America*. Writ. Michael Kantor and Laurence Malson. PBS, 2008. DVD.

72. *Man of La Mancha*. Dir. Arthur Hiller. Pref. Peter O'Toole, Sophia Loren, James Coco. PEA, 1972. Film.

73. Mauldin, Bill. *Up Front*. New York: W.W. Norton & Company, 2000. Print.

74. McCaffrey, Donald W., *Assault on Society: Satirical Literature to Film*. Maryland: Scarecrow Press, 1992. Print.

75. McChesney, Robert W., *Rich Media, Poor Democracy: Communication Politics in Dubious Times*. New York: The New Press, 2000. Print.

76. McGregor, Michael A., Paul D. Driscoll and Walter McDowell. Head's Broadcasting in America: A Survey of Electronic Media. 8th ed. Boston: Allyn & Bacon, 2010. Print.

77. Mcluhan, Marshall. *Understanding Media: The Extensions of Man*. New York: McGraw-Hill, 1965. Print.

78. Moyers, Bill, perf. "Jon Stewart Interview ." *Bill Moyers Journal*. PBS: 27 Apr 2007. Web. <http://www.pbs.org/moyers/journal/04272007/watch.html>.

79. Murrow, Edward R., perf. *See It Now*. CBS: WCBS, New York, 1951-1958. Television.

80. Nader, Ralph. *In Pursuit of Justice: Collected Writings 2000-2003*. New York: Seven Stories Press, 2004. Print.

81. Nader, Ralph. *The Reader*. New York: Seven Stories Press, 2000. Print.

82. *Nashville*. Dir. Robert Altman. Pref. Keith Carradine, Karen Black, Ronee Blakley. ABC Entertainment, 1975. Film.

83. Navasky, Victor S., *The Art of Controversy: Political Cartoons and Their Enduring Power*. New York: Alfred A. Knopf, 2013. Print.

84. Nichals, John and Robert W. McChesney. *Tragedy & Fate: How the American Media Sell Wars, Spin Elections, and Destroy Democracy*. New York: W.W. Norton & Company, 2005. Print.

85. *Night of the Living Dead*. Dir. George A. Romero. Pref. Duane Jones, Judith O'Dea, Karl Hardman. Image Ten, 1968. Film.

86. O'Connor, Rory and Cutler, Aaron. *Shock Jocks Hate Speech & Talk Radio: America's 10 Worst Hate Talkers and the Progressive Alternatives*. San Francisco: AlterNet Books, 2008. Print.

87. *Old School*. Dir. Todd Phillips. Pref. Luke Wilson, Vince Vaughn, Will Ferrell. DreamWorks, 2003. Film.

88. Orwell, George. *Animal Farm*. New York: Penguin Group, 1983. Print.

89. Parker, Trey, writ. "Cartoon Wars: Part 1." Writ. Matt Stone. *South Park*. Comedy Central: 05 Apr 2006. Television.

90. Parker, Trey, writ. "Osama Bin Laden Has Farty Pants." Writ. Matt Stone. *South Park*. Comedy Central: 07 Nov 2001. Television.

91. Parker, Trey, writ. "Red Hot Catholic Love." Writ. Matt Stone. *South Park*. Comedy Central: 03 Jul 2002. Television.

92. Parker, Trey, writ. "200." Writ. Matt Stone. *South Park*. Comedy Central: 14 Apr 2010. Television.

93. Parker, Trey, writ. "201." Writ. Matt Stone. *South Park*. Comedy Central: 21 Apr 2010. Television.

94. Parker, Trey, writ. "About Last Night..." Writ. Matt Stone. *South Park*. Comedy Central: 05 Nov 2008. Television.

95. Parker, Trey, writ. "Best Friends Forever." Writ. Matt Stone. *South Park*. Comedy Central: 30 Mar 2005. Television.

96. Parker, Trey, writ. "Bloody Mary." Writ. Matt Stone. *South Park*. Comedy Central: 07 Dec 2005. Television.

97. Parker, Trey, writ. "Britney's New Look." Writ. Matt Stone. *South Park*. Comedy Central: 19 Mar 2008. Television.

98. Parker, Trey, writ. "Cartman Gets an Anal Probe." Writ. Matt Stone. *South Park*. Comedy Central: 13 Aug 1997. Television.

99. Parker, Trey, writ. "Cartoon Wars: Part 2." Writ. Matt Stone. *South Park*. Comedy Central: 12 Apr 2006. Television.

100. Parker, Trey, writ. "Casa Bonita." Writ. Matt Stone. *South Park*. Comedy Central: 12 Nov 2003. Television.

101. Parker, Trey, writ. "Death." Writ. Matt Stone. *South Park*. Comedy Central: 17 Sep 1997. Television.

102. Parker, Trey, writ. "Douche and Turd." Writ. Matt Stone. *South Park*. Comedy Central: 27 Oct 2004. Television.

103. Parker, Trey, writ. "Eek, a Penis! ." Writ. Matt Stone. *South Park*. Comedy Central: 09 Apr 2008. Television.

104. Parker, Trey, writ. "Ginger Kids." Writ. Matt Stone. *South Park*. Comedy Central: 09 Nov 2005. Television.

105. Parker, Trey, writ. "I'm a Little Bit Country." Writ. Matt Stone. *South Park*. Comedy Central: 09 Apr 2003. Television.

106. Parker, Trey, writ. "Make Love, Not Warcraft." Writ. Matt Stone. *South Park*. Comedy Central: 04 Oct 2006. Television.

107. Parker, Trey, writ. "Margaritaville." Writ. Matt Stone. *South Park*. Comedy Central: 25 Mar 2009. Television.

108. Parker, Trey, writ. "Night of the Living Homeless." Writ. Matt Stone. *South Park*. Comedy Central: 18 Apr 2007. Television.

109. Parker, Trey, writ. "Rasins." Writ. Matt Stone. *South Park*. Comedy Central: 10 Dec 2003. Television.

110. Parker, Trey, writ. "Scott Tenorman Must Die." Writ. Matt Stone. *South Park*. Comedy Central: 11 Jul 2001. Television.

111. Parker, Trey, writ. "The Snuke." Writ. Matt Stone. South Park. Comedy Central: 28 Mar 2007. Television.

112. Parker, Trey, writ. "You're Getting Old." Writ. Matt Stone. *South Park*. Comedy Central: 08 Jun 2011. Television.

113. Pinker, Steven. *The Better Angels of Our Nature: Why Violence Has Declined*. New York: Viking Adult, 2011. Print.

114. Pont, Simon. *The Better Mousetrap: Brand Invention in a Media Democracy*. London: Kogan Page Limited, 2013. Print.

115. Price, David A., *The Pixar Touch: The Making of a Company*. New York: Alfred A. Knopf, 2008. Print.

116. Rodman, George. *Mass Media in a Changing World*. 4th ed. New York: McGraw-Hill, 2012. Print.

117. Schiffrin, Andre. *Dr. Seus & Co. Go to War: The World War II Editorial Cartoons of America's Leading Comic Artists*. New York: The New Press, 2009. Print.

118. Schudson, Michael. *Discovering the News: A Social History of American Newspapers*. New York: Basic Books, 1978. Print.

119. Scott, James. *Satire: From Horace to Yesterday's Comic Strips*. Delaware: Prestwick House, 2005. Print.

120. Semiatin, Richard J., *Campaigns on the Cutting Edge.* 2nd ed. Los Angeles: CQ Press, 2013. Print.

121. Shakespeare, William. Barnet, Sylvia, ed. *All's Well That Ends Well.* New York: Signet Classic, 1965. Print.

122. Shakespeare, William. Farnham, Willard, ed. *Hamlet.* New York: Penguin Group, 1970. Print.

123. Shakespeare, William. Mowat, Barbara A., and Paul Werstine, ed. *Twelfth Night.* New York: Washington Square Press, 1993. Print.

124. Shakespeare, William. Mowat, Barbara A., and Paul Werstine, ed. *King Lear.* New York: Washington Square Press, 1993. Print.

125. Shakespeare, William. Sargent, Ralph M., ed. *As You Like It.* New York: Penguin Group, 1970. Print.

126. Shakespeare, William. *The Four Histories.* New York: Penguin Group, 1968. Print.

127. Shakespeare, William. Mowat, Barbara A., and Paul Werstine, ed. *Titus Andronicus.* New York: Washington Square Press, 2005. Print.

128. Sicko. Dir. Michael Moore. Pref. *Michael Moore.* Dog Eat Dog Films, 2007. Film.

129. Simon, David, writ. *The Wire.* HBO: 2002-2008. Television.

130. Smith, Harriet Elinor. *Autobiography of Mark Twain.* 1. Los Angeles : University of California Press, Print.

131. Smothers, Dick Smothers, Pat, perf. Perf. Tom Smothers, and Dir. Bill Davis. *The Smothers Brothers Comedy Hour.* CBS: WCBS, New York, 1967-1969. Television.

132. Spade, David, perf. "Hollywood Minute." Dir. Dave Wilson. *Saturday Night Live.* NBC: WNBC, New York, 03 Oct 1992. Television.

133. Stewart, Jon, David Javerbaum and Ben Karlin. *America (The Book): A Citizen's Guide to Democracy Inaction.* New York: Warner Books, 2006. Print.

134. Stewart, Jon, David Javerbaum, Rory Albanese, Steve Bodow and Josh Lieb. *Earth (The Book): A Visitor's Guide to the Human Race.* New York: Grand Central Publishing, 2010. Print.

135. Stewart, Jon, perf. *The Daily Show with Jon Stewart.* Comedy Central: New York, 20 Sept 2001. Television.

136. Stewart, Jon, perf. "Barack Obama Interview." *The Daily Show with Jon Stewart.* Comedy Central: New York, 18 Oct 2012. Television.

137. Stewart, Jon, perf. "Chaos on Bullshit Mountain." *The Daily Show with Jon Stewart.* Comedy Central: New York, 19 Sept 2012. Television. <http://www.thedailyshow.com/watch/wed-september-19-2012/chaos-on-bulls--t-mountain---the-entitlement-society>.

138. Stewart, Jon, perf. "Democalypse 2012- Bain Damage." *The Daily Show with Jon Stewart.* Comedy Central: New York, 16 Jul 2012. Television. <http://www.thedailyshow.com/watch/mon-july-16-2012/democalypse-2012---bain-damage>.

139. Stewart, Jon, perf. "Have Gun will Grovel ." *The Daily Show with Jon Stewart.* Comedy Central: 24 Sept 2007. Television. <http://www.thedailyshow.com/watch/mon-september-24-2007/have-gun-will-grovel>.

140. Stewart, Jon, perf. "Hope and Change: The Party of Inclusion." *The Daily Show with Jon Stewart.* Comedy Central: New York, 05 Sept 2012. Television. <http:// http://www.thedailyshow.com/watch/wed-september-5-2012/hope-and-change-2---the-party-of-inclusion/>.

141. Stewart, Jon, perf. "March of Dumbs." *The Daily Show with Jon Stewart.* Comedy Central: New York, 01 Oct 2013. Television. <http://www.thedailyshow.com/watch/tue-october-1-2013/march-of-dumbs>.

142. Stewart, Jon, perf. "Marco Rubio Interview." *The Daily Show with Jon Stewart*. Comedy Central: New York, 25 Jun 2012. Television. <http://www.thedailyshow.com/watch/mon-june-25-2012/exclusive---marco-rubio-extended-interview-pt--1>.

143. Stewart, Jon, perf. "Mormon Mo Problems." *The Daily Show with Jon Stewart*. Comedy Central: New York, 02 May 2012. Television. <http://www.thedailyshow.com/watch/wed-may-2-2012/mormon--mo--problems>.

144. Stewart, Jon, perf. "The Road to Jeb Bush 2016." *The Daily Show with Jon Stewart*. Comedy Central: New York, 28 Aug 2012. Television. <http://www.thedailyshow.com/watch/tue-august-28-2012/rnc-2012---the-road-to-jeb-bush-2016>.

145. Stewart, Jon, perf. "Sen. McCain Interview." *The Daily Show with Jon Stewart*. Comedy Central: New York, 24 Apr 2007. Television. <http://www.thedailyshow.com/watch/tue-april-24-2007/sen--john-mccain-pt--1>.

146. *That's My Bush: The Definitive Collection*. Writ. Trey Parker and Matt Stone. Viacom and Comedy Central, 2001. DVD.

147. *The Birth of a Nation*. Dir. D.W. Griffith. Pref. Lillian Gish, Mae Marsh, Henry B. Walthall.

148. *David W. Griffith Corp. and Epoch Producing Corporation*, 1915. Film.

149. *The Boondocks: The Complete First Season*. Writ. Aaron McGruder. Sony Pictures, 2005. DVD.

150. *The Boondocks: The Complete Second Season*. Writ. Aaron McGruder. Sony Pictures, 2008. DVD.

151. *The Daily Show with Jon Stewart: Indecision 2004*. Writ. Jon Stewart, John Oliver, Rob Corddry, Ed Helms and Samantha Bee. Viacom and Comedy Central, 2005. DVD.

152. *The Lion King*. Dir. Roger Allers, Rob Minkoff. Perf. Matthew Broderick, Jeremy Irons, James Earl Jones. Walt Disney Pictures, 2004. Film.

153. *The Little Mermaid*. Dir. Ron Clements, John Musker. Pref. Jodi Benson, Samuel E. Wright, Rene Auberjonois. Walt Disney Pictures, 1989. Film.

154. *The Third Man*. Dir. Carol Reed. Perf. Joseph Cotten, Alida Valli, Trevor Howard, Orson Welles. The Criterion Collection, 1999. DVD.

155. Thompson, Hunter S., *Fear and Loathing in Las Vegas: A Savage Journey to the Heart of the American Dream*. New York: Random House, 1998. Print.

156. Thompson, Hunter S., *Fear and Loathing on the Campaign Trail '72*. New York: Simon & Schuster, 2012. Print.

157. Timpane, John, and Tirdad Derakhshani. "How the media can defang poisonous political discourse." 11 Jan 2011: n. page. Web. <http://articles.philly.com/2011-01-11/news/27021867_1_discourse-violence-media-fight>.

158. *Toy Story*. Dir. John Lasseter. Pref. Tom Hanks, Tim Allen, Don Rickles. Pixar Animation Studios and Walt Disney Pictures, 1995. Film.

159. Trudeau, Garry, writ. Dir. Robert Altman, and Perf. Michael Murphy. *Tanner '88*. HBO: New York, 1988. Television.

160. Twain, Mark. *Adventures of Huckleberry Finn*. New York: Dover Publishing, 1994. Print.

161. *Up*. Dir. Pete Docter, Bob Peterson. Pref. Edward Asner, Jordan Nagai, John Ratzenberger. Walt Disney Pictures, Pixar Animation Studios, 2009. Film.

162. Van Gelder, Sarah. *This Changes Everything: Occupy Wall Street and the 99% Movement*. San Francisco: Berrett-Koehler Publishers, 2011. Print.

163. *WALL-E.* Dir. Andrew Stanton. Pref. Ben Burtt, Elissa Knight, Jeff Garlin. Pixar Animation Studios and Walt Disney Pictures, 2008. Film.

164. Weinbrot, Howard D., *Eighteenth-Century Satire.* New York: Cambridge University Press, 1988. Print.

165. Weinstock, Jeffrey Andrew. *Taking South Park Seriously.* New York: State University of New York Press, Albany, 2008. Print.

166. Weisenburger, Steven. *Fables of Subversion: Satire and the American Novel 1930-1980.* Georgia: University of Georgia Press, 1995. Print.

167. West, Darrell M., *Air Wars: Television Advertising and Social Media in Election Campaigns 1952-2012.* 6th Ed. Los Angeles: CQ Press, 2014. Print.

168. *Who Framed Roger Rabbit.* Dir. Robert Zemeckis. Pref. Bob Hoskins, Christopher Lloyd, Joanna Cassidy. Touchstone Pictures, 1988. Film.

169. Wilson, Joseph C. "What I Didn't Find in Africa." *New York Times* [New York] 06 Jul 2003, Opinion. n. pag. Web.

170. *You're Welcome America: A Final Night with George W Bush.* Writ. Will Ferrell. HBO, 2009. DVD.

171. Zinn, Howard and Anthony Arnove. *Voices of a People's History of the United States.* New York: Seven Stories Press, 2004. Print.

172. Zinn, Howard. *On History.* New York: Seven Stories Press, 2001. Print.

173. Zinn, Howard. *On War.* New York: Seven Stories Press, 2001. Print.

174. Zoglin, Richard. *Comedy at the Edge: How Stand-Up in the 1970s Changed America.* New York: Bloomsbury, 2008. Print.

IMAGE CREDITS

1. p. 3: "The Emancipation of the Negroes." Thomas Nast / *Harper's Weekly* (1863) / Public Domain.
2. p. 4: "Santa Claus." Thomas Nast / *Harper's Weekly* (1881) / Public Domain.
3. p. 24: "Jon Stewart as Don Quixote." Courtesy of Meredith Caraher.
4. p. 63: "Thomas Nast." *Harper's Weekly* (1867) / Public Domain.
5. p. 63: "Peace Insecure." Thomas Nast / *Harper's Weekly* (1875) / Public Domain.
6. p. 64: "Peace Secure." Thomas Nast / *Harper's Weekly* (1875) / Public Domain.
7. p. 64: "A Gallant Color Bearer." Thomas Nast / *Harper's Weekly* (1862) / Public Domain.
8. p. 65: "Victory and Death." Thomas Nast / *Harper's Weekly* (1865) / Public Domain.
9. p. 66: "Into the Jaws of Death." Thomas Nast / *Harper's Weekly* (1878) / Public Domain.
10. p. 66: "The Political Death of the Bogus Cæsar." Thomas Nast / *Harper's Weekly* (1864) / Public Domain.
11. p. 67: "The American River Ganges." Thomas Nast / *Harper's Weekly* (1875) / Public Domain.
12. p. 67: "Der Fuhrer's Face." Copyright © 1943 by Walt Disney Productions.
13. p. 101: "To the Victor Belongs the Spoils." Thomas Nast / *Harper's Weekly* (1871) / Public Domain.
14. p. 102: "Shadow of Forthcoming Events." Thomas Nast / *Harper's Weekly* (1870) / Public Domain.
15. p. 106: "Under the Thumb." Thomas Nast / *Harper's Weekly* (1871) / Public Domain.
16. p. 107: "Can the Law Reach?" Thomas Nast / *Harper's Weekly* (1872) / Public Domain.
17. p. 112: "Southern Chivalry." Thomas Nast / *Harper's Weekly* (1863) / Public Domain.
18. p. 115: "Uncle Sam's Thanksgiving." Thomas Nast / *Harper's Weekly* (1869) / Public Domain.
19. p. 116: "Another Such Victory." Thomas Nast / *Harper's Weekly* (1877) / Public Domain.
20. p. 117: "What That 'Ere 'Honorable Thomas Nast / *Harper's Weekly* (1867) / Public Domain.
21. p. 120: "The Tammany Tiger Loose." Thomas Nast / *Harper's Weekly* (1870) / Public Domain.
22. p. 121: "Tweed-le-dee and Tilden-dum." Thomas Nast / *Harper's Weekly* (1876) / Public Domain.

CPSIA information can be obtained
at www.ICGtesting.com
Printed in the USA
LVOW02s1755040216

473741LV00001B/4/P

9 781609 272609